AF292026

STALIN'S
TOP SPIES

STALIN'S TOP SPIES

From WW2 into the Cold War

NORMAN RIDLEY

FRONTLINE
BOOKS

STALIN'S TOP SPIES
From WW2 into the Cold War

First published in Great Britain in 2025
by Frontline Books
An imprint of
Pen & Sword Books Ltd
Yorkshire - Philadelphia
Copyright © Norman Ridley
ISBN 9781036146573

Typeset by Lapiz Digital
Printed and bound in the UK by CPI Group (UK) Ltd,
Croydon, CR0 4YY.

Printed on paper from a sustainable source by
CPI Group (UK) Ltd, Croydon, CR0 4YY

The Publisher's authorised representative in the EU for product safety is
Authorised Rep Compliance Ltd., Ground Floor, 71 Lower Baggot Street,
Dublin D02 P593, Ireland.
www.arccompliance.com

For a complete list of Pen & Sword titles please contact
PEN & SWORD BOOKS LTD
47 Church Street, Barnsley, South Yorkshire, S70 2AS, England
E-mail: enquiries@pen-and-sword.co.uk
Website: www.pen-and-sword.co.uk
or
PEN & SWORD BOOKS
1950 Lawrence Rd, Havertown, PA 19083, USA
E-mail: uspen-and-sword@casematepublishers.com

Oh what a tangled web we weave when first we practice to deceive.

Sir Walter Scott

CONTENTS

LEOPOLD TREPPER AND THE RED ORCHESTRA

I propose that you come and work with us, because we need you. Not here in the central organisation, this is not your place. I want you to lay the basis of our activity in Western Europe.

GRU director to Leopold Trepper[1]

Leopold Trepper was the central character on what would later be known as the Rote Kapelle, the Soviet Red Orchestra spy network in Europe just before and during the Second World War. Trepper, a Polish Jew, was born into poverty in 1904 in Nowy Targ a small town in the Austro-Hungarian Empire close to what would later become the southern border between Poland and Czechoslovakia. When, during the first weeks of the First World War, rumours that Cossack horsemen were gearing up to plunder the town in one of their periodic antisemitic pogroms, Trepper's family fled with other Jews to seek some measure of security in Vienna. Still only 10 years old, Trepper started to take a keen interest in politics and began to question how his family's religious convictions could be reconciled with what was happening all around him. With his father driven half-mad as the war took one son and left another badly wounded, the young Trepper challenged the notion of religion as a spiritual foundation and instead looked for salvation in what he thought of as the human spirit. When his father suffered a heart attack and died it left him with a deep anger towards what he saw as the hypocrisy of religion. He abandoned his faith completely and searched for salvation within himself rather than what he called 'some hypothetical beyond'.[2]

After the foundation of the Polish state at the end of the First World War, despite Polish President Ignacy Paderewski signing the Minority Protection Treaty, protecting the rights of minorities, there was a resurgence of antisemitism. The treaty had been signed under pressure from the Western Powers but, in practice, when several political parties in Poland openly declared themselves to be antisemitic, the treaty was effectively ignored, and prejudices were legitimised by government decrees such as the ones forbidding Jews taking up government employment. Despite his rejection of religion, rather than turn away completely from his Jewish heritage, Trepper found that the political climate encouraged within him a determination to cling to his cultural identity. He joined a secular Jewish youth movement with strong Marxist leanings, the Ha-Shomer Ha-Za'ir (The Young Guard), that worked towards the liberation of young Jews through emigration to Palestine where they could experience the communal life of the kibbutz.

The young Trepper was a bright student but any hopes he might have had of an extended formal education studying history and literature at the Jagiellonian University of Kraków had been crushed when his father died, and his family was forced to move to Dombrova in the heavily polluted environment of the Silesian coalfields. Rather than work in the mines, he turned to petty crime smuggling alcohol between Kraków and Dombrova and spending what free time he had feeding his 'insatiable intellectual curiosity' by getting involved in working class political movements.[3] He got caught up in militant revolts against the appalling working conditions in the mines and, for his troubles, he was thrown in jail for eight months where his treatment would have made the mines seem benign by comparison.

At the age of 20 with a bleak future ahead of him now that he was tainted as a left-wing agitator and revolutionary, the penniless Trepper took the only course open to him and signed up to seek a new life in Palestine using the first of his many aliases, Leiba Domb. With a few other recruits to the Zionist cause, he took a train first to Vienna and then to Brindisi where he boarded a ship for Palestine. In Jaffa, the Mediterranean sun dazzled him and he was captivated by the noisy, jostling, gesticulating crowds that were so unlike anything he had known. The narrow, winding streets with their pungent odours and incessant noise did not repel him, but instead enthralled him. The sense of delight was short-lived, however. There was work to be had but anyone who gave any sign of left-wing tendencies was sidelined and only given the sort of jobs that no one else wanted. Trepper found himself 'doing the work of animals' from dawn to dusk with his 'feet in the muck' draining swampland and lying awake at night 'devoured by thousands of mosquitos'.[4] He lived in circumstances little better than those he had known in Poland living in a shack in Tel Aviv with eight other communists including Zofia (Zosha) Poznańska, Léon Grossvogel and Hillel Katz, all of whom would go on to play major parts in the story of the Rote Kapelle.[5] After long, hot days of heavy toil, they would gather together 'exhausted but happy', living on 'the idea of revolution and a few tomatoes' as they pooled their meagre wages to survive and talked about politics and what might constitute a 'just society'.[6] It was not only they who were exploited. Unprotected by trade unions, many local Arab agricultural workers lived and worked in the most appalling conditions on estates owned by rich Jewish landowners. Seeing all this at first-hand and recognising it as a betrayal of the ideals that had brought him to Palestine in the first place, Trepper found his old revolutionary spirit rekindled. It was an easy step to join the PKP (the Palestine Communist Party). He mingled with members of other kibbutzim identifying potential recruits for the group Ichud (Unity) that served as a legal façade for communist activity, forbidden by the British.

At the end of 1925 things had improved somewhat to the point where Trepper was able to gain employment at an electrical engineering factory in Tel Aviv. His new circumstances allowed him to rent a small room which he shared with Sarah Orschitzer, another Polish Jew who had arrived in 1925 on SS 'Romania'. She had been part of a communist group in Lviv and had been forced to flee to Palestine using the name Luba Brekson after one of their number was hunted down by the police on a charge of murder. In 1927, she was arrested by the Palestinian police and charged with taking part in an illegal demonstration. The punishment was two months' hard labour.

By 1928, Trepper had become a member of the Central Committee of the PKP whose primary aim was to unite Jews and Arabs against the British administration. Together Trepper and Orschitzer took part in demonstrations against British rule that were brutally suppressed. They organised political work, wrote tracts and manifestos and attended meetings, which brought them to the attention of the police. Arrests followed and again Trepper saw the inside of a prison cell this time at the medieval fortress of Saint Jean d'Acre.

It was also a time when he took his first steps along a road that led to a career in espionage. He encouraged a comrade, Anna Kleinmann, to take up employment as housekeeper to the chief of police in Tel Aviv where she surreptitiously went through his papers to find information about whom the police were targeting. In this way Trepper was able to warn them and keep them out of harm's way. Kleinmann later joined the French Resistance during the Second World War and was eventually arrested and murdered by the Nazis at Auschwitz. Arrested and imprisoned for a third time, Trepper incited a hunger strike amongst other prisoners. When London newspapers picked up the story, questions were asked in the British House of Commons. Eager to avoid drawing attention to the issue, the British authorities in Palestine were ordered to release the hunger strikers all of whom were carried out of the prison gates on stretchers, too weak to walk.

By 1929, there was a fierce backlash against Jewish immigration culminating in the massacre in Hebron of around seventy Jews by *fellaheen* (Arab peasants) incited to violence by the Grand Mufti of Jerusalem. The British authorities evacuated all the surviving Jews from Hebron to Jerusalem. Many Jewish immigrant returned to Europe and those deemed to be troublemakers were deported to Cyprus. His experiences in Palestine convinced Trepper that the Jews, desperate to escape the antisemitic pogroms in Eastern Europe, would find no salvation there. Their fate, he believed, was now inexorably tied to the class struggle in Western Europe, a move that had been accentuated by the US Immigration Act (the Johnson-Reed Act) of 1924 restricting the number of Jews who were allowed to emigrate to the New World.

In his memoir, *The Great Game*, Trepper says that he travelled to Marseilles on the strength of a tourist visa, living and sleeping on deck of a lumbering tramp steamer. He worked in that city illegally as a kitchen porter just long enough to scrape together enough money to buy some decent clothes and a train ticket to Paris, where he met up with an old friend from Palestine, Alter Ström. They shared a tiny louse-infested garret with sometimes as many as three other people. This was the beginning of what the Glavnoye Razvedyvatelnoye Upravlenie, (GRU, Soviet military intelligence) Central Office in Moscow called the 'Jewish network', a generation that had deserted the ghetto for the Promised Land, then left Palestine by political decision to finally end up in the West.[7]

For Trepper, Zionism was a dead end, the solution to the Jewish question would not be in the world as it was but in the one that would soon give birth to the revolution. At the time Paris was one of the main human centres of Yiddish culture with as many as 90,000 Jews living in the city. A letter of recommendation from the PKP meant that Trepper was able to get help from the French communists but only on the understanding that he would engage in militant action on their behalf. That was certainly no impediment to him. He found intermittent work as a night-time cleaner in the big Parisian department stores or as a porter loading freight trains at the Gare de la Chapelle. More regular work could be had on construction sites on the basis of handing over a percentage of his wage to the foreman, who would turn a blind eye to his lack of a legal work permit.

However, a file KV 2/2074 in The National Archives gives an alternative version of Trepper's life during the 1920s that differs in many respects from the one he, himself, gave in his memoirs. It quotes the FBI saying that Trepper attended the Universities of Lviv and Kraków in 1922 and from 1926, spent four years at the Red University in Moscow studying political and economic world revolution. He also underwent military training. The file goes on to say that during 1929 and 1930, Trepper went to Egypt, Palestine, India and China spreading communist propaganda. Another file states that Palestinian police records show that Trepper arrived at the port of Jaffa on 21 February 1924 on the SS 'Asia' travelling on a Polish passport No. 30/45253 and finally left in the autumn of 1930.

Meanwhile, Luba had been arrested again in 1928 while still under a two-year probation order. This time, she got another two months in prison but a deportation order as well. One version has it that legal arguments delayed the deportation process long enough for her to marry a Palestinian Joseph Orschitzer which gave her British citizenship and she was given leave to stay in Palestine. Trepper claimed that Luba had acquired British citizenship by adopting her sister's name, Sarah Orschitzer before entering into an illegal marriage of convenience with a Palestinian. Whatever the truth of that, Palestinian police records show that she had changed her name to Delia Yerushaimi to avoid police detection but acquired a Palestinian passport in the name of Orschitzer allowing her to leave the country on medical grounds. She arrived in France on her British passport in 1930 and together she and Trepper lived in a Parisian apartment where their first son, Michel, was born.

By now Trepper was the virtual leader of the Jewish section of the Parti communiste français (French Communist Party, PCF) with both he and Luba involved with the illegal *Rabcors* (*rabotniki correspondent*). This organisation collected information about working and living conditions in France and sent it to Moscow via its leaders, two more Polish Jews, Isiah Bir and Alter Ström, who had recently transitioned into espionage. Bir was hunted by the French police but remained at large thanks to his legendary elusiveness that earned him the nickname of 'Phantôme (Fantômas)'. It was from Bir that Trepper learned many of the essential skills a spy needs to survive in a hostile environment and ones he would employ with such aplomb in the years to come.

Bir lived in a cheap hotel and usually only communicated with his group through a trusted accomplice. His network of informants was strictly compartmentalised to reduce the risk of a single security lapse contaminating the whole.

Rabcors thrived for much of the 1920s but was eventually dismantled by the French police in 1932 after one of its members betrayed them to the police. Seven of the group, including Bir and Ström were given stiff jail sentences, but Trepper avoided arrest by travelling to Berlin on a Polish passport where he contacted the Soviet Embassy. The Soviets were sufficiently impressed by his story to send him to Moscow and enrol him in a GRU (Soviet military intelligence) school to train as a spy under General Orlov. His wife and two sons, the second, called Edgar, were able to join him in 1933. The GRU, under the leadership of Jan Karlovich Berzin, was one part of the Soviet intelligence network, the Comintern and the Narodnyy komissariat vnutrennikh del (NKVD) being the other two. The GRU and the NKVD tended to compete with each other which was a serious weakness. The Comintern, an international communist organisation working for the overthrow of capitalism had a presence in all the major countries of the world and, during the days when the Soviet Union did not have diplomatic relations with these countries, was an important channel for the sort of intelligence normally garnered 'legally' through embassies.

In 1935, having obtained a history degree from Prodrovsky University, Trepper was made technical director of Soviet intelligence in Western Europe covering Belgium, France, Spain, Portugal and Britain and was given the nickname 'Big Chief'. His first big assignment was to return to Paris and find out who had betrayed the *Rabcors* organisation which he did under the name of Sommer. Intensive investigation uncovered the culprit, a Dutch Jew named Svitz who had headed a Soviet spy ring in the US before being trapped and 'turned' by the FBI. For the next two years, Trepper lived in Paris making contacts and laying the foundations for an espionage network to cover northern Europe. A keen judge of people, he built up a significant body of potential and working sources of intelligence in the West and had consequently acquired a reputation and was given a modicum of freedom to carry out this work.

Another file SF.422/Gen/3. Vol. 17 of BAOR (British Army on the Rhine) and dated 5 August 1947 ostensibly compiled from Gestapo reports, seems to confirm the FBI report up to 1930 but says that Trepper remained in Palestine until 1934 after which he was ordered to go to Paris to assist in the release of three Soviet citizens being held on espionage charges. It is implied that Trepper effected their release by employing bribery. At the same time, now holding the rank of colonel, he worked with Department 111 of the Red Army staff and the military attaché in Paris to lay the foundations of a spy network covering the whole of Europe.

In early 1938, he returned briefly to Moscow for a meeting with Berzin to get new instructions but it was Berzin's deputy Alexander Korin who received him. It was at the height of the Stalinist purges when tens of thousands of top Red Army and GRU personnel were facing the firing squads. Berzin had disappeared from view. As a protégé of Berzin, a Pole, a Jew, an expatriate, a journalist and someone who had spent many years outside the Soviet Union, Trepper was on more than one list of 'people of interest' to Stalin's executioners. Berzin was arrested on 13 May and would be shot on 29 July 1938. 'I saw all my friends vanish one by one,' Trepper later said, and 'I knew my turn was bound to come', but it didn't.[8] Once Korin had introduced Trepper to his coding procedures based on the Balzac novel *La Femme de Trent Ans* and explained to him the details of what he was ordered to do, it was an intense relief for Trepper to get out of Moscow and move to Brussels. In the best Soviet tradition, however, his son Michel remained in Moscow to ensure Trepper was not tempted to defect. The two would not be reunited until years after the war.

Throughout his espionage career, Trepper had used many aliases. To cover his tracks on this occasion, he had travelled through Finland, Sweden and Denmark where he was given the Canadian passport, No. 43781, issued in Ottawa 12 July 1937, that showed no indication of him ever having been in the Soviet Union. Canada was one of the few countries which issues passports by mail and did not require a personal appearance before an official. Luba and Edgar, also with Canadian passports, accompanied him. Trepper's papers identified him as Adam Mikler, a Canadian industrialist, born 5 April 1903 in Rudki, Poland. His father was André Mikler, born in 1875 in Rudki; his mother was Maria Jagodrinski, born in 1870 in Tarnów, Poland; and his wife was Anna (née Orschitzer), born 25 May 1908 in Drohobucz, Poland. They were married 15 May 1928 in Rudki. Their son, Edgard Mikler, was born 4 December 1936 in Vancouver, Canada. The family's address in Canada was given as 131 Rue St Louis, Québec (the address was fictitious). In Brussels, they lived 198 Avenue Richard Neyberg. Trepper's wife had Canadian passport No. 45584, issued in Ottawa on 5 August 1937. Her son travelled on her passport.

Both passports were authentic Canadian passports which had been illegally altered by the Soviets. The genuine Canadian passport No. 43671 had been issued to Michael Dzumaga, born in Winnipeg on 2 August 1914. Canadian passport No. 45584 had been issued on 5 August 1937 to Mrs William Syme, née Agnes Lockie. Dzumaga had his passport confiscated by the Soviets during the Spanish Civil War when he had signed up as a volunteer in the Mackenzie Papineau Brigade, part of the International Brigade. Members invariably had their passports confiscated 'for safekeeping' when they arrived in Spain, and usually these had been 'lost' when they wanted to return home. The Soviets invariably tried to obtain genuine passports and visas through fraudulent means, as was the case of Spanish Civil War confiscations but they were not always successful when converting them to fraudulent use. Trepper insisted that the documents should be in a name which was native to the country of origin and in common use which made police investigations and inquiries that much more difficult.

Belgium was chosen as a centre for the planned operation because it was conveniently close to both Britain and Germany and was quite relaxed about foreign espionage agencies operating on its soil as long as they shared some of their intelligence with the Belgian intelligence agencies and did not threaten Belgian interests. The Belgian Penal Code provided penalties only for espionage conducted against the Belgian government itself. The country was widely used throughout the 1930s by the Soviet Union, along with other European countries as a training ground for espionage personnel. The Abwehr was well aware of the existence of a Soviet spy network in northern Europe but believed that the GRU was constrained by the Nazi-Soviet Pact of August 1939 and would restrict its activities to collecting intelligence about Britain who they believed would be the Soviet Union's enemy in the next war.

Trepper's objective was to set up a cover organisation through which he would assume rigid control of the existing agent groups, reorganise them, and start the work of setting up a new radio network. Communications had been revolutionised by radio. With a soldering iron and a collection of spare parts now available in retail shops groups had been trained in the manufacturing and maintenance of radios during the Spanish Civil War. Upon arrival in Brussels, Trepper met up with Johannes Wenzel and Léon Grossvogel, the latter whom he had known in Palestine. Born on 9 March 1902 in Danzig, Johannes Wenzel, who had laid the foundations for Trepper's Belgian network, was a communist political agitator of long standing. He was a member of the Soviet-inspired Internationale der Seeleute und Hafenarbeiter (International of Seamen and Dockers) an early resistance and propaganda movement set up to oppose National

Socialism in Germany. It had been founded in Hamburg in 1930 and later established branches in France, Belgium, the Netherlands, and Scandinavia. He probably came into contact with Henri Robinson, a Belgian communist who had been working for the GRU since the 1920s and who would later work closely with Trepper. Up until 1935, Wenzel had worked for the clandestine military section of the German Communist Party (KPD) but in that year he was ordered to report to the GRU in Moscow to be intensively trained in wireless telegraphy (WT) and subsequently returned to the Low Countries as a technical advisor for a network the GRU was organising there.

Posing as a German communist refugee, Wenzel had entered Belgium on 29 January 1936 on a one-month tourist visa, later extended by the Belgian Ministry of Foreign Affairs until 8 October 1937. At the end of this term, he was denied any further extension despite his application to enrol on a mechanics course. He returned to Moscow for additional training and there was given a new assignment, to set up a new network in Belgium. He re-entered the country illegally early in 1938, staying in a safehouse run by Franz and Germaine Schneider in Brussels under the alias Hegenbarth. In terms of espionage, Germaine was by far the most involved of the couple. Having lived in Brussels since 1920, she had been very active in the communist movement and was well known to the Belgian police. She was probably the most important Rote Kapelle courier working the Berlin-Brussels link. Wenzel quickly earned a reputation as 'the professor' establishing a number of W/T transmitters relaying economic information to Moscow and a network of couriers and informants including the Schneiders, Abraham Rajchmann, Malvina Gruber (née Hofstadjerova), and Grossvogel. The transmitters were the most vulnerable aspect of all the Rote Kapelle operations, beset as they were by numerous problems not least of which was recruitment and training of operators and the selection of suitable clandestine sites for transmitting.

Trepper's assignment was to create, under cover of trading companies, a Europe-wide Soviet espionage network in preparation for the European war that was clearly coming. While it had been agreed that Trepper's new organisation would benefit from commercial cover, a practice that the Soviets had established in other countries, it was a bonus that the espionage networks should be self-financing which would give them resilience during time of war when the transfer of funds from Moscow might be interrupted. Each country in which a network was established would be built up around three leading agents. There would be a leader, not necessarily a Soviet citizen, a W/T technician and a military specialist to evaluate intelligence.

Crucial to Trepper's plans was Grossvogel, a French Jew of Polish origin and a former Comintern agent who had entered Belgium from Strasbourg in 1926 having returned from a period in Palestine. Two years later he was embroiled in a police investigation into adultery and received a punishment of eight days in prison. At the same time, he had been found guilty of aggravated assault and battery. He fled from France to Belgium to avoid further harassment for failing to complete his military service. Officially he was described as an electrical engineer but, in Brussels, he soon gained a reputation as a 'dandy' in high society.[9] His easy-going manner and generous nature had seen him integrate seamlessly into Belgian society and when he became an employee of the raincoat manufacturer Roi du Caoutchouc the following year, his flair, his great capacity for representation, organisation and social ease saw him made manager of the distribution network of the company.

Actually, he was lucky to still be employed by them because he had annoyed his employer with his communist background and pro-worker sympathies during a strike in 1938. It may be that being related to one of the owners of the business, Louis Kapelowitz, saved him and, at Trepper's suggestion, he proposed and was allowed to set up a subsidiary company, the Foreign Excellent Raincoat Company, in the same line of business. It was Trepper's idea to use the new business as a cover for espionage. Roi du Caoutchouc even stumped up half the seed capital in return for a half share in the company. The other half was held by Grossvogel himself.

Trepper's plan was to grow the export side and infiltrate it with communist personal in positions such as shareholders, business managers and department heads. It was Trepper's intention that persons engaged in the purely commercial aspects of the business were to be kept in complete ignorance of its true purpose. The Soviet intelligence networks in Europe at this time focussed on the US and all the countries of Western Europe, particularly England. In the beginning they were primarily engaged in establishing and building up agent nets, installing radio and other communication facilities, and training the various units to gather intelligence about the development of aviation in the Western countries, the development of heavy weapons and comprehensive information about the great fortification lines in the West. The objective was to set up a special apparatus of thoroughly trained and qualified intelligence officers, agents, and auxiliary workers, and an entirely original system of intelligence transmission services. It was with this in mind that Trepper's primary objective was to establish trading offices in

Norway, Sweden, Finland and Denmark, all along the North Sea coast to Boulogne. By now, he was an experienced intelligence officer who had mastered his craft completely. Disciplined and meticulous, he spoke only when it was absolutely necessary. Drawing him into conversation was almost impossible. His manner was modest, but his greatest strength was his ability to ingratiate himself into important social groups.[10]

In March 1939, the GRU agent Mikhail (Michel) Varfolomeevich Makarov, codename at that time 'Chemnitz', arrived from Moscow and was made manager of the Foreign Excellent Raincoat Company's Ostend branch, where his undercover objective was to set up a W/T transmitter establishing communication with an agent in England. Having served as an air gunner fighting on the side of the Republicans during the Spanish Civil War, Makarov later trained in Moscow as an intelligence officer specialising in forgery and the preparation of false documents. He arrived in Belgium carrying a Uruguayan passport No. 4652 in the name of Carlos Alamo, issued in New York on 16 October 1936, indicated that Alamo had been born in Montevideo on 12 April 1913. Trepper was decidedly unimpressed with this boastful 'impetuous amateur' who seemed not to have acquired even basic espionage tradecraft.[11] He was surprised to find that Makarov seemed to have access to substantial funds and he was deeply concerned about his habit of going around spending his money recklessly.

One of Makarov's tasks was to act as a *shoemaker*, in the jargon of Soviet spying someone who provides *Kennkartes* (false identity papers) for agents operating inside the Third Reich, but Grossvogel had already enrolled the expert forger, career criminal and revolutionary militant Abraham Rajchmann in that role. As early as 1934, Rajchmann had been active working with Grossvogel forging passports for people trying to leave Germany illegally. In 1939, he again met up with Grossvogel, who was now a well-respected and successful businessman and who put pressure on Rajchmann to work for him again. Rajchmann was introduced to Trepper but it was not fake passports Trepper was after, he was looking for someone who had the skill and experience to vet official documents and ascertain their validity. Before anything could come of it, however, Rajchmann was arrested as a foreign alien on 16 September 1939 and interned at Saint-Gilles Prison. Upon his release from a few week's custody, he met up with Makarov who arranged for him to lay low in Rue du Progrès with a Jewish family named Rybski.[12]

Rajchmann was given just enough information to let him know that he was now working for the Soviets and Makarov arranged for him to adopt a new identity. Members of Rajchmann's Polish family had been killed by the Germans during the invasion of September 1939 and it was commonly understood that, at some point in the not too distant future, Germany would attack the Soviet Union. On that basis, it didn't take much to convince him to cooperate. Because Rajchmann was already in place, Makarov was assigned to act as liaison between him and Trepper.

In Ostend on 17 July 1939, Makarov had been joined by Anatoly Markovich Gurevich another GRU officer who was masquerading as Viktor Sokolov (Sukolov). Born to Jewish parents in Kharkiv, Gurevich was a proficient linguist and had also served with the Soviet forces during the Spanish Civil War as a translator at the headquarters of international teams. When he returned to the Soviet Union, he had joined the GRU and trained as a radio operator and cryptographer. On 15 April 1938, he was sent to France to start work as an agent. Taking on the identity of a Mexican tourist he travelled through Finland, Sweden, Norway and the Netherlands, before finally arriving in Paris where he exchanged his Mexican passport for a Uruguayan one. This new passport had been issued in New York on 17 April 1936, in the name of Vincente Sierra, whose date and place of birth were given as 3 July 1911 in Montevideo and his permanent address as Calle Colon 9, Montevideo. One of his tasks at that time was to contact the Luftwaffe officer Harro Schulze-Boysen and act as liaison between him and Moscow. Sierra's persona was that of a rich South American language student traveling through Europe, with temporary Belgian residence permit. He enrolled as a part-time student at the Université Libre in Brussels. Using this cover he was able to make a trip to Switzerland shortly after his arrival in Belgium. There he made contact with Alexander Radó to whom he passed on $3,000 to finance a Soviet spy ring there.[13]

Makarov was supposed to train Gurevich to take over the Foreign Excellent Raincoat Company's Denmark branch but the outbreak of war contrived to see him end up as an assistant to Trepper performing routine tasks which included being a cipher clerk, deciphering instructions from Soviet intelligence, and preparing reports with information for the Soviet Trade Representative of Belgium. As Trepper's assistant, Gurevich became known colloquially as the 'Little Chief' but, for the purposes of radio communications with Moscow also had the codename Kent. While Trepper's wife adored Makarov who could do no wrong in her eyes, Gurevich seemed to her to be far too fond of luxury to be trusted. When he set himself up in an apartment at 106 Avenue Émile-de-Béco and proceeded to establish himself within the social fabric of the city, his sybaritic lifestyle was an affront to the central core of the group who had endured such deprivations to get where they were and had grown somewhat spartan and iron-hard as a result.

Six days after the Germans had launched their invasion against Poland, unbeknown to Trepper at the time, another network was set up in Belgium by the tall, blond blue-eyed Konstantin Lukitsch Yefremov who arrived via Zurich on a Finnish passport in the name of Eric Jernstroem. The passport, issued in New York on 22 June 1937, showed that Jernstroem had been born in Vaasa, Finland and had lived in the US since 1932 but there is no record of Yefremov ever having set foot on US soil. It is likely that he had lived in the Netherlands between 1936 and his arrival in Brussels. Masquerading as a chemistry student at the École Polytechnique, he had also been instructed to meet up with Wenzel, whom he had known previously, and set up another network.

Little was done in the way of actual espionage at this time and contact between the groups and Soviet diplomatic staff was kept to an absolute minimum. By the spring of 1940, there was an efficient W/T organisation at Moscow's disposal in northern Europe supplemented by small-scale but efficiently functioning auxiliary agent, courier and radio network, independent from the political intelligence service of the Comintern, which served as an alternate routing system for messages, via London and Stockholm. Alongside this but of fundamental importance, was the developing Foreign Excellent Raincoat Company's export business methodically built up, step by step. The expectation was that the radio network would come into play in the event of a Nazi-Soviet conflagration but before Trepper was able to make much headway in the trenchcoat venture, Hitler's forces struck with devastating impact against France and the Low Countries on 10 May 1940. Belgian police were rounding up all German nationals. The Treppers, posing as Mikler, were suspected of having German affiliations and had been forced to flee their apartment to avoid being interned as potential enemy aliens. Luba and Edgar latched onto the Soviet delegation and were driven to Marseilles under diplomatic cover to be repatriated to the Soviet Union while Trepper went to Grossvogel's house and quickly adopted an alternative French identity as Jean Gilbert.

On 19 May, Grossvogel had persuaded Durov, the Bulgarian consul in Brussels, and fellow Bulgarian diplomat named Petrov to take Trepper along with him on a three-week journey through Belgium ostensibly so that Trepper could ascertain the level of damage sustained by various 'Trenchcoat' branches during the fighting. The shop in Brussels had been destroyed by a bomb in May. He later recalled,

> During this journey, I was able to study the advance of the German troops in great detail. I paid particular attention to the problem of German supply and its organisation. I also analysed the reasons why anti-tank defences and fortifications had not played their role. The intervention of paratroopers was also a new phenomenon, which is why I was interested in it. You could still see the traces of combat and learn from them. How was it that the British had suffered such a crushing defeat? The journey also allowed me to see the traces left by the crossing of the Maginot Line near Sedan. Further on, I saw the battlefield of Abbeville where tanks had intervened shortly before: it was the first major tank battle of the war.[14]

When they arrived back in Brussels, the three men, along with other diplomats from pro-German neutral countries, were taken on an official tour of the Western theatre of operations by Reich government officials. They saw the traces left by the withdrawal of British troops between Ostend and Dunkirk and engaged in discussions with military personnel who were eager to boast about the German offensive in the West. Their reception was always warm because of the good relations between Germany and Bulgaria. There was ample opportunity to obtain information about the war from excellent sources as well as about the morale of the German troops. Afterwards, they were given a compendious dossier proudly explaining how the German Blitzkrieg had smashed the Allied forces. This document with campaign maps and photographs soon found its way to Moscow. Days later, among the flood of refugees heading west ahead of the advancing Wehrmacht was Durov, with two passengers in his car. Diplomatic immunity allowed them to avoid scrutiny by German units they met along the way which was just as well since the consul's companions were none other than Grossvogel and Trepper, the latter gripping a large suitcase containing his radio transmitter which would soon be his sole means of communicating with Moscow.

In 1939, after his wife and son had been repatriated to Moscow, Trepper had taken a mistress, a '21-year-old, auburn-haired beauty with sparkling eyes, graceful bearing and a perfect figure', Georgina 'Georgie' de Winter.[15] Now pregnant, she joined Trepper in Paris. Georgie was completely in thrall to Trepper with whom she went to restaurants and cabarets almost every evening describing her time with him as 'a wonderful life' and saying, 'I can honestly say I've never been happier'.[16] Under the cover name of Elisabeth Thevenet, she had given birth to a boy, Patrick de Winter, on 29 September 1939. Many accounts claim that Patrick was Trepper's son but in his memoir *The Great Game*, Trepper refers to Patrick as 'Georgie's son' which implies that he was not Patrick's father.[17]

When Trepper moved to Paris in the summer of 1940 with Georgie de Winter and Patrick, he was returning to a city he knew well but now he found that 'flags bearing swastikas floated over the city and men in grey-green uniforms filled the streets'.[18] They took up residence at 6 Rue Fortuny and set about establishing a second network in Paris. He went to the Soviet Embassy and was taken onto the staff as a minor functionary which had the benefit of allowing him free travel between the occupied part of France and Vichy. At once, he set about building an espionage organisation with military intelligence targets. He began making contacts within the local left-wing groups recruiting agents for the new network while still retaining some control over the Belgian network now run by Gurevich. When Trepper travelled to Belgium he used his Jean Gilbert identity which identified him as a French businessman. It had begun to play on his mind that his time was almost up in Western Europe and he anticipate a recall to Moscow which was not at all what he wanted. He thought about getting permission from Moscow to take Georgie, whose father was the American actor George de Winter, and Patrick with him to the US which was becoming a prime targets for Soviet espionage. The task of creating a new identity (legend) for Trepper proved far too difficult under the circumstances, however, and the idea was scrapped.

Now in the unoccupied part of France with Grossvogel, Trepper found contact with Moscow difficult to maintain. In later testimony, he said that, at the time, he was struck by the discrepancy between the clear evidence of German battlefield dominance he had witnessed in Belgium and northern France and the information that Soviet diplomats were sending back to Moscow either through fear of being accused of exaggeration or simply a refusal to face reality. Trepper ensconced himself in the Hotel Cecilia that was frequented by officers from the German Ministry of War and picked up what gossip he could. A post as a Soviet diplomat in Vichy allowed him to move freely across the whole of France but when the Soviet military attaché had left, all diplomatic connections were severed, and Trepper had to rely solely on W/T communications through the PCF.

Gurevich, with his Uruguayan identity, had no problems with the German authorities and had been left to run the Belgian Rote Kapelle network which he reorganised in Trepper's absence, but he still conferred with Trepper occasionally on fundamental points of policy.

With agents all across Belgium, including Isidore Springer, Gurevich was keeping Makarov extremely busy on his transmitter so, in the summer of 1941, Moscow sent Makarov an assistant, David Kamy (Kamenomotski) who arrived under the alias Albert Desmets. Kamy was the son of a wealthy Jewish banking family from St Petersburg, who had emigrated to Palestine after the Bolshevik Revolution. A polyglot and expert mechanic, Kamy returned to Europe and fought with the Lincoln Brigade in the Spanish Civil War. Married and living in Paris, he joined the Polish Brigade of the French army when the Germans attacked on 10 May 1940. After the French surrender, he became involved with the resistance and joined the PCF specialising in radio communications which is where Trepper first came across him.

Under Gurevich's supervision, Makarov and Kamy set up their transmitter operating from a safehouse located at 101 Rue des Atrébates in Brussels. This was the home of Isidore Springer and his mistress, Rita Arnould-Bloch, nicknamed Juliette on account of Springer having been allocated the codename Romeo, both of whom acted as couriers and recruiters for the ring. Zofia Poznańska whom Trepper had known in Palestine was the station cipher clerk now working under the alias of Anna Verlinden.[19] Poznańska had been born on 8 June 1906 in Łódź, Poland and lived later in Kalisz where, at the age of 20, she joined the Ha-Shomer Ha-Za'ir movement and emigrated to Palestine. She had met Trepper and lived alongside him at the Afula kibbutz. Trepper had become a great admirer of her commitment to revolutionary ideals based on egalitarianism and freedom and a lasting resolution to the Jewish problem. They shared a common disdain for British imperial rule of Palestine and had both joined the Ihud, a communist front movement, and later the PKP. Since leaving Palestine in 1930, she had lived in Paris and Brussels doing a variety of humanitarian jobs and working with other Jewish left-wing Eastern Europe immigrants and continued her communist political activity. It was not, however, a communism in the Stalinist mould but much more of a utopian ideology based on humane, egalitarian concepts. For her, espionage was not what Trepper called his 'great game' but a cause. She had obtained a visa for her great friend Sonia Kestner to emigrate to the US but refused to go herself saying she 'had a job to do'.

Trepper made contact with Rajchmann, who had fled to Montréjeau with his Belgian wife and had been briefly interned at the Saint-Cyprien internment camp as an alien. He was now in Revel, a town where many Belgian refugees had concentrated and contemplating flight to Portugal but Trepper ordered him to go to Toulouse to meet the Soviet agent Malvina Gruber who had repatriation permits that would allow them both to return to Belgium. When they tried to cross the demarcation line, however, they were turned back and went instead to Bordeaux where they crossed successfully. When they got back to Brussels, Rajchmann and Gruber became lovers and became part of a small group under Gourevitch that included a new recruit, Hermann Izbutski (Bob) who had fought in the Botwin Company of the International Brigades. In January 1941, Rajchmann managed to get a temporary identity card in his own name which was a mistake because it alerted the Belgian police who arrested him again a few weeks later for violating his expulsion order. He served two months in prison.

Trepper had also met up with an old acquaintance with whom he had shared a cell and gone on hunger strike in Palestine and who had followed him to France where he had become active in the Young French Communists under the alias of André Dubois. The son of a learned schoolmaster, he generally, the 'young, short [slightly built] … unfailingly optimistic' and 'utterly devoted' Hillel Katz, whose 'glasses took up half his face'.[20] Katz would go on to become Trepper's indispensable right-hand man and liaison with Henri Robinson. Grossvogel was also in Paris using all his business acumen to establish a financial basis for espionage there. His responsibilities including the renting of apartments in Rue Fortuny and Rue de Prony and a dozen premises in the suburbs to be used as 'safehouses'. In a very short time, under cover of an impeccable social persona, he had recruited agents to act as cutouts and couriers to handle information.

With Grossvogel being Jewish, the Roi du Caoutchouc business had been sequestered by Belgian administrators in the pay of the Germans and the Foreign Excellent Raincoat Company hastily liquidated, on 13 January 1941, Katz helped Gurevich and Grossvogel to establish a new business called Simex (Societé importacion exportacion) in Paris with a sub-branch in Marseilles as a cover organisation for their espionage activities with funds substantially supplied by Moscow. It was Grossvogel's task to develop the firm on a sound and respectable foundation while Trepper concentrated on the development of the clandestine side. Simex headquarters were in the Lido building on the Champs Élysées while a sister company, Simexco was set up at 192 Rue Royale in Brussels.

Simex and Simexco were both official civil and military engineering providers, general dealers and contractors supplying black market materials to the Nazi Todt Organisation, that used slave labour on building contracts resulting from the German occupation. The companies built accommodation and even provided furniture, but also supplied earth-moving equipment, concrete mixers and rail lines. It was a near perfect trojan horse operation working at the very heart of the Nazi economy. Representatives were able to travel throughout the whole of German-occupied Europe which had the added bonus of making available security passes for Simexco representatives to sensitive construction sites. The company was also given unlimited telephone and telex communication facilities that came in very useful for clandestine work. Both flourished and made substantial profits. Simexco's main investor was Willy Thévenet, a Belgian communist and informer, who was fully aware of the companies true purpose and actively took part in operations. Margarete Barcza used her contacts to find additional shareholders among whom were the nightclub owner, Robert Christen, travelling salesman Jean Passelecq, the publisher Henri de Ryck, and Henri Seghers, the owner of a cigarette factory.

The key man in Simexco was a French national, Alfred Valentin Corbin who became the company's commercial director in September 1941. Corbin was a friend of Hillel Katz with whom he had served in the French Foreign Legion and it was Katz, in his role as recruiter for the Rote Kapelle, who had introduced Corbin to Trepper. Corbin ran a small poultry feed business that was running into difficulties under the occupation and had no difficulty in agreeing to run Simex. It was not a great surprise to discover the covert side of the business and he had no qualms about getting involved with that also eventually serving as a courier with the networks in Lyons and Marseilles, using as cover his business journeys to the unoccupied zone. Corbin also had feed supplier in Ghent that gave him a legitimate excuse to travel to Belgium.

The Simexco operation, developed 'on the hoof' and with Moscow preoccupied with the German advance, was far from soundly based, however. If agents working within it were caught and suspicion fell on the company, all those whose names appeared as employees or who had any contact with it at all would be rounded up for questioning. The exposure of Simex would endanger Simexco and vice versa. It was something of a disaster waiting to happen.

Aside from Simexco, Trepper set up seven completely independent networks of agents in France supplying intelligence to the GRU. He maintained contact with each group through its leader, who was the only one aware of Trepper's identity. Meetings between Trepper and each of the leaders was strictly according to a prearranged protocol in predetermined locations and no other contact was permitted. Operations in France after 1940 were financed by Simex profits and regular injections of capital from Moscow brought by a courier through

Switzerland. Trepper made his requests for funds by radio direct to Moscow. In reply he was told how the cash, usually US dollars, would be assigned to him and where, when and in what circumstances the money was to be collected. The wireless message from Moscow also gave a description of the person, Aenis Hanslin, who would hand over the money, the password and any other necessary details to ensure that the transfer was safely effected.

Before the war Trepper's remuneration had been about $350 a month, which was reduced to $275 when his family returned to Moscow. Grossvogel initially got rather less, £175 dollars a month but that was increased until he was on a par with Trepper. Local agents were not paid a regular amount but rewarded according to their level of activity. Trepper had at least two emergency funds, one of which consisted of gold sovereigns, to the value of about $1,000. There is no doubt that Trepper and Grossvogel both dipped regularly into the funds to finance a lavish lifestyle which they justified by claiming that it was necessary to live up to their image as successful businessmen in order to acquire intelligence. There were, of course regular payments to agents and rents for at least three flats in Paris and a villa at Sèvres. It is also believed that Trepper maintained flats in Amsterdam and Lyons to avoid having to stay in hotels when going there.

Grossvogel took on a supervisory role for all communications for Trepper's network and was responsible for finding safehouses and lodgings which could be used as rendezvous sites, letter drops, and temporary accommodation for couriers. Grossvogel also took on the role of training W/T operators. Lucienne Giraud later expanded her involvement to act as liaison and cutout between Trepper and Käthe Völkner. Trepper had been particularly pleased with this arrangement. Giraud had no German and Völkner spoke no French. All transactions and exchanges were carried out according to prearranged protocols in metro stations. There was no danger of them getting into any sort of conversation that might involve the inadvertent exchange of personal details that might prove fatal if either one was picked up and questioned.

Trepper and de Winter lived a very high life indeed, untroubled by the German occupation forces. Through the Simexco black market operations, Trepper was able to siphon off substantial funds and had first choice of all manner of luxury items that Parisians were selling off. Not for him the privations of living under the jackboot. It was almost as if Trepper and Gurevich were vying to outdo each other in the hedonistic lifestyle department. Gurevich was, by now, well known throughout Brussels and travelled freely all the time collecting intelligence to satisfy the Moscow's demands which came to him through the radio network established in a safehouse where agents and couriers met. A typical message read:

> Need report regarding Swiss army in relation to possible German invasion [of Switzerland]. Armed forces in the event of a general mobilisation, Stop. Nature of fortifications. Quality of weaponry. All details concerning aviation, armour and artillery.[21]

Gurevich would undertake such missions personally but did not have to worry about other requests such as the one for information about German troops assigned to the Atlantic Wall defences. A quick look at the Simexco accounts would tell him all he needed to know about that since they provided much of the construction materials.

The Germans responded to the discovery of illicit radio signals by creating the Funkabwehr des Oberkommandos der Wehrmacht, an Abwehr radio counterintelligence organisation in 1940 under the command of Hans Kopp, to monitor illicit radio broadcasts sent by secret agents and resistance groups who were communicating with other agents or sending intelligence from inside German occupied territory to Germany's enemies. Their method was to use direction finding (DF) equipment to locate where a radio source originated. Initially they used a vehicle with a circular metal antenna about 1 metre in diameter on top but when that proved to be too conspicuous and easily spotted they went on to develop a device that could be carried in a suitcase or inside a closed van. The location of an illegal radio source could be determined by triangulation measuring its direction from two or more locations.

New techniques were developed such as narrowing down the location of a transmitter by cutting off the current sub-district and noting when the clandestine transmission was interrupted. The searchers would then concentrate their efforts on the sub-district affected, and hope to track down quickly at least the block, if not the building, the set was working from. Long transmissions in a large town would probably bring a detection van to the door within thirty minutes and operators risked their lives for every second they stayed on the air beyond a few short minutes. All this meant that the 'pianist' (Morse code operator) became the Achilles' heel of the illicit operation and good tradecraft was meant to ensure that organisers and wireless operators saw as little of each other as possible.

The Soviets, with their usual eye on the long game, had set up a wireless centre in Brussels, but Trepper left it essentially moribund as he concentrated on recruiting a team of informers, and enlarging his contacts with the world of business, the military and diplomacy. Only after May 1940 did he turn to radio as his primary method of communicating with Moscow. Until the outbreak of war with Germany, most communications between the Rote Kapelle networks and Moscow were directed through the official Soviet installations. Couriers and postal links connected the networks with these installations. From there the information went by wireless or by diplomatic pouch from the Soviet Embassy and the Soviet Chamber of Commerce in Belgium to Moscow. Communicating with Moscow by radio was a complicated business. Transmission times were normally restricted to between the times of 23.00 and 02.00 hours but this directive would be increasingly ignored as more and more information was acquired and the number of connections decreased. Frequencies and call signs were changed by Moscow at regular intervals and some wavelengths were reserved for particular agents.

After the Germans launched the invasion of the Soviet Union, Operation Barbarossa, the level of diplomatic and military radio communications traffic exploded but so did illicit radio traffic. Once the Nazi-Soviet alliance was shattered, Trepper's network was brought into play. On 26 June 1941, the Funkabwehr monitoring station at Cranz in Hamburg intercepted a series of radio transmission sent from somewhere in northern Europe to Moscow. The messages were recorded but, of course, could not be read since they were in code. The Germans were fairly sure that the messages were of significant importance to the Soviets but had they been able to decipher them they would have been apoplectic. Whoever was sending them clearly had access to very sensitive information.

2 July 1941 to the director No 34. Rdo (very urgent) Urals objective by Moscow entered into force. Stop. Lateral movements diversionary manoeuvres.

3 July 1941 to the director No. 37 Daily production of dive-bomber aircraft currently 9 or 10 devices. Average daily aviation losses on Eastern Front 40 aircraft.

5 July 1941 to the director No. 44 German aviation workforce 21,500 first and second line aircraft plus 5,250 transport.

27 July 1941 to the director No. 92 Plans thrust on Arkhangelsk and Murmansk Stop. In the event of modification I will receive precise information within 48 hours.[22]

All across Wehrmacht-held territory, Funkabwehr direction-finding teams were put on high alert. There was a flurry of excitement that got the attention of the director of the Reich Security Main Office, Reinhard Heydrich and his deputy Walter Schellenberg. With this level of interest a new special counterintelligence unit Sonderkommando Rote Kapelle was set up jointly by the Abwehr and the Gestapo under the command of SS Obersturmbannführer Friedrich Panzinger. Kapelle was an Abwehr term for counter-espionage operations against clandestine radio stations and Rote was used to identify the Brussels network. The term Rote Kapelle is commonly translated as Red Orchestra.

Its function was to locate the radio stations and either put them out of action or try to utilise them in *Funkspiel* operations. This was when controlled information was transmitted over a captured agent's radio in such a way that the agent's parent service had no knowledge that the agent was working for the enemy.

On 10 October 1941, Gurevich received a coded message in Brussels ordering him to go and find out what was happening in Berlin. Gurevich did as he was instructed and went to Berlin where he arranged for an extra transmitter and another 'pianist' and, thinking that was enough, then travelled on to Prague. When he eventually got back to Brussels on 21 October, he got news that the Berlin network had gone off the air again piling the pressure onto Brussels which was also handling intelligence arriving by courier from Paris. Trepper had the foresight to have couriers already available to operate between Berlin and Brussels. The Belgian capital was now at the very centre of a complex Europe-wide network of Soviet spies stretching from Bulgaria and Czechoslovakia, where Trepper had made contacts in 1937, to Portugal and many of their networks all funnelling intelligence back to Moscow through Brussels.

By 7 September 1941, Funkabwehr analysts at Cranz had narrowed a major source of transmissions to somewhere in the Brussels area broadcasting from 02.00 to 05.00 hours, without interruption. On 30 November, a team of experts led by Feldpolizeikommissar Heinrich Piepe from the Ghent branch of the Abwehr IIIF, who had been put in charge of the Belgian Funkabwehr moved into Brussels equipped with both mobile and suitcase detectors. With this level of surveillance, it was soon established that there were three sources of transmission. One in Uccel, another in Laeken and a third, the one emitting the strongest signal, from 101 Rue des Atrébates in Etterbeek. Closure of the Berlin transmitter had piled enormous pressure on Brussels and the sheer volume of traffic it was now handling meant that it had to stay on the air much longer than was prudent and did not have time to periodically relocate the transmitter all of which had serious implications for security. The net was about to close. A house close to the suspect property was taken over as an observation post and plans were made to launch a raid. On the night of 12 December 1941, the transmission was so strong from 101 Rue des Atrébates that it interfered with normal radio broadcast of a concert. Bauer, who had joined Piepe, confirmed the location. After curfew, the road was sealed off by auxiliary police and a dozen armed Abwehr agents got into position ready to break into the house.

For weeks, Poznańska, whom Trepper had known in Palestine and whom he described as someone who showed 'rare qualities of courage and intelligence' had complained to him about the arrangements Gurevich had made for her and Kamy after their arrival from France. She had been obliged to bed down at the Rue des Atrébates house where she worked when she should have been given secure accommodation well away from there at all other times. Normally, those involved with the actual transmission of intelligence such as radio operators and coders would know nothing about the overall organisational structure of the group even when members of a radio team and members of an agent team lived on the same street and even in the same building. Before the war the networks had been kept isolated from one another and had been successful in maintaining the necessary level of compartmentalisation, but wartime had eroded these security measures.

When told of the incident, Ivan Bolchakov who had, at one time been the GRU *rezident* in Brussels and who had returned to Moscow, could not believe that three agents from the same service could have been in this clandestine hideout all at the same time.[23]

Kamy was lodged with Makarov when again he should have had his own private accommodation. Both Poznańska and Kamy were regularly exposed to contact with friends of Gurevich who nobody seemed to know anything about. Trepper feared that the two had been badly compromised and posed a risk to the operation so he decided to send them back to France and leave Gurevich to find his own replacements. Trepper had arranged to meet Makarov, Poznańska and Kamy at 101 Rue des Atrébates around noon on 13 December to tell them of his decision but before he could do that, disaster struck.

The house was stormed at 02.30 hours on that day and when Piepe reached the garden of the house he heard a gunshot followed by a scream. Kamy had tried to escape by jumping over the wall behind the house and had been caught a short time later in a neighbouring property. Breaking into the room, Piepe discovered what he described as a 'forger's paradise'. There were blank passports, official forms and stamps as well as chemicals to make 'invisible ink'. What struck Piepe most of all was that all the documentation was in German. It was clearly the workshop of a very sophisticated organisation with wide-ranging associations and one that was much bigger than he could possibly have imagined. Two photographs, no doubt ready to be incorporated into false passports showed the faces of two men Piepe did not recognise but who would soon become well known to him.

Arnould and Poznańska were arrested in the property, and it soon became clear to Piepe that Arnould wanted to cooperate so, according to his later testimony, he 'had one of his men fetch a bottle of wine' and they sat down to talk.[24] Arnould was simply a housekeeper, she said, and, although she knew about the clandestine radio, she knew very little detail about the people who came and went and who they were sending messages to. Having no real allegiance to the group and fearful of the police, she told Piepe all she knew which wasn't much except for the revelation of a hidden room behind a partition on the ground floor. When Piepe showed Arnould the picture of Trepper she claimed not to know him but the other man, she said, lived close by on Boulevard Brand Whitlock and could often be seen walking his dog there but she didn't know his name. Arnould was taken to Berlin-Moabit Prison. She was tried by the Berlin *Kriegsgerichtshof* in April 1943, sentenced to death, and executed on 20 August 1943 at Plötzensee Prison. After months of gruelling interrogation Poznańska, committed suicide by hanging herself on 29 September 1942 in Saint-Gilles Prison. She was buried in a mass grave in San Jill, where a tombstone with the epitaph 'Resistante' would be erected in her memory in 1985. A commemorative grove was dedicated to her in 1983 in the Eshtaol Forest, on the way to Jerusalem, and the State of Israel awarded her a posthumous Fighter Against the Nazis Citation.[25]

On the day after the raid, Makarov, unaware that the Abwehr had raided it, went to the house while Piepe's men were searching it from top to bottom. He was quickly ushered inside and questioned. He showed his Uruguayan passport in the name of Carlos Alamo and claimed to have come to the house to arrange a supply of black-market luxuries. He was detained. Next to arrive was Trepper, himself. Coming face to face with a policeman, Trepper says that he 'had the definite sensation that [his] heart stopped beating'.[26] He was unceremoniously pulled into the house and the door firmly closed behind him. The house was in a mess after the police search. Trepper caught a glimpse of Makarov in another room. Without waiting to be questioned, he took out official documents which identified him as Monsieur Jean Gilbert, a businessman with connections to the Todt Organisation and said he was scouring the area for scrap metal. He knew that there was an abandoned garage on the opposite side of the street, and he claimed to have come to the house to see if anyone could tell him who owned it. Anyone getting in the way of his official business, he said, would have to answer to higher authority. After the policeman had made a quick call to Piepe, Trepper was back on the street and on his way. Trepper must have made a very great impression on the guards because normally in these circumstances, everybody who had any connection at all to a suspected building would be arrested.

Other members of the group were warned about what had happened and it was assumed that anyone taken prisoner would almost certainly talk under torture. Gurevich frantically made arrangements with Rajchmann to have his mistress, Margarete Barcza and her son, Rene, sent to France. Piepe still didn't know Gurevich's identity so he had time to wind up his interest in Simexco, on the pretext that he wanted to avoid internment as a South American national now that Germany was at war with the United States, and he was able to cash in his investment. He followed Barcza to France sometime in mid-December along with Springer. The Brussels network was in tatters.

Piepe now went after the other two transmitters still operating but they had been closed down. Informants told him that although some agents had fled to Marseilles and Nice couriers were still active between the French capital and Simexco. In Paris, Trepper was left with no direct communication to Moscow since Soviet Embassy staff had taken their transmitters with them when they left. Moscow instructed him to re-establish the Brussels link as a matter of urgency. At the end of March 1942 he was instructed to arrange a meeting at the Schneider safehouse with Yefremov, still living under cover as Eric Jernstroem.

Trepper had hitherto been unaware of Yefremov's very existence in Belgium and when he made enquiries about him, he was not reassured. Yefremov, he was told, had peddled gossip he had picked up in nightclubs frequented by the Wehrmacht and concocted elaborate intelligence reports 'based largely on his own imagination'. Moscow told Trepper to give 100,000 Belgian francs to Yefremov and hand over to him what was left of the Brussels network. Trepper was not happy about putting his veterans Wenzel, Izbutski and Rajchmann in the hands of someone whose qualifications were 'a three-month course at the intelligence school'.[27] None of the Brussels old guard were enthusiastic about the idea either but 'Professor' Wenzel was ordered to get the transmitters up and running again in view of the desperate need to send intelligence being couriered in from the Schulze-Boysen group in Germany. The trouble was that Piepe's mobile units were all over Brussels each night scanning for signals and Wenzel could not start transmissions again until secure arrangements were made and that would take time. Through Belgian Police Inspector Charles Mathieu, the Gestapo soon became aware of a clandestine group in Brussels but had no clues about its location and were not certain that it has any connection to Moscow.

Meanwhile, Trepper's only option was to use an auxiliary link in Paris that was technically reserved specifically for use only by the PCF. The GRU were seriously concerned because their links with the PCF were extremely sensitive and should on no account be compromised. Trepper had serious concerns about Gurevich whom he suspected of having lost his nerve after the Rue des Atrébates incident. Leaving him in play in Paris would never do so Trepper arranged for him to go south to Marselles in the unoccupied Vichy zone where Jules Jaspar had already relocated to. Together they could set up a branch of Simex where there was less of a German presence.

With all Brussels transmitters off the air, Piepe was getting a lot of criticism for having jumped in too quick to silence the Rue des Atrébates station especially given evidence that the spy network was active inside Germany itself. Better by far, his critics said, would have been to keep the location under surveillance to identify all who went there and spring the trap when the catch was much bigger. Stung by the rebukes, Piepe called in experts and sent men to collect up all the coded messages that had been intercepted during the previous six months. The trouble was that few survived. Most had been binned or lost but his men managed to rescue a few hundred which was nowhere near enough for his codebreakers to make much headway breaking the cipher. It seemed as if the trail had gone completely cold but there was one clue.

The Germans had found in the fireplace of the Rue des Atrébates house a charred piece of paper covered with numbers; it was obviously an enciphering worksheet and miraculously it had been preserved. It was known that such encoding grids were always used with reference to a publication that is available at both ends of the communication channel and one that was not readily available to the general public.

Decoding was a laborious and painstaking job. When a few words had been decoded, it was necessary to find exactly where those words appeared in the book. Sometimes they did not appear at all. SS Hauptsturmführer Karl Giering had centred his *Funkspiel* efforts on

Breendonk prison, halfway between Brussels and Antwerp. The key to success was breaking the Soviet encryption codes. The encryptors used different reference books, which served as enciphering keys, known as 'Talmud'. Several French books were employed, Balzac's *The Thirty-Year-Old Woman*, Léon Daudet's *When My Father Lived*, Prosper Mérimée's *Colomba*, Antoine Saint-Exupéry's *Terre des hommes* and Guy de Téramond's *Le Miracle of Professor Wolmar* none of which had been printed in any great quantity and were quite rare. Trepper had already complained to Moscow about having to use a code that had been operational unchanged since 1935. When he was not taken, he decided to change it himself in 1940 and adopted a new book, *Quand vivait mon père*, by Léon Daudet. It is a measure of just how cavalier Moscow was concerning agent security by losing their copy of this book and failing to decode over forty of Trepper's telegrams before telling him. He was forced to fall back on the old cipher after that. Then when Moscow arranged for a new cipher in June 1941 for use by the André network, Trepper was told to pass it on to the Belgians so that they could use it also but he claims to have refused to do so. Nevertheless, the whole GRU espionage operation in Western Europe was riddled with examples of different networks using the same ciphers which made life a lot easier for the Gestapo when they eventually broke the codes.

German cryptanalysts got to work on deciphering the code and deduced that the numbers related to part of a sentence in French that seemed more like a fragment of text containing the word 'proctor'. The overlay of characters on the recovered page indicated that decryption was taking place in the house at the time of the raid which means that the publication must also have been in the house at the time but when Piepe went back to look for possible sources a few days after the raid he found it deserted. No police guard had been left. If there ever had been a book or magazine that had been used in the coding and decoding process it was no longer there.

Nothing daunted, Piepe questioned Arnould who remembered that there had been a number of books lying around whenever Kamy was coding. She recalled the names of some of them. Copies of all but one were found in Brussels bookshops but scrutiny of the texts did not produce the word or name 'proctor' anywhere between the covers. The missing volume was Téramond's 286-page science-fiction novel, *Le Miracle du professeur Wolmar*. It had never actually been published for sale and had been given away as a supplement for subscribers to a book club. Piepe sensed that this was the book he was looking for. After a wide search, a copy was eventually found in a Parisian second-hand bookshop on 17 May 1942 and revealed that the special word did in fact appear in there. The Téramond key could now be used to work out the rest of the code and Piepe began to unlock all the existing messages but first he was introduced to his new boss, the 'tall, thin, cadaverous looking' Karl Giering and his right-hand man, the 'short, plump' Willy Berg 'whose strong hands could hit hard'.[28] Clearly Heydrich felt that the Abwehr component of Sonderkommando Rote Kapelle did not have the stomach for the kind of investigations that were now required to root out this 'cancer' of Soviet espionage that was growing in the Reich. Giering was a member of Amt IV, Abteilung II of the RSHA and had spent the past half dozen years hounding communists on behalf of the Nazis. Hitler, himself, was making more frequent references to the Soviet intelligence network and, no doubt, looking for more scapegoats to blame for the Wehrmacht's increasing military setbacks on the Eastern Front.

The existence of Soviet informers so close to the beating heart of the German military establishment coming soon after the assassination of Heydrich on 4 June 1942 in Prague sent shockwaves through Berlin.[29] It took the teams until July 1942 to actually decipher a single whole message and it landed on Giering's desk like a bombshell. Dated 10 October 1941, it was the message containing the addresses of three members of the Berlin group working under Harro Schulze-Boysen, Arvid Harnack and Greta Kuckhoff.

KLS from RTX. 1010. 1725. 99 wds qbt.b
from the director to Kent, Personal

Immediately go to Berlin to the three addresses indicated and determine the causes of the radio link failures. Stop. If interruption occurs again, undertake transmissions personally. Stop. Work [of] three Berlin groups and transmission of information of vital importance. Addresses: Neuwestend, Altenburger Allee 19, third right. Coro – Charlottenburg, Frederickstrasse 26a, Second left. Wolf. Friedenau, Kaiserstrasse 18, fourth left. Bauer. Send 'Eulenspiegel' back here. Password: Director. Stop. Report progress before October 20. New plan, repeat new, in force for three stations. Qtb ar. KLS from RTX.[30]

Meanwhile, Izbutski hid a reserve transmitter and entrusted it to Rajchmann who, in turn, hid it at 65 Avenue des Tilleuls in Uccle, the home of his friend, Inspector Charles Mathieu. Rajchmann had come into contact with Mathieu during an incident concerning false identity papers at some time in 1940 when Mathieu had hinted that he belonged to the Belgian Resistance but, in fact, he was a Gestapo informer.

In early June 1942, Grossvogel returned to Brussels to hand over 3 million Belgian francs to the Yefremov to finance his network there but the Gestapo were starting to put the pieces of the Rote Kapelle puzzle together. It was the French police who followed the clues in Vichy because the Sonderkommando did not have the facilities or legal authority to do so. The first important lead came on 9 June after Hersch and Miriam (Myra) Sokol were arrested with their transmitter in Maisons-Laffitte. Subsequent surveillance of the property led to the questioning of a man who turned up asking for the Sokols. When the house agent who had handled the rental, was given a description of the man, he was identified as someone who had made numerous enquiries about various empty properties and had left a contact address in Brussels. It was the offices of the Roi du Caoutchouc where several arrests had already been made as a result of the Rue des Atrébates raid.

By mid-June at least one of the Brussels transmitters was back on the air and was operating at full capacity all through the night trying to make up for lost time. Moscow controllers pressured the operators to ignored security. For the GRU, the acquisition of intelligence was far more important than the safety of its agents. Piepe was sparked back into life. He soon located the source of transmissions to be in the Laeken district. It was close to an electric rail line which might have shielded it had the Funkabwehr technicians not continued to improve their equipment. Their more powerful detectors were now able to filter out even loud background 'noise' and homed in on a property at 12 Rue de Namur, occupied by Germaine Schneider's brother-in-law a cobbler, Jean Janssens, who because of his trade, had been incorrectly identified in accounts of the incident as Kurt Schumacher.[31] Then, in the early hours of 30 June 1942, Piepe raided it. Janssens tried to delay Piepe by saying that Germaine was upstairs conducting an illicit love affair with another man. On hearing the commotion, Schneider stripped off her clothes and jumped into bed where Piepe found her. He was evidently embarrassed and confused because he allowed her to dress and leave the house. Only then did he realise that there was an attic where his men found a transmitter, still warm, and a bundle of documents in German but no 'pianist'. He had fled through a dormer window and when police pursued him over rooftops, he fired at them but Piepe forbade his men to fire back; he wanted the fugitive alive. Eventually he was cornered in a nearby house and taken into custody.[32]

Wenzel, using the name Albert Verhoeven, was caught *in flagrante* along with two messages that were awaiting encryption. Piepe was staggered to find that the uncoded messages included details about *Unternehmen Blau* (Case Blue), the Wehrmacht plan to launch a major assault in the direction of Stalingrad. Germaine Schneider fled to Paris days later where she reported the news of Wenzel's arrest to Trepper. Schneider would later be interned by the French in Lyons. Sent to Ravensbrück concentration camp she was liberated by the Red Army at the end of the war but by then she was gravely ill with cancer. She died in a sanitorium in Zurich six months later.

Wenzel was quickly broken through torture and gave up details of the codes he used and the identities of his collaborators. When applied to transmissions previously intercepted, the decoded messages began to show the extent of the network's reach. Warned by Trepper about Wenzel's arrest, Yefremov asked Rajchmann to provide him with new identity cards as a matter of urgency, one for him and another for Trepper.

In the meantime, using the name, Hoffmann, Yefremov took shelter at 25 Rue Alfred Orban in the house of Ernst Bomerson, a friend of Franz Schneider where he patiently awaited his new papers from Rajchmann, but Rajchmann had been under Gestapo surveillance for some time owing to his connection with Mathieu. Trepper had repeatedly warned Rajchmann to steer clear of Mathieu but his warnings had gone unheeded. Rajchmann made a new passport and gave it to Mathieu to pass on to Yefremov but it ended up with Piepe allowing his agents to identify Yefremov and arrest him as he made his way to a meeting with Mathieu, ostensibly to receive the documents, on 22 July 1942. This meant that the arrest could take place without Yefremov's fellow agents knowing about it and without compromising Mathieu's cover.

The arrest of Yefremov was particularly damaging because it revealed his connection with Simex and Simexco which were henceforth put under close surveillance. Piepe was astounded to discover that Simexco had offices in the same building as his unit and when he saw Yefremov he exclaimed 'My God, I've met him on the stairs, and I've even tipped my hat to him'.[33] In all more than thirty people were arrested as a result of information Yefremov provided.[34] In some cases innocent family members of those he had betrayed were executed according to the Nazi code of *Sippenhaft*.

Throughout the whole of 1941 Trepper had tried to establish a wireless network in France. He had acquired a transmitter and had call-signs and codes to hand but found himself without a 'pianist' after Wenzel, who was supposed to leave for Paris the next day, was arrested in Brussels on 12 December 1941. So, by the spring of 1942, Trepper's work was essentially limited to ensuring the successful operation of Simexco, run by Gurevich in Brussels and Simex in

Paris where it thrived thanks to its business manager Maria Likhonin who maintained its links with the Todt Organisation. Despite its reputation as a major source of intelligence through its contacts with German industry and the convenience of an agent transport (couriers) between Paris and Brussels, Simex's importance to the Rote Kapelle was primarily its financial contribution to its operations. Central to the Brussels-Paris link was Simone Margarete Pheter, administrative secretary of the Belgian Chamber of Commerce in Paris who was very close to Grossvogel. Very intelligent and very bright, Pheter had a very calm demeanor and a laughing, friendly manner.[35] Pheter, together with Suzanne Spaak, however, was linked with another organisation run by Pastor Paul Vergara, director of the La Clairière social center, that sheltered Jewish children who had managed to escape the Vel' d'Hiv roundup of Jewish families on 16–17 July 1942. Surveillance of Pheter resulting from her association with Vergara would lead the Sonderkommando to the door of Simex. She would be arrested on 29 November 1942 and executed by guillotine on 20 August 1943.

When the Sokols were arrested in April 1942, the lines from Paris to Himmler's Reich Security Main Office in Berlin buzzed with intensity. The link between the Brussels and Paris radio transmission stations had been uncovered. Giering and Berg were soon on their way to the French capital with a task force of Sonderkommandos with Piepe having been left behind in Brussels. Elements within the French police known to have strong anti-communist views were taken into Giering's confidence and instructed to send special agents in to penetrate the French Resistance groups and keep a lookout for links to Trepper and Grossvogel. This was at a time when Sonderkommando operations were having marked success against these groups. By the end of September 1942 Trepper and Grossvogel were known to the men of Special Brigade No. 1 but there whereabouts was unknown. The French Resistance was beginning to regret getting mixed up with the Rote Kapelle network.

Investigations confirmed that Simex had contacts in Paris but some intercepted signals went as far afield as Prague. The operation was proving to be much bigger than expected using Polish, Czechs, Bulgarian and Swiss agents all under the control of the GRU but rather than close Simex down, Giering allowed it to continue under close observation hoping to discover the full extent of the operation. He instructed Yefremov, who was now in play as a Gestapo stooge, to get in touch with Franz Schneider and try to discover the whereabouts of his wife Germaine who had so cleverly slipped through their fingers on 30 June 1942 when Wenzel was arrested at Rue de Namur. That was an embarrassment that Giering was anxious to wipe from the record.

The discovery of the Sokol transmitter clearly indicated that Trepper's French network had failed to appreciate the level of sophistication achieved in Paris by the Funkabwehr who had brought in their small portable detectors and so could move around the city without arousing suspicion. The shortage of transmission sites had also contributed to the capture since the Sokols were obliged to remain in one location far too long and remained on air much longer than it was wise to do so. For the Germans, it had given their investigations a significant boost by presenting them with documents allowing them to reconstruct large parts of the Rote Kapelle network. So much so that by the end of September they had set up surveillance on the home of the man they knew as Gilbert but Trepper had abandoned his Rue Fortuny residence and moved into a villa rented by Georgie de Winter at 27 Route de la Borde, in Le Vésinet. Grossvogel had also decamped and gone to live in Avenue Wagram.

The Gestapo and their French allies had discovered a great deal about Simex and Simexco but before making a move they wanted to find out the full extent of the network. Feeling the heat, Trepper wanted Gurevich to relocate to Algeria. He even sent false papers and travel documents but Gurevich resisted fearing that it was a precursor to his recall to Moscow where he would have to answer for the failure of the Brussels operation. At the end of October the net began to close in on the Marseilles group. The only real evidence that the head of the Gestapo in France, SS-Sturmbannführer Karl Bömelburg, had to work with was the photo found at Rue des Atrébates but that did not help to locate Gurevich. There were clues, however. Investigations carried out in Brussels had revealed that Gurevich was renowned in the city's restaurants for his prodigious appetite and Barcza was an eccentric dresser, often being seen in a top hat. It need hardly be said that neither of these distinguishing features were conducive to a clandestine existence. Temptation and ego had not loosened their grip. Waiters in the better restaurants of Marseilles had noticed them and soon they were on Bömelburg's radar.

On 9 November 1942, at around 01.00 hours and under the utmost secrecy, French police in civilian clothes broke into Gurevich's apartment and arrested him and Barcza. They were taken by car to the Boulevard d'Athènes and the next day taken separately to Paris where they were held at the Sûreté, Rue des Saussaies. The rest of the Marseilles network was allowed to operate, although it was generally ineffective, so that the arrests would go undetected by other members for a while at least. Jaspar and another Simex associate, Marguerite Marivet, would not be taken for another three weeks.

Three days later Gurevich and Barcza were in Breendonk and fully aware of their situation. Neither of them was at all prepared to stand up to interrogation. They did not know how far Bömelburg's investigation had gone. When told that others in their organisation had been detained, they had no way of knowing if it was true. With no formal training to withstand close questioning, they had no idea what to say to protect themselves and others. Gurevich starts by indignantly claiming Uruguayan nationality and refusing to admit any involvement with the Rote Kapelle but his testimony is quickly refuted when he is brought face to face with other detainees such as Izbutski, broken by torture, who identify him as their former leader. He was read the confessions of Makarov and Peper and shown copies of decoded telegrams written in his own handwriting. He admitted that he was the Soviet agent known to his colleagues as Kent and that his real name was Sokolov, without revealing that it was really Gurevich.

Gurevich admitted to having had contact with Harro Schulze-Boysen who at that time was facing trial in Berlin. Faced with evidence of more than sixty telegrams signed 'Kent', Gurevich admitted that the German contacts had provided him with the exact coordinates of Hitler's *Wolfsschanze* headquarters in the Forest of Gierloz in Poland. The level of detail in the questions Gurevich was now facing convinced him that the Germans had one or more leading Rote Kapelle agents in custody and were getting significant amounts of information from them. It was clear to him that Trepper's whole network was being systematically broken up by the Germans so he made a calculated decision to offer his cooperation and hoped that might give him scope to manage the intensity of interrogations and allow him to some extent, to control the amount of information he would have to divulge.

There now followed an incident that convinced the Germans that it was time to step up the pressure on Simex and roll up the whole Soviet network that was operating under its cover. A man that Georgie de Winter referred only as 'Edgar', who was most likely Trepper, had been entrusted with 'two or three million worth of industrial diamonds' by a friend who had fled to America. That seems unlikely and the diamonds were probably part of Trepper's war chest that he now wanted to convert into ready cash and most likely had originated in the Soviet Union which was one of the world's largest producers of industrial diamonds and had been smuggled in through the Brussels diamond trade. He wanted to sell them on the black market and asked Maria Likhonin to act as a go-between with relevant German authorities who might be interested in buying the diamonds. After Likhonin had made contact with someone in the Todt Organisation, Trepper changed his mind when he realised the importance of industrial diamonds in the armaments industry where they were used to make precision cutting machines and tried to call off the deal.

When Bömelburg learned from Todt that they had been offered the diamonds and then told they were no longer for sale, he made the connection to Simex and indicated that they should get back to Likhonin and try to resurrect the deal. Likhonin was probably never keen to try to sell the diamonds in the first place but got quite nervous with the renewed level of interest. She went to Brussels which is where the diamonds were and was shocked to learn that the Gestapo had identified Trepper and Grossvogel as persons of interest and were actively looking for them. Bömelburg asked Likhonin to send someone to Brussels with authority to close the deal. The person they recommended was a man called Jean Gilbert. This indicated to Trepper that the great game was almost up but rather than alert his agents and give them time to go into hiding, he did nothing.

Bömelburg, meanwhile, rattled Simex's cage with increased surveillance, not always covert, and arrested the Simex executives, Alfred Corbin and Waldemar Keller on 9 September along with Suzanne Juliette Cointe and Juliette Mignon. Corbin's wife, daughter Denise and brother were also taken into custody a week later and put in Fresnes Prison to rack up the pressure on Corbin who was thought to be the most likely to crack and the one who might divulge the most information. Trepper later claimed that it was Corbin who gave Bömelburg the information he needed to find him but there is no corroborating evidence to back that up.[36] The relationship between the two men had become strained prior to Corbin's arrest. Trepper had developed a quiet contempt for Corbin, a businessman he referred to as a 'trader' who worked for the Soviet network but whose bourgeois sensibilities really left no room for communist sympathies.

The raid on Simex premises on 20 November produced little of any use in tracking down members of the spy network. Staff members were arrested nevertheless and thrown into Fresnes but none could reveal very much information about 'Monsieur Gilbert'. Trepper had been careful to ensure that he kept a discrete distance from the everyday activities of Simex. Some employees, such as Juliette Mignon, were soon allowed to go free in the hope that they might lead Giering's men to Trepper and Grossvogel. These two men, meanwhile, met with Simone Pheter at the Belgian Chamber of Commerce in Paris. Germaine Draily, a close friend of Jeanne Grossvogel, was also there having just arrived from Brussels. Jeanne Grossvogel was anxious to warn her husband that Rajchmann had just been arrested. Draily said that she had gone straight to the Simex offices where she was told by someone who 'smells of the Gestapo' that the offices were closed. Trepper seemed unconcerned by this news and, clearly unaware of the extent to which Rajchmann and Gruber had helped Bömelburg to penetrate his organisation, tried to calm everyone down.[37] Nevertheless, Pheter was sent to Brussels to tell Nazarin Draily to bring his family to Paris without delay but, like Trepper, he chose not to fully appreciate the dangers and ignored the advice with the result that he was arrested by the Gestapo on 22 November along with Jeanne Grossvogel and other shareholders of Simexco.

Trepper was now faced with the gravity of the situation and considered what could be done to prevent further damage and also what might be done to help those already taken. The worst thing now would be for him to be arrested as well because if he is exposed as an officer of the GRU all the pieces of the jigsaw would come together and the fate of all those in custody or who would soon be guests of the Gestapo would be sealed. At a crash meeting on 23 November at Katz's house in Verrières-le-Buisson, he, Trepper and Grossvogel agreed that it was close to time for issuing a '*sauve qui peut*' signal and scatter the remnants of the organisation to the four winds but first they would wait a few days to see if those in custody might be released. Georgie de Winter found Trepper very depressed and began to worry about him when he failed to turn up for two rendezvous in a restaurant near Rue La Fontaine. Trepper prepared to flee to a safehouse in Royat near Clermont-Ferrand where he might still be of use to the GRU but first he had a minor issue to attend to. It was not urgent and could well have waited for a less perilous moment but either vanity or carelessness caused him to go visit Dr Albert Maleplate, his dentist, at 13 Rue de Rivoli to have two gold crowns fitted.

Trepper later said that Maleplate had been recommended to him earlier in the year by Marie-Louise Corbin and it was probably her or her husband who had given up that information to their interrogators in Fresnes thinking that it was of little value to them. Bömelburg sent men to question Maleplate and found an appointment in his diary for a man galled Gilbert on 25 November. It was a curious lapse of security on Trepper's part which is all the more interesting when he was seen to start cooperating with the Germans almost immediately after his arrest. There is a temptation to think that he deliberately allowed himself to be taken perhaps because he believed that his arrest was inevitable with so many of his agents now in custody. He had possibly calculated that he would have more chance of survival by making himself useful to the Gestapo but in such a way that he could control the agenda and spin a tale that they could accept at the same time as concealing as much as possible. Whatever the truth of this, it was clear at the time and has been proved to be the case subsequently that Trepper was a survivor. He would go on to survive imprisonment and avoid execution by the Soviets after the war and then emigrate to Israel where he died in 1982.

Giving evidence to the British in 1949, one of Trepper's German interrogators immediately after the arrest, Karl Heinrich Gagl, said that Trepper began by congratulating his captors on their success and indicated that he was eager to cooperate with them.[38] It is clear from Gagl's testimony that he gained a very favourable impression of Trepper as a 'true great leader', and a man 'as charismatic as he is calm'.[39] Answering to the Soviets on 27 August 1945, Trepper said that when he was arrested by the Gestapo he had created a favourable impression by confessing to being a GRU agent and named some others. He told the Germans that he had been forced to work for the Soviet under duress and he praised the power and technical strength of the German army. Giering checked Trepper's statements against the known facts and found a convincing correspondence.[40]

There is a 280-page dossier of Gestapo interviews, all pages signed by Trepper, confirming the extent of his cooperation.[41] Trepper's plan was to try and protect his family back in Moscow by convincing his GRU bosses that the closure of Simex and Simexco was nothing to do with anything he had done and that their agents were still operational. To the Germans, he portrayed himself as the central player in the whole Rote Kapelle operation and in so doing made himself indispensable to the Gestapo's *Funkspiel* efforts thereby ensuring his survival. At the same time, he hoped to manipulate the signals going back to Moscow in such a way as to indicate to his Soviet handlers that he had not, in fact, gone over to the enemy and was still playing the 'great game' on their behalf. For this to work it was essential that other central figures, especially the 'pianists' who were the ones who made the actual contacts with Moscow, were prevented from informing the GRU that their prize assets were being rounded up. The problem was that many of them were still at large. Try as they may, the men of BS1 still could not locate Katz or Grossvogel.

Two addresses Trepper had given the Germans had failed to turn up Grossvogel so on 26 November, he arranged with his captors to send a message to Grossvogel through an intermediary, Modeste Erlik, a young schoolteacher and friend of Katz in the Parisian Young

Communists, telling him to break off all contact with Moscow and to surreptitiously warn him not to make any contact with Pheter whom he now knew to be under Gestapo surveillance.

Katz, meanwhile, was on his way to the Château de Billeron in Cher with his 18-month-old son Jean-Claude while his wife, Cécile (Seskia), was still in a clinic at 219 Rue Vercingétorix in the 14th arrondissement where she had just given birth to their daughter, Annette. Katz wrote a letter to Jean-Claude hoping that he would be able to read it when he grew up.

> On 25 November 1942 I took you to Paris to stay with a friend. You slept with me in the same bed. It was very cold. I held you close to me to give you all my warmth. The next morning, I gave you something to eat and drink and took you to the Gare de Lyon. I think it was the saddest moment of my whole life. I hope that you will be as upright and honest as your mother, very courageous and virile, modest and good, and that you will love me as much as I love you.[42]

In the commune of Lugny-Champagne in the Cher, Jean-Claude was taken care of by Anna Maximovitch who would later be sentenced to death in Paris and executed in Berlin-Plötzensee on 20 August 1943.

De Winter had met Katz in something of a panic but Katz tried to calm her and said that Trepper had sent a message to him saying that he was ill and would not be around for a few days. Two days later, Simone Pheter was arrested and forced to divulge the whereabouts of Grossvogel who was picked up in front of the restaurant La Courcelles, on Boulevard de Courcelle where Pheter had previously arranged a rendezvous with him. Franz Schneider was the next one to be taken, this time in Brussels where he was subjected to torture in Breendonk. Pheter's friend Renée Alice Barro came across her in Saint-Gilles Prison looking 'terribly thin and sad'. Barro said that Pheter took her in her arms and began to cry, saying: 'It's my fault, this is where I've led you.' Pheter, with head shaved and hands tied behind her back was executed by guillotine on 20 August 1942 in Plötzensee along with seven other women including Anna Maximovitch, Rita Arnould and Marguerite Marivet.[43]

In his memoirs, Trepper accused Otto Schumacher of betraying Katz but one of his interrogators, Heinz Pannwitz, claimed that it was Trepper who sent a message inviting Katz to a rendezvous at Erlik's home at 14 Square Port-Royal, Rue de La Santé, in the 13th arrondissement, on 2 December where he was arrested by the Gestapo.[44] Surviving Gestapo files make it clear that, in fact, Trepper denounced the great majority of the Parisian group, almost all of the Lyon group and most of the executives of Simexco and Simex. Much of what he said was, in fact, put forward as evidence for the prosecution of those he had betrayed in Berlin trials. He may not have been aware of the trials but it was surely disingenuous of him to inquire of his Soviet hosts in January 1945 about the whereabouts of Grossvogel, Makarov, Robinson and Sokolov when there were 200 pages and 40,000 words of his confessions in Gestapo files for February 1943.[45] A few weeks later when interrogations continued after a few weeks pause, all the Gestapo were interested in was Trepper's life story, his recruitment by the GRU and anything he could tell them about the workings of Soviet intelligence. They clearly felt that they had exhausted his supply of information and it must have been clear to Trepper at that time that what amounted to little more than 'fireside chats' indicated that the Gestapo had rounded up his whole network.

As a result of his denunciations, many French members of Trepper's network were arrested, including Robert Giraud and Jeanne Ponsaint, each one a new source of information for Bömelburg allowing him to widen his search. Giraud was taken from his home in Rue de Sablonville while his wife Lucie was out shopping. She returned to find the street cordoned off and, fearing the worst, fled the scene. Robert would be executed by guillotine on 28 July 1943 but Lucie survived the war and died in the year 2000 in a rest home in southern Paris. There were still enough of his contacts still out there to make Trepper uneasy about what his GRU bosses in Moscow knew or did not know or guessed. He was wise to worry because on 22 December, unbeknown to him, Moscow got a message saying that Trepper and one of his lieutenants had not been seen for a couple of weeks. His misgivings compelled Trepper to find a way of reassuring Moscow that all was well and that any problems he was experiencing were minor ones.

The Germans now saw no value in allowing any of the network to remain at liberty. In a coordinated effort across Paris and Brussels, there were wide-ranging arrests including those of Charles Draily who was the head of Simex, Anna and Basile Maximovitch and Isidore Springer. Giering, who conducted Trepper's interviews, found him very talkative and as a result was able to draw up charts of the structure of Simex and Simexco. His value to the Germans was such that Trepper was transferred from Fresnes to the premises of the Sonderkommando, 11 Rue des Saussaies, a building belonging to the Ministry of the Interior which housed the German Security Police in Paris. Giering issued orders that 'Any possibility of escape, suicide attempt or any other attempt by the prisoner to enter into contact with the outside world must be prevented under all circumstances.'[46] At every turn, the testimony of Trepper in Paris and Gurevich in Berlin were scrutinised for discrepancies. On more than one occasion Gurevich was incensed by the way that Trepper's version of events put him in an unfavourable light.

After the war, Trepper played down any responsibility he might have had for betraying his fellow spies but GRU archives contain a detailed description of the way in which he gave up his agents one after the other.[47] Having denied any responsibility for betraying Basile and Anna Maximovitch he was upbraided by Soviet interrogators in November 1946, who had been particularly aggrieved at the loss of two NKVD agents. Demanding that he stop lying to them, they read to him from a captured German document based on his depositions to the Gestapo, dated 2 December 1942. Trepper was forced to admit that he had given their names but was adamant that he had not divulged their addresses. That was somewhat disingenuous given that he had denounced other members of his network, such as Hillel Katz, who knew perfectly well where they lived. Backed into a corner, Trepper now changed tack tried to curry favour by saying that the arrest of the Maximovitchs would lead the Gestapo to their intelligence sources in the émigré white Russian community. Although these people such as General von Pfeiffer, chairman of the Franco-German armistice commission, were aiding the Rote Kapelle they were nonetheless anti-communists and enemies of the Soviet Union.

The Germans began their radio game at the end of December 1942 and seemed to convince Moscow that all was well. GRU archives contain a telegram dated 26 December 1942 confirming that direct connection with Trepper was established. The fact that they had not heard from him for twenty-six days previous to this apparently seems not to have disturbed them too much. However, they made, sometimes less than convincing, excuses to justify their faith which suggests that doubts had started creeping in.

By the end of 1942, Giering was sure that he had found and neutralised all of Trepper's radios but he still did not know much about Robinson's operations. Questioned about Robinson, Trepper told Giering that 'Harry' was about 50 years old, of sickly appearance and had a limp due to a rheumatic condition. With no photographs to go on, it was all the Germans had to locate Robinson but Trepper further told Giering about certain places where Robinson usually made rendezvous with his agents. Trepper also collaborated with Giering to entrap Robinson although he would later insist that it had been Franz

Schneider who, under torture, had divulged the name of Merdado Griotto, a close friend of Robinson, and it was through the Italian that Robinson was caught.

What actually happened was that Malvina Gruber had been sent to Brussels, under German supervision, to bring Rajchmann back with her to Paris. Gruber had been arrested in October a few days after Rajchmann had been taken. Both had been subject to torture or threats of torture and were now cooperating with their captors. In Paris, Rajchmann was given a note written by Trepper and told to take it to the Griotto's flat on 20 December. The note asked Robinson to meet Rajchmann, a man whom he had never met, at 14.30 hours on the following day at the Ségur metro station. By now Robinson was on high alert. He was aware that Trepper had dropped out of circulation but did not know much more about his current whereabouts so went to the flat of Cécile Katz for help. He asked her to go to the proposed rendezvous early and see if she could identify the man he was supposed to meet. She did so and recognised Rajchmann. Unaware that Rajchmann had been compromised she reassured Robinson who now went to keep the rendezvous.

In Rue Pérignon, some 30 metres away from where Rajchmann stood was a car facing away from the metro station. Inside the car observing the scene through the rearview mirror was Trepper along with two Gestapo officers. He confirmed that the man walking past the entrance was Robinson who had continued to walk on. It was standard procedure when he had a meeting for both participants to walk past each other without acknowledgement so that each could scan for followers and then return minutes later. As Robinson turned into a side street to come round again to the station entrance a second car pulled up next to him. Gestapo men jumped out and grabbed him. In his memoirs, Trepper claimed that he had hoped to warn Robinson 'by making a noise of some kind'. 'I watched Harry's arrest', he wrote, '[but] without being able to do anything about it'.[48] When he was brought into Gestapo headquarters at Rue des Saussaies Robinson saw the Griottos who had been arrested earlier in the day. Nina Griotto later described how Robinson was supported under the arms, unable to stand, with his face all bruised. The guards let him go and he fell in a heap on the floor in front of her. This is what awaits your husband, the Germans told her, if she did not tell them all she knew about Robinson.

The most important thing for Giering now was to show his prisoners on the streets of Paris to dispel rumours of their arrest. Successful implementation of the *Funkspiel* would, they believed, open a door for them right into the heart of the communist section of the French

Resistance movement. The most glaring omission from their arrest list was Germaine Schneider, an experienced W/T operative with her own code and someone particularly well versed in clandestine operations. They had already sent a signal to Moscow, supposedly from Trepper, implying that she had become an Abwehr agent to compromise any information that she might have been able to transmit during the previous few weeks.

Rajchmann, trawling Rote Kapelle 'letterboxes' under German supervision learned that Schneider was looking for a rendezvous with Trepper. Rajchmann contacted Schneider and said that this could be arranged through a man called Kurt Abraham, one of Giering's men. Schneider had been hiding at 49 Rue de la Chapelle, the home of her friend Marcelle Capré. When she came to the rendezvous on 13 January 1943, she was arrested.

Cécile Katz was hiding out with her new baby at the home of Arlette Humbert-Laroche, Otto Schumacher's mistress, where she had gone to try to find out what had happened to her husband and where she had stayed having nowhere else to go. When the couple were arrested at the Iéna metro station on 14 January, the police came to their flat to find Katz and the child both of whom were taken and sent to join her son Jean-Claude at the Château de Billeron where they were kept out of sight. Hillel had suffered weeks of torture and, after the latest blow of his wife's arrest, now agreed to play the radio game with Trepper. Grossvogel, meanwhile was resolutely refusing to divulge any information to the Gestapo even under extreme torture. When confronted with the threat that his wife and new-born child would be shot if he continued to resist, he was reputed to have replied 'Go on then and shoot them'.[49]

It was a critical time for Giering and his *Funkspiel* operation. Although he had ensured that his prisoners were allowed out on the street from time to time to give the impression that they were still free agents and information was still flowing from their radios through the ether to Moscow, the longer the deception continued, the more likely that Moscow would smell a rat. Archives which became available after the fall of the Soviet Union revealed a GRU report written in June 1943 analysing over 100 telegrams received by Moscow purporting to be from Trepper but in reality the product of *Funkspiel*. Over half contained nothing of any real value and only four were considered important with another seven categorised as being of moderate value.[50] Although Trepper claimed that Moscow had been alerted to Giering's deception by something he had managed to slip into one of his messages, there is no hint of this in the above report.

Giering found himself struggling with conflicting objectives. On the one hand, he wanted to stage a huge public trial of all those he had rounded up to embarrass the Soviet Union and enhance his own prestige but, at the same time, he needed the GRU to believe that their agents were still operational, which was necessary for the success of his *Funkspiel* operation. The trials would go ahead but behind closed doors.

On 8 March, the trial of Alfred Corbin and Waldemar Keller opened in the Roger & Gallet building, at 62–64 Rue du Faubourg-Saint-Honoré where they were subjected to an 'accelerated Luftwaffe procedure court martial'. Manfred Roeder prosecuted having already '[left] a trail of blood behind him. After obtaining the heads – he boasted – of about sixty members of the Berlin network, he [had gone] to Brussels with his judicial arrogance, sending the executioner a new cartload of convicts. Now he was in Paris to settle the accounts of the French network.'[51] Keller was given three years' hard labour but Corbin, emaciated, very pale, with almost total loss of voice, was condemned to execution by guillotine.

Then, in April, the Rote Kapelle prisoners were told that they had been pardoned and were being taken to work in Germany. They were taken from Fresnes to the Gare du Nord railway station in Paris and loaded into railcars with locked doors and windows. They had simple benches to sit on and given no food or water. The train went first to Brussels where it picked up more prisoners then continued to Berlin where it arrived on the morning of Sunday, 17 April 1943 when the prisoners were taken and chained up in a prison in Berlin-Alexanderplatz.

It is worth asking what exactly Giering was hoping to achieve. He had stopped the flow of clandestine intelligence by the arrests so the only extra benefit he could achieve through *Funkspiel* would be to misinform or misdirect. The Wehrmacht, however, had resolutely refused to give him any military intelligence that might be remotely useful to the Red Army over a timespan that included three major turning points in the war, Stalingrad, the second Battle of Kharkiv and the Battle of Kursk. It seems that his objective from this point was to manipulate the link with Moscow to infiltrate the French Resistance movement. Trepper agreed to arrange a meeting with Fernand Pauriol around 20 April near the Rueil-Malmaison station but Pauriol failed to show up.

The GRU in Moscow, it seems, was oblivious to the subterfuge being played on it but Giering was in no position to enjoy his achievement. He was by now seriously ill with cancer and on the verge of being replaced. This was not welcome news to Trepper who felt that he had established an amicable working relationship with his jailer and hoped that it would stand him in good stead for the future, whatever that might bring. Trepper was further discomforted by the arrival of Gurevich at Rue des Saussaies in mid-April. Gurevich had been in Gestapo custody for several months which would have been a surprise for the GRU who had promoted him to captain at the end of March.

In a bid to put psychological pressure on both men, Giering had them placed in adjoining cells. The two men responded to their proximity by ignoring each other. It was clear to both men that each had been closely interrogated about the activities of the other. Gurevich, in particular, was repeatedly told that Trepper had been denouncing him to Moscow as a traitor in his *Funkspiel* communications but that he would be given a privileged status while in captivity, similar to that enjoyed by Trepper, if he agreed to cooperate in similar fashion by also engaging in *Funkspiel*. This was designed to appeal to Gurevich's vanity which had been severely bruised by seeing how much better Trepper was being treated in Rue des Saussaies. Karl Heinrich Gagl, an interpreter at Gestapo headquarters later said that Gurevich was incensed by seeing Trepper 'always clean-shaven and [wearing] becoming suits' often being allowed out to take walks in Paris, albeit accompanied by a discrete police escort and evidently trusted more than he was.[52] Trepper had indeed told Giering a great deal about Gurevich. For instance, he told about Gurevich's involvement in the Spanish Civil War as a translator on a submarine, he told about his trips to Switzerland and, more seriously, about his missions to Germany at the Leipzig fair and to Dresden, where he deposited money intended for German illegal immigrants.

Before he left for Berlin, Giering began to see progress with his plan to infiltrate the French Resistance. On 6 May 1943, Gurevich received a request from Moscow to make contact with Waldemar Ozols, codename Zola. Ozols was a Latvian who had fought for Russia during the First World War and later took part in the Spanish Civil War where he held the rank of general in the International Brigades. In 1938 he had gone to Paris where he mixed in French intellectual while maintaining close relations with the NKVD. By 1943, he had become involved with Paul Legendre one of the leaders of the Marseille section of the Anglo-French Mithridate military intelligence network.

Trepper's main concern was that Gurevich might undermine his standing with the Germans at a time when it was becoming clear that Giering would not be in charge for much longer and he would have to develop a new relationship from scratch with Giering's interim replacement, Josef Heinrich Reiser. A secondary, but no less important, issue was Trepper's fear that if the *Funkspiel* operation collapsed, he would become surplus to Gestapo requirements and face the hangman or the guillotine. This prompted Trepper to make plans to try and contact Moscow directly, around 28 May, through Juliette Moussier, who worked at the Jacquin chocolate shop situated at 12 Rue Pernelle.

It seems that Gurevich had been elevated by Giering to run the *Funkspiel* operation and now that he had been instructed to make contact with Ozol, Trepper feared that he would use that link to pass information about Trepper's betrayals to Moscow through the French Resistance. The German military reversals at Stalingrad and Kharkiv on the Eastern Front had emboldened him into believing that the Red Army might prevail against the Wehrmacht and that his future might depend more on his relations with Moscow and less on those with Berlin. If indeed he ever did get back to Moscow there would also be the matter of putting forward his version of events before Gurevich could muddy the waters for him.

On 16 September 1943, Trepper evaded his German escort in a pharmacy near St Nazaire railway station. He met up with de Winter and hid at 27 Route de la Borde, in Le Vésinet. When the police issued a wanted notice with Trepper's picture they move to Rue de Beaujolais where Suzanne Spaak agreed to provided them with temporary accommodation, via the Jewish rescue network to which she belongs. On 28 September, they move again to La Maison Blanche boarding house at 15 Boulevard Carnot, in Bourg-la-Reine. When the police tracked them down de Winter was arrested in Bronville but Trepper got away and remained at large until 8 January when he fled from Paris to Moscow under the identity of Vladislas Ivanovitch, along with Alexander Foote, travelling as Alfred Feodorovitch Feodorovich Lapidus, and Sándor Radó, known as Ignati Iakovlevitch Koulicher.

Trepper was interrogated by GRU and held in custody until 1955. When he was released, he went to Warsaw with his wife and three sons under one of his aliases Leiba Domb. There he devoted himself to Jewish affairs getting elected to run the Yiddisher Kultur-Gezelshaftlekher Farband and also running its publishing house, Yiddish Bukh. In 1974, after much agitation, he was eventually granted permission to leave Poland and settle in Jerusalem where he died eight years later.

Chapter 2

URSULA KUCZYNSKI: THE ATOMIC SPY

very much a red-bloodied woman ... determined to live life to the full, have lovers and bear children, which she did in the most adverse of circumstances.[1]

At the end of the Second World War one of the greatest Soviet female secret agents of the twentieth century was living quietly with her husband and three children in a stone farmhouse called The Firs in the small Cotswold village of Great Rollright. Known to her neighbours as Ursula Burton, this thin, elegant and friendly but reserved housewife had immersed herself in village life since arriving in 1940 and despite speaking with a distinct foreign accent, which might otherwise have singled her out for suspicion given that the country was at war, had settled comfortably and gained a reputation within the community for the quality of her baking. That particular skill was not something that she was lauded for in Moscow's headquarters of Red Army intelligence, however, where she was better known as Colonel Ursula Maria Kuczynski, codename Sonya. Here it was her fifteen-year career that had included operating espionage rings in China, Poland and Switzerland that would eventually see her twice awarded the highest Soviet military honour, the Order of the Red Banner. She always objected to being called a spy, which to her implied capitalist lackey, preferring instead the description *Kundschafter* intelligence operator, a much less pejorative term.[2]

Ursula had been born on 15 May 1907 to secular Polish-Jewish middle-class parents in Berlin both of whom had suffered a serious decline in status from their bourgeois origins but were still comfortably-off, nevertheless. The second of six children, her siblings were Jürgen (b. 1904), Brigitte (b. 1910), Barbara (b. 1913), Sabine (b. 1919) and Renate (b. 1923). Because of her small, pointed face and long nose, this 'gawky child, inquisitive and restless in a way her mother found perfectly exhausting' was given the family nickname of 'mouse'.[3] Resigned to her unflattering looks, Ursula wrote in her diary that she doubted that this ugly duckling would ever turn into a beautiful swan but that did not curb her enthusiasm for the opposite sex quite a few of whom were later to be beguiled by her 'powerful sexual allure'.[4]

Ursula's father, Robert, a strong supporter of the Social Democratic Party of Germany, was well respected and well connected within Berlin's left-wing intelligencia that included Karl Liebknecht, the artist Käthe Kollwitz, Walther Rathenau, and Albert Einstein. Her memories of the early post-war conditions in Berlin were of 'hunger, scarcity and widespread poverty of which she was, even as a child, acutely aware.'[5] All the time she was reading Maxim Gorky and Jack London and growing up within a domestic atmosphere of intellectual political radicalism and human rights advocacy that saw her, by the age of 16, joined up with the Kommunistischer Jugendverband Deutschlands, the Young Communist League taking part in marches and demonstrations. This brought her into conflict with the Weimar government who had narrowly avoided a nationwide civil war in Germany partly instigated by the new Bolshevik regime in Russia and had little tolerance for agitators on the streets. The growing influence of the Nazis in Berlin, which they saw as 'the reddest city after Moscow' was consolidated when Nazi propagandist Joseph Goebbels became his party's Gauleiter for Berlin in the autumn of 1926.[6] Both state police and nazi brown-shirted thugs were usually on hand to discourage illegal protests with violence if need be.

It was during a May Day parade of 1924 celebrating the Russia Revolution, in which she was taking part that Ursula witnessed first-hand the full force of state repression when the march was broken up by a police charge. Protestors were beaten and dragged off into trucks to face further maltreatment away from the public gaze. Ursula was thrown to the ground and struck by a police truncheon but made it to a doorway to recover before rejoining the chaos fired up with righteous fury at state brutality. Returning home that night with her battle scars, instead of sympathy, she was roundly berated for mixing with bad company. Her father knew where street violence could lead. He had seen Liebknecht and fellow revolutionary Rosa Luxemburg bludgeoned to death by Freikorps reactionaries and their bodies thrown into the river. His friend Rathenau who had become German foreign minister had been assassinated by ultra-nationalists after signing a treaty with the Soviet Union. He wanted to protect his daughter from such a fate at all costs but Ursula's determination to challenge what she saw as the iniquities and injustices of the capitalist regime remained undimmed.

Hoping to harness her love of literature and channel her enthusiasm in what he hoped was a positive direction, Robert found Ursula a position with the R.L. Prager Bookshop on Mittelstrasse. Her new employer, however, had no intention of allowing her to spend time reading. It was soon clear that this was not going to work especially as her brother Jürgen was, by this time, gaining a reputation as a published writer turning out left-wing political material. Sibling rivalry would never allow her to tolerate such a sublimation. Much more was required of her. She set up the Marxistische Arbeiterbibliothek (Workers' Marxist Library) in Berlin becoming its director and increased her activism by joining the Kommunistische Partei Deutschlands, the German Communist Party (KPD) which, under the leadership of Ernst Thälmann, was turning more and more to Moscow for support and inspiration. Here she learned to handle firearms. At the same time she met and fell in love with a young Jewish architect, Rudolf 'Rudi' Hamburger, despite his liberal and progressive political outlook falling some way short of her own radical views. It became something of a challenge to Ursula to convert Rudi to her way of thinking and, while she had a modicum of success, he baulked at signing up to membership of the party.

Ursula's frustration with Prager boiled over and she walked out to join the Jewish firm of Ullstein Verlag, publishers, as an archivist but when she began getting articles printed in the left-wing newspaper *Die Rote Fahne,* her new employers marked her down as a potential troublemaker. Unwilling to compromise, Ursula was forced out by Ullstein who worried that she might bring the company to the unwanted attention of the growing body of antisemitic authoritarian organisations such as the Nazis.

There seemed little scope in Berlin for either personal or professional advancement which prompted her to look across the Atlantic to where Jürgen had recently gone to study architecture at the Brookings Institute in Washington DC. Rudi did his best to persuade her to stay in Berlin but all to no avail. Her mind was made up. It was an incredibly bold decision for a young woman and one that was in no way applauded by her parents, who did all they could to change her mind but, in the end, they financed her passage to Philadelphia in September 1928 where she found work teaching German. Moving on to New York, she took up employment at the left-wing Prosnit Bookshop in upper Manhattan.[7]

Contacts she made through her work led her to the American Communist Party, CPUSA, which she quickly joined. For a time she lived, rent-free, in the Henry Street Settlement at 256 Henry Street, and helped out at this refuge for homeless Jews. Amongst those she met was the writer and fervent communist Michael Gold whose real name was Itzok Isaac Granich, the son of immigrant Romanian Jews who had earlier been briefly acquainted with Ursula's parents. Although energised and exhilarated by American culture, Ursula could not settle and longed both for her home and for Rudi who was patiently waiting for her to return to Berlin. When Ursula responded to the homing call, she and Rudi quickly married in October 1929 but with little money and a determination to reject any sort of financial assistance from their families, found themselves spending the bitter winter in an unheated flat.

Their political life was anything but impoverished, however. Touring the streets of Berlin pulling a handcart, Ursula collected left-wing books and pamphlets from sympathetic publishers which were accumulated into a sort of lending library operated by the KPD. Rudi, meanwhile, having completed his own architectural studies tried to find gainful employment. The couple were struggling to survive and, with the Great Depression crushing the economic life out of Germany, saw little likelihood of better times ahead if they stayed where they were.

Help came from an unlikely and unexpected source when Rudi received a letter from a childhood friend, Helmuth Woidt, who had emigrated to China. The letter contained an advertisement inviting applications for a position with the Shanghai Municipal Council as an architect. China, and Shanghai in particular, was experiencing a construction boom and the Chinese government under Chiang Kai-shek was particularly keen to encourage his country's links with Germany whose industrial power was still considerable despite its pariah status in Europe. Shanghai was a booming industrialised city and a busy centre of trade. It was also 'a veritable witch's cauldron of international intrigue [and] a focal point of Communist effort'.[8] Rudi applied and was quickly accepted. Ursula was excited by the prospect of travel and saw only advantages in new opportunities to expend her revolutionary energies in a new environment, but it soon became apparent that she knew precious little about the political climate within which she hoped to do that.

The couple left for Moscow in July 1930 where they boarded the Trans-Siberian Express bound for Dalian. There they took a steamer for the last leg of the journey. Setting foot on land, the social conditions of most citizens they encountered in Shanghai were shocking, even by the standards she had already witnessed in Berlin and New York. The level of poverty, pollution and human suffering appalled her. Here, surely, there seemed to be the sort of conditions ripe for exploitation in the service of revolution but any prospect of becoming involved with the local Chinese Communist Party were immediately dampened when she discovered that it had been made illegal and was systematically harassed and persecuted by the capitalist Kuomintang regime. Then came a further shock when she discovered that she was pregnant.

Both Rudi and Ursula were made welcome in a Bohemian social circle of wealthy expats in Shanghai centred around a sprawling manor house called the Concordia. Life here was a world away from that which they had witnessed on the quayside and in the streets of Shanghai. Within the wealthy and privileged Western expat communities they attended cocktail parties in salubrious apartments and shopped in fashionable stores but Ursula, in particular, soon became bored by the dull, mindless chatter and trivial preoccupations of their new acquaintances. This was not what she had expected and decidedly not something that would satisfy her revolutionary spirit. She began to crave any sort of excitement and intellectual stimulus but most of all she needed an opportunity to make contact with local communist organisations and forge links between them and Moscow.

Ursula took a job as secretary to the Far East correspondent of a news agency called the *Wolff Telegraphic Bureau* through which she found salvation in the form of a woman whose book *Daughter of Earth* had already become a cornerstone of her political philosophy. This woman was also known to Ursula through an accidental meeting with her estranged husband at a book fair in Berlin some months previously. The woman was Agnes Smedley, an American journalist working for the *Frankfurter Zeitung*. A fluent German speaker, Smedley had lived in Berlin during the Weimar period and been recruited there by the Comintern's Otdel Mezhdunarodny Sviasy, OMS, the Comintern's clandestine International Liaison Department. Her various homes in Shanghai provided a rendezvous for other journalists, communists and fellow agents including the future head of MI5, Roger Hollis, who would have responsibility for hunting down Soviet spies in Britain after the Second World War. When Ursula met Hollis, he was an employee of British American Tobacco and later became a freelance journalist.[9]

The two women were introduced by a mutual acquaintance and Ursula found Smedley to be a hugely complex, conflicted and unstable character but one unquestioningly committed to the communist cause. Ursula was immediately impressed with this feminist anti-fascist advocate of free love, someone with such a passionate temperament but even that paled into insignificance compared to the thrill of learning that Smedley was also a spy heavily involved on behalf of the Soviets supporting the Chinese communists in their desperate struggle to avoid extermination by the nationalist government. Smedley introduced Ursula to another side of Shanghai, a city that had become the thriving hub of international espionage in the Far East.

Smedley contacted her handlers in Moscow for permission to recruit Ursula. They responded by arranging a meeting between Ursula and Smedley's current lover; a man with 'a slender head, thick wavy hair, his face already deeply furrowed, his intense blue eyes framed by dark lashes, his mouth beautifully formed'. Sporting a pronounced limp and speaking with a pronounced German accent, with three fingers of his left hand missing, this man who called himself Richard Johnson 'radiated charm, and danger'.[10] Tall, well-built and handsome, a man whose face was scarred from previous fights, he made an immediate impression on Ursula.[11] Having confirmed to the man that she was more than willing to be recruited to the cause, she was put under surveillance for a few days by Soviet agents and, having passed scrutiny, was allocated the codename Sonya, meaning 'wisdom' in Ancient Greek. She was instructed to put her flat at the disposal of the man Johnson, whom she now knew as Richard Sorge, where he could hold meetings with both Chinese and European communists. Although he had been introduced to Sorge as a friend of Smedley, all this time Rudi was quite unaware of these clandestine meetings which were conducted during his working hours. Although sympathetic to left-wing politics, Rudi was still far from being a communist and Ursula realised that she would be required to lead a double life and conceal her activism from him.

It was exciting and invigorating. Now with a sense that she was actually doing something positive and making a real contribution, Ursula sensed that she had found her true calling. It soon was made apparent to her that it brought with it danger. Sorge had emphasised to her the need to do everything possible to avoid attracting attention to herself but, in this regard, Smedley was not a reliable associate. She drank copiously and was subject to extreme mood swings. This was hardly the sort of temperament that enhanced security of their activities. If there was a breach Smedley's American passport might save her from arrest but German nationals had no such guarantees and Ursula would face the harshest punishment. The German government would not lift a finger to help avowed communists inciting insurrection in a foreign land. They, along with the British and French were actually doing all they could to help the Chinese authorities to track down and arrest them. It was a priority for them to stem the spread of communism throughout the East where it was seen as a direct threat to colonial interests. A major situation arose when, with the birth of her child approaching, Ursula received news that members of the group meeting at her flat had been arrested, tortured and executed.

Michael Pitt 'Misha' Hamburger was born on 12 February 1931 and the family moved into more spacious accommodation in Avenue Joffre. Their new house was ideally situated to host secret meetings that continued unabated. It was surrounded on three sides by a large garden and had a separate servants' staircase allowing discreet access to the drawing rooms on the second floor.[12] Ursula's position as a new mother and wife of a German bourgeois government employee was cover of the highest order and she was encouraged to consolidate it by her dress, demeanour and general behaviour in relationships with others in the Bohemian community of wealthy expats in Shanghai.

Through Rudi and her acquaintances at Concordia she had access to politicians, journalists, businessmen, and bankers, listening in on their conversations. Immersing herself in Chinese culture, she set about learning Chinese, which she managed to do to a reasonable standard, so that by the end of her stay, in 1936, she was capable of holding an intelligible conversation and reading documents.[13] At the same time, through Smedley, Ursula met another Soviet agent who was to play a major role in Second World War and Cold War espionage operations including the US Atomic Manhattan Project and the defection of the British spy Kim Philby.

Katherine 'Kitty' Harris had been born into a Russian Jewish émigré family in Whitechapel, London at the beginning of the twentieth century. The family then moved on to Winnipeg in Canada. By the age of 30, Kitty was married to Earl Browder, the leader of the CPUSA and had joined the Soviet Communist Party. The couple had been despatched to Shanghai in 1927 to operate on behalf of the Comintern and had become well-integrated into the Chinese communist movement running a parallel operation to the one in which Ursula was involved. There does not appear to have been significant contact between Ursula and Kitty primarily because the main link, Smedley had little time for Kitty who, like her, was highly-strung and temperamental.

Meanwhile Ursula and Sorge had become lovers, and they moved closer in their conspiratorial relationship also. She was far from Sorge's only lover, however, but that did not dim her enthusiasm for the relationship. Ursula was introduced to other members of Sorge's operations and grew close to one especially. Married to a Chinese communist, Irene Wiedemeyer was a 23-year-old German Jew who ran the 'Zeitgeist' bookshop, a cover where Comintern agents were able to meet and exchange messages. Ursula stepped up her monitoring of conversations across her dinner table where the guest list included a wide range of German and Chinese industrialists.

Then in the middle of June 1931, the British spy catcher Inspector Patrick 'Tom' Givens working with the Special Branch of the Shanghai Municipal Police and acting on a tip-off, arrested Professor Hilaire Noulens and his wife, Gertrude. Givens soon established that Noulens was, in fact, Jakob Matveyevich Rudnik, a central figure in the Far East operations of OMS and his wife was Tatiana Moissenko.[14] A search of their house uncovered six passports in various names and a large quantity of coded messages which, when deciphered, provided copious amounts of intelligence about subversive communist activity. Moscow reacted swiftly by closing down all Comintern activity in Shanghai and launching a world-wide propaganda campaign to get Noulens freed.[15]

Smedley fled to Hong Kong. Others went back to Germany. Sorge, however, stuck it out. He gambled that he was not known to Noulens' networks, but he put Ursula and others on standby for a rapid evacuation should the need arise. Rudi had to be told and when he was enlightened about the extent of his wife's complicity in espionage, he was furious but knew that, however reluctantly, he would do what he had to do to protect Ursula and little Misha.

When interrogation of Noulens failed to provide more information, police activity diminished somewhat and Smedley returned to Shanghai. Moscow sent of a new cadre of operatives to rebuild the network. Another new acquaintance made through Sorge was a 'dark-eyed, dark-haired' man described by Ursula as 'funny and vivacious'.[16] Assigned to act as courier between Sorge and this man, whom she knew only as 'Fred', Ursula became infatuated with him and confided in him about the unhappy state of her marriage. Unbeknown to her, Fred was an important Soviet agent called Manfred 'Moses' Stern who had recently arrived in China after several years working in the USA where he had been the GRU leader of an espionage group stealing US military secrets. Stern, who was now military adviser to the Chinese Communist Party, had been assigned by Moscow to make a final evaluation of Ursula's potential to become a fully-fledged Soviet agent. While he was setting Ursula a series of tests, however, the whole of the Far East was shaken by the Japanese invasion of Manchuria. By January 1932, Japanese forces were at the gates of Shanghai. Hoping that two European women would remain safe from harassment, Moscow ordered Sorge to send Ursula and Irene Wiedemeyer up to the battle front to report on the situation.

Rudi was appalled by the carnage wreaked by Japanese forces. His politics took a decided turn to the left and he committed himself to the communist cause as a rejection of what he saw as a 'capitalist' aggression. He was also trying to bridge the rift that had opened up in his marriage to Ursula but it was too little and too late. Ursula had become fully enthralled by the prospect of a career in espionage. She was exhilarated by the adventure of clandestine work and enthralled by the glamour of the agents she had met in Shanghai. All her ambitions in that direction, however, seemed to hit a wall when Sorge informed her one day by phone that he was returning to Moscow immediately on orders from the Comintern. Ursula had already been shaken by a split in her relationship with Smedley who had become increasingly unstable.

Separated from her two enigmatic and inspirational role models, and working now under a new more mundane taskmaster, much of the thrill had gone. Misha was suffering chest infections brought on by the climate and the thought of taking him back to Germany was challenged by news of Hitler's appointment as chancellor in January 1933. Nazi thugs had menaced the Kuczynski family forcing Robert to go into hiding in Czechoslovakia while trying to get passage for his family to England. Jürgen chose to remain in Germany and join the anti-fascist resistance. Led by Givens, the authorities were also stepping up their purge of communists in Shanghai. The situation was becoming intolerable when word came through from Moscow that she was being 'brought in from the cold'.

The problem was that her handlers refused to even consider allowing Ursula to bring Misha with her to Moscow. For them it was just an unnecessary complication and a hindrance to what operations they had in mind for her. She was faced with what appeared to be a terrible dilemma but really such was her commitment to the cause of communism that, in the end, the decision was a foregone conclusion although one that would haunt her for the rest of her life. 'The thought of giving up my work never occurred to me', she later said, and the prospect of being reunited with Sorge was appealing on a professional level as well as an emotional one.[17] Moscow had other ideas, however.

Sorge was already being readied for another assignment in the Far East and the two would never meet again.

Ursula and Rudi were now faced with the problem of what to do about Misha. With all other options discounted, they decided to take him to stay with Rudi's parents who had fled Germany and were now living in the village of Grenzbauden in Czechoslovakia. For Rudi who was staying in Shanghai, it was a devastating blow to lose his son but he clung to the hope that the family might soon be reunited and that the marriage might be salvaged from the wreckage around them. On 18 May 1933, Ursula and Misha left for Vladivostok to take the long train ride to Moscow and then to Grenzbauden. Rudi's parents were delighted to see their grandchild and happily took him in on the understanding that it was purely a temporary arrangement. Ursula's father, Robert, had meanwhile left for Britain and his family, apart from Jürgen, who risked his life by remaining in Berlin, were in the process of joining him.

With a heavy heart, Ursula left Misha and returned to Moscow determined to serve the cause to the full extent of her capabilities in order to justify the pain of the separation. Back in Moscow, she was assigned to an intensive training course at the Radio Training Laboratory of the People's Commissariat of Defence, codenamed 'Sparrow', located in the woods on the Moscow river near the village of Vorobyeva and run by Alexandr 'Jakob' Abramov-Mirov. Previously she had simply passed on her intelligence to others such as Sorge for transmission to Moscow but now she would learn to do it for herself. Over the next six months, she studied wireless telegraphy and techniques of repairing and constructing radio transmitters and proved to have high aptitude for the work. In what must have been an extremely intense few months, Ursula also trained in combat techniques, sabotage and the use of explosives, surveillance and counter-surveillance, and other tradecraft vital to survival in the espionage jungle.

This prepared her for her first major assignment which was again in the Far East but this time in Mukden in the Japanese-occupied region of north-east China and Inner Mongolia known as Manchuria. Mukden was a less glamorous microcosm of Shanghai, where foreigners lived in their own enclave well away from the surrounding slums. It was a town awash with adventurers, crooks, opium-dealers, criminals and prostitutes.[18] There it would be Ursula's task to liaise with and assist in whatever way she could the communist partisans and provide radio communications between them and Moscow but first, she collected Misha from his grandparents and went back to Shanghai for a brief liaison with Rudi. Any hopes Rudi might have had for a reunion, however, were dashed when Ursula told him that she was taking 3-year-old Misha with her to Manchuria and asked him for a divorce. Rudi was adamant that he would not agree to a dissolution of the marriage, but Ursula abandoned him anyway, and left with Misha travelling to Mukden under cover as the representative of Evans & Co., an American educational bookseller.

Manchuria had been turned into a nominally independent, but in reality a puppet state by the invading Japanese who renamed it, Manchukuo. When the League of Nations effectively turned a blind eye to the illegal occupation, Chiang Kai-shek attempted to form an alliance of convenience with the leader of the communists, Mao Tse-tung, but neither would trust the other and the Chinese nationalist government spent more time attacking Mao than the Japanese.

Ursula was now accompanied by and was working under Johannes Patra, codename 'Ernst'. Their mission was to make contact with partisan groups fighting Japanese forces in the mountains, establish a communication link between them and Moscow and supply them with explosives for their espionage activities.[19] The two agents were to take up residence in Mukden posing as a couple in an illicit relationship fleeing from their past in Shanghai. Patra overcame his initial opposition to having Misha on the mission and became extremely fond of the boy. As a result of his own personality, his acceptance of Misha and the proximity of their working environment, the relationship between Ursula and Patra soon grew into something more than professional. Rudi visited them to see the child and must have known that Ursula and Patra were lovers but he made no fuss. He had, by now become an ardent communist also and managed to keep his personal feelings out of party affairs. Maintaining his relationship with his son Misha was his first priority.

They settled down to their mission sending news of the Chinese partisans, reporting on sabotage, and Japanese counter-insurgency measures. For Moscow the fate of China and the possibility of a communist government there were, at the time, of equal importance to events taking place in Nazi Germany. Meanwhile Japanese intelligence agents had begun scouring the airwaves for radio transmissions. Every day and every message Ursula sent back to Moscow increased the risk of exposure causing her to begin experiencing periods of great tension. It was not only her but her child who would suffer if they were caught. The situation became critical when one of the partisan leaders, Feng, was taken prisoner by the Japanese in April 1935, Ursula and Patra were ordered to leave Manchuria immediately to avoid being swept up as a result of information obtained from Feng under torture.

Evacuating to Beijing, they set about re-establishing communications with Moscow but then Ursula discovered that she was pregnant with Patra's child; something she chose not to share with him. Before her physical appearance could alert him to her condition, however, Moscow ordered Ursula to come home. Givens had arrested a man going by the name of Joseph Walden and discovered that he was really a Soviet agent Yakov Bronin. In his apartment, Givens found a reference to Ursula Hamburger. It was not conclusive evidence of her involvement in a spy ring but it was enough to initiate her immediate extraction. Rudi left with her, fully committed now to the communist cause.

Before leaving China, however, he had urged Ursula to abort Patra's child which would have been relatively easy to arrange in Shanghai, but Ursula refused to consider it. Rudi respected her decision and, although he knew that his marriage to Ursula was effectively over, he agreed to stay with her and welcome the baby into their marriage as his own. Moscow would be none the wiser. As far as Ursula's GRU handler Colonel Gaik Lazarevich Tumanyan was concerned, they were a happy family and so when Ursula's new assignment was confirmed, Rudi was ordered to accompany her and as a good comrade did not argue. Ursula, however, was not happy about the arrangement. She knew Rudi well enough to understand that he would make a poor spy and would constitute a serious risk to their security.

Before that Ursula requested permission to travel to England with Misha to visit her family who had all, including Jürgen, taken up residence there in a 'dowdy three-roomed flat' in Belsize Park. It was the first time that she had seen them in five years.[20] Robert was teaching at the London School of Economics but the left-wing proclivities of the whole family were well known to MI5 who kept a close watch on their activities. Ursula's brief visit did not go unnoticed.

She confided to her family that her new mission was in Poland. The family nanny, Olga Muth, who had looked after Ursula and her siblings since childhood begged Ursula to take her along. She no longer had a role in the family, the youngest Renate was almost in her teens, and Olga was crammed into the tiny flat with nothing much to do. She could be useful looking after Misha and the second child when it was born, she argued, and Ursula, seeing the logic of it agreed. Olga was quite well aware that Ursula was going to Poland to carry out espionage work of some description but she never asked about it and fully intended to devote herself entirely to the welfare of the children. The four of them left for Warsaw in January 1936 and a month later settled in the suburb of Anin.

Rudi found work as an architect and Ursula set about building a radio transmitter. Her contact in Poland, a man called Stoyan Vladov, who ran a network of informants, was less than welcoming. For whatever reason he was surly and uncooperative. Whether it was the idea of working with a woman or just a certain resentment that Moscow had decided that he needed any help at all is not clear. Such work as Ursula was called upon to perform was quite mundane and she soon became bored. After her experiences in China, this new situation was very much a come-down and she felt distinctly over-qualified for the work she was asked to perform. Rudi, however, was quite at home and constantly requested Moscow to call him in for more training so he could play a greater part. Moscow was having none of it. He was not what they considered ideal espionage material and anyway he was needed as a non-activist to act as cover for Ursula. Janina 'Nina' was born on 27 April 1936.

In the summer of 1936, under orders from Moscow, Ursula, Olga and the children moved to Danzig while Rudi remained in Warsaw. The port city of Danzig, with its disputed sovereignty, was one of the European 'powder kegs' waiting to have its 'fuse' lit by the Nazis. She made contact with a communist cell operating in the shipyards reporting on the shipment of arms to the fascist insurgents in Spain. Walking around the city pushing a pram was excellent cover. The work there was humdrum and routine but not without its risks. Ursula, however, still considered that her role was far beneath her capabilities and continued to make known to Moscow that she would be happier in a more challenging scenario and one that, perhaps, would benefit from extra training in other espionage skills than radio.

Eventually Moscow submitted to her entreaties and recalled her but first she went to Czechoslovakia where she left the children and Olga in the care of their grandparents. Rudi remained behind in Poland still vainly pleading with Moscow to be sent back to China. Much to her surprise, on 15 June 1937, Ursula was ushered into the Kremlin to receive the first of her two awards of Order of the Red Banner. She was then rewarded by another period at the Sparrow espionage training centre where she spent several months studying the manufacture and application of explosives as well as other techniques of operational espionage.

How much Ursula was aware of the great Stalinist purges that saw tens of thousands of military and political personnel executed is not clear. Very little according to her own testimony but she noted that 'comrades in leading positions changed frequently at that time'.[21] It must have been clear to her what was going on when many of her old friends disappeared either to gulags or to a more permanent exile but she chose to ignore the implications and her commitment to the cause of communism seems to have remained undimmed.

Exactly how she, as a German-born member of the intelligence community who had spent many years abroad mixing with foreign groups, survived is a mystery. Many of those she served with in China were recalled to Moscow and never seen again. Sorge survived by having the sense to ignore orders and remain in the Far East. Survive she did, however, and was sent back to Poland where she was reunited with Rudi and the children while Moscow, growing ever more confident of her abilities, debated how best to utilise them.

Switzerland was already one of the most important centres of espionage in Europe and after the start of the Second World War probably became the most important hub of all. The diplomatic missions of every country were operating their own professionally equipped radio stations from their embassy buildings. The Soviet Union, however, did not yet have diplomatic relations with Switzerland and was therefore compelled to employ covert personnel and equipment. It was here that Ursula would play out the next act of her career establishing a small group of activists to be infiltrated from Switzerland into Germany to gather military information and conduct sabotage but first she was ordered to go to England, ostensibly to visit her family but, in reality, to scout for potential recruits to go with her to Switzerland. England was considered a rich source of left-wing sympathisers ripe for exploitation having seen many of them travel to Spain and fight for the nationalists in the civil war. Before she left Moscow, however, she met an agent who had been assigned to work alongside her.

Franz Obermanns, codename 'Alex' was another German communist, one who, as a member of the communist resistance in Berlin, had felt the rough edge of fascist persecution but three years in a Nazi prison had done little to dim his political fervour. A former waiter who had served with the International Brigade in Spain, he had undergone espionage training in Moscow and was now a competent radio man. He would follow Ursula to Switzerland travelling separately on a Finnish passport, under the name Eriki Noki even though he knew nothing of the country and certainly did not speak the language.

Liverpool-born Alexander Allan Foote had served under Fred Copeman as part of the British contingent of the International Brigade in Spain where he had come into contact with communists like Dave Springhall, a political commissar. The men had stayed in contact when they returned home after the war in 1938 and it was during one reunion dinner that Copeman hinted to Foote that he had an assignment that might interest him. Springhall, he said was on the lookout for someone to go to Switzerland on behalf of the Comintern. A further meeting to ascertain his suitability for the mission was arranged with Brigitte Lewis, which was the married name of one of Ursula's sisters.

Suitably impressed, Brigitte thought Foote an acceptable candidate and recommended to Moscow that he be recruited. It may be that Foote was flattered by the attention he was getting or simply eager for adventure, but, according to his and Ursula's account, he readily agreed to put himself at the disposal of the party.[22] When Ursula arrived in Switzerland she took over a Soviet espionage network, later known as the Rote Drei that had been established in Zurich in 1937 by Henry (Henri) Robinson and Maria (Mira) Josefovna Poliakova who had returned to Moscow from where she continued to direct the Swiss operations. Ursula moved into an isolated house called La Taupinière (the Molehill) near Caux, above Montreux under the name of Ursula Schultz where she began assembling a radio transmitter-receiver for direct links with Moscow.

Despite the vagueness of the offer made to him and the uncertainty over who he would actually be working for, Foote, who, according to Sándor Radó, the Red Army intelligence resident director in Switzerland, had a 'total lack of political education', joined Sonya at La Taupinière.[23] Right from the start, Radó had serious doubts about Foote and suspected him of being an agent of Britain's secret foreign intelligence service SIS (MI6).[24] There was certainly a discrepancy between Foote's account of his earlier RAF career and official records. It is clear that Foote had joined the service on 26 July 1936 but by December of that year he had left the country on a one-day excursion ticket and gone to fight in Spain. However, there is no record of his desertion. His RAF discharge papers state that Foote's services 'were no longer required – at his own request', and his character was identified as being 'VG'. Significantly, no attempt was made to arrest him when he returned to Britain on 16 September 1938. His application for a passport was approved in double quick time on 12 October which, given his history was remarkable. The clear implication is that Radó's suspicions were well founded. It is possible that SIS was hoping to exploit the Rote Drei spy ring in Switzerland to pass to Moscow disguised intelligence derived from British ULTRA intercepts of German radio traffic.

On 29 September 1938, Ursula had made her first test message to a station in Dymovka forest near the Polish Ukrainian border. Poliakova acknowledged it and the link was established. Foote was assigned to go to Munich on a one-year tourist visa, learn to speak German and make as many friends as possible especially at the BMW aircraft engine factory. Ursula gave him 2,000 Swiss francs and told him to report back after three months but before he left, she asked him who else among his civil war companions, she might usefully contact.

Foote and Ursula met again, as planned, three months later when Foote received further finance and told not to compile reports on political and economic conditions in Germany and prepare for a possible sabotage operation. Meanwhile, on Foote's recommendation, an old comrade of his from Spain, Leon (Len) Charles Beurton, had been contacted by Copeman and he also had agreed to go to Switzerland to meet Sonya. He was given a payment of £10 and instructions to rendezvous with Ursula outside the Uniprix shop in Vevey, Switzerland.

There he was given a similar assignment to the one Foote had undertaken but in his case the target was the I.G. Farben factory in Frankfurt. Enthused by his new assignment, Beurton, a man whose nervous system 'operated efficiently under stress', was no less captivated by Sonya with whom he instantly fell in love.[25] It was a great surprise for Beurton to find that it was Foote whom he was instructed to meet in Munich in April 1939. It was an even greater surprise when they went to lunch at the Osteria Bavaria and discovered that one of the other tables was occupied by Adolf Hitler, Unity Mitford and Eva Braun.

German Abwehr and RSHA agents were swarming all over Switzerland searching for enemies of the Reich. A crisis arose in December 1939 when Obermanns was arrested by the Swiss police and a search of his flat uncovered radio parts. There was a direct link between him and Sonya because, on one occasion when he had been visiting her at La Taupinière a Swiss policeman had turned up having been informed by neighbours that various men had been seen visiting the property from time to time. Nothing much came of the encounter except that the policeman had taken note of Obermanns' 'Noki' identity papers and the location where he had been questioned, information that was now on file at police headquarters. All radio equipment at La Taupinière was hurriedly wrapped up and buried in nearby woods.

On top of this Ursula's German passport, issued in Shanghai in 1935, was due to expire in May 1940, and her status as a Jew meant that she was unlikely to get a new one. Deportation to Germany along with her two young children, and all that entailed, stared her in the face. Marie Ginsberg, the librarian at the League of Nations, was a Polish

Jew actively spiriting Jews out of Germany on false passports offered to provide her with a Honduran (Bolivian) passport for 2,000 Swiss francs. It was not foolproof but better than nothing.

Then on 22 August 1939, the world was stunned by the announcement that Germany and the Soviet Union had signed a non-aggression treaty which completely altered the way in which the GRU was constrained to operate. On the following day, Ursula got a telegram from Poliakova telling her to 'Cease all activities against Germany, pull all [illegal] agents out and break all contact with any remaining resident agents.'[26] She was to stay in Switzerland and bring her two main agents up to speed with radio. She chose to make it plain to Foote and Beurton that they were working for the GRU something that had never actually been spelled out to them before but which probably came as no great surprise to them. The radio reports to Moscow contained little of interest and the Swiss network was left in limbo to mark time as best it could until new orders came through. Meanwhile both the Gestapo and the Swiss police stepped up their search for illicit radios while Ursula's money supply from Moscow all but dried up. Meanwhile the GRU had decided that arrangements should be made to infiltrate Ursula into Britain as a deep penetration agent, probably to initiate the transmission of purloined atomic weapons research to Moscow, as the Soviet Union had solid contacts with those carrying out atomic research in British universities at the time. But they were not the only intelligence agency keenly interested in Ursula.

It is a perennial problem when trying to reconstruct the history of spies, especially when the bulk of written evidence comes from their own testimonies, to separate fact from fiction. This is very much the case when considering the events surrounding the relationship between Ursula and MI5 in 1939 and beyond.

Professor Anthony Glees, emeritus professor at the University of Buckingham specialising in intelligence matters, says that many of Sonya's claims in her memoir *Sonjas Rapport* have been shown to be false 'by simple inspection of time and space', or by other records that have come to light that show persons she talks about were simply not where she said they were at the time, or by knowledge of the *modus operandi* of her employer, the GRU.[27]

Sonya and Rudi were in Switzerland with their two children and their nanny in the summer of 1939 facing deportation to Germany because their visas were about to expire. Honduran passports which they had acquired were of poor quality and would be of little use. Ursula's account of what happened next, says Glees, is illogical and inconsistent. So too is the account of her time there given by Alexander Foote in his book, *Handbook for Spies*.

Foote claimed that Ursula saw her salvation as escape to Britain but that was seen to be impossible because of her German nationality. Moscow, he said, hatched a plot whereby she would divorce Rudi, whom Foote erroneously says was in a Chinese jail, and marry Len Beurton thereby getting a British passport. Exactly how the Soviets imagined that they could install and run in England the German-born Ursula with the sort of reputation she had got, under the noses of MI5 has never been explained. Her family were already suspected by the British authorities of being dangerous subversives. Her rabble-rousing brother Jürgen, the leader of the exiled KPD had been interned in Warner's Camp, Seaton, Devon. Furthermore, Moscow should have realised that trying to operate an illicit radio transmitter in a country known for its expertise in detection of alien wireless traffic would be a high-risk operation. This all throws into doubt the idea that Ursula's move to Britain was undertaken primarily at Moscow's behest. Moscow may well have been introduced to the idea by Sonya herself who raised the possibility after prompting by a third party, namely MI5. Th Soviets may not have been particularly enthusiastic about it but may have concluded that it was the best of a number of disagreeable outcomes if Ursula was forced out of Switzerland. They were already suspicious of Britain's research programme into atomic weapons and were on the lookout for a competent radio operator to relay intelligence about it. Using Ursula was a risk, given her background but she certainly knew how to operate an illicit radio.

Evidence suggest that Beurton had been recruited by SIS and was operating under instructions from Victor Farrell.[28] Farrell, was an experienced SIS officer who had previously served in Budapest before heading the Geneva Station where he was instrumental in recruiting sources of German intelligence. He would later become the passport control officer (PCO) in Geneva in February 1940. The PCO was widely recognised as being run for and on behalf of SIS. He dealt with escaping prisoners, organising routes through southern France and across the Pyrenees into Spain, then Portugal and so to Britain, besides liaising with the French and with other agents working in the ILO and similar institutions in Geneva, on behalf of the SIS. He also looked after the smuggling of arms and strategic materials such as industrial diamonds. His main preoccupation was to monitor the Rote Drei network into which he had infiltrated Rachel Dübendorfer, a middle-aged Polish Jew who was then working in the League of Nations' International Labour Office as a secretary and translator. Farrell had his own radio transmitter/receiver, through which he could contact both Berne and London.[29]

Ursula, meanwhile, says that Rudi was in Switzerland with her but getting ready to return to China on orders from the Comintern. She claims that two of them came up with the idea of divorce and Ursula's remarriage to an Englishman, preferably Foote who, at first agreed to the plan but soon afterwards changed his mind and suggested that Beurton take his place. The idea was that the Hamburgers would divorce once safely in England. Foote later claimed that Ursula's sued for divorce against Rudi's wishes, and it was he who had supplied false evidence of Rudi's adultery with one of Ursula's sister in a London hotel.[30] Professor Glees presents a theory that what actually happened owes much more to the involvement of SIS, in particular Farrell.

Glees asserts that Foote, had been recruited by SIS to infiltrate the Soviet Rote Drei spy ring so when he told his MI5 handlers about Ursula's plan for him to marry her, Glees believes that his boss Claude Dansey, the head of the shadow Z network within SIS, rejected the idea instantly but, at the same time, saw an opportunity to manipulate Ursula. SIS boss Stewart Menzies had authorised Dansey's organisation to run in absolute secrecy quite separately from all other intelligence agencies. It was Dansey, says Glees, who came up with the suggestion of replacing Foote with Beurton as Ursula's new husband and proceeded to facilitate the production of evidence to support Ursula's divorce process.

This begs the question of how exactly Dansey hoped to use Ursula. The Molotov-Ribbentrop Pact of 23 August 1939 had placed the Soviet Union and Britain of different sides of the impending cataclysm of war. The sort of constructive espionage roles for Ursula in such a situation seemed to be rather few and far between except in the one of double agent, or controlled enemy agent, unwittingly feeding false information to her masters in Moscow.

Documentary evidence shows that the divorce was granted on 29 December 1939 and the marriage to Beurton took place soon afterwards on 23 February 1940. On 11 March, the British Consulate in Geneva transmitted Ursula's application for a passport to the passport office in London which included references given by Dr Churchill, D.M. Macrae-Taylor and Mr Blelloch. When the passport office submitted a request for information about the applicant they were told that 'MI5 had no records of Ursula Beurton' and only a possible trace of her ex-husband who had 'a communistic smell'.[31]

The British Consul in Geneva H.B. Livingston, however said that Ursula did not claim to know any British subject in Switzerland who could vouch for her and had got Mademoiselle Ginsberg, assistant librarian at the League of Nations, and a member of Jewish intelligence, to vouch for her. This was the person who had supplied Ursula with her Honduran passport, and Len with a Bolivian one. Livingston further told London that the application stated that Ursula was 'not a British subject' and 'there is reason to suspect that the main purpose of the marriage was to confer British nationality on the applicant to enable her to enter the U.K., the local Swiss authorities having refused to extend her residence permit'.[32]

Evidence now shows that MI5 certainly did have records of Ursula Kuczynski. A memo on file records an anonymous but strong opinion that Ursula should not be granted a passport. On 25 May 1940, despite recommended that Ursula should not be given a passport because her husband, Beurton, was on the Central Security War Black List of persons whose opinions or associations were deemed politically inconvenient, it was granted. Strange to say that Alexander Foote, whose political profile matched that of Beurton, was not on this list. The passport head office in London decreed on 24 April, a week after Jürgen had been released on the grounds that membership of the KPD was not sufficient grounds for internment, that it was now too late to decline Ursula's passport application. This was either an example of gross incompetence or an exercise in looking the other way for some larger political reason, when MI5 failed to respond in a timely manner about any concerns they had about the genuineness of Ursula's marriage and passport application. It did not help that, at the time, MI5 was riven with internal divisions and rivalries for control of the organisation.[33] The inference is that Dansey, whose influence within the security services was considerable, applied pressure to ensure that the application was approved but there was no guarantee that the children, still considered to be German citizens, would be allowed entry into Britain. Again, documentary evidence shows that Victor Cazalet informed MI5 that his committee on refugees had 'no objection to the names of Mrs. Ursula BEURTON's children being added to her passport and the children accompanying their mother to this country'.[34]

It is hard to say just what Moscow thought of the seemingly effortless process by which Ursula was granted a passport by British authorities. Naïve the Soviets were not and the speed with which all applications were approved must have called them to question why. Of course it meant that they would now have Ursula installed and ruthlessly exploiting her new British citizenship for espionage purposes but to an outside observer their insouciance must have verged on stupidity unless they simply concluded that MI5 and SIS were hopelessly inefficient.

Of course, MI5 was desperately struggling during this period with so many investigations into suspected aliens. Alternatively, the Soviets may well have suspect the British of subverting Ursula as a double agent and hoped to exploit that for their own ends. Another possibility exists whereby the Soviets already had agents in British intelligence who were in positions to facilitate Ursula's entry and protect her while she set up her network in the country.

Later in November 1940, when negotiations were undertaken to have Ursula's children added to her passport, a cable from Geneva indicates that Farrell enabled Len Beurton to acquire a passport under a false name in early 1942.[35] Ursula claimed that her new husband's chequered history of the civil war would have prevented him accompanying her through Spain and Portugal, which was the default route for couriers between Switzerland and Britain, and so he was forced to stay behind when she left with the children. The difficulties Ursula encountered travelling across occupied France in December with two young children in an 'unheated bus', and waiting in 'icy cold' outside custom houses was described by her in a letter she wrote to her parents. Train travel across Spain was a little easier but the last leg of the journey to Lisbon in Portugal, which ended on Christmas Eve, was again traumatic and hazardous.[36]

Lisbon was a city swarming with refugees desperate for passage to the US. The British Consulate in Lisbon, while issuing an exit visa to Ursula and the children on 31 December, proved to be in no hurry to find them a place on a ship. She had to use money provided by Moscow to pay for hotel accommodation in the Grande Hotel in Estoril while they waited. Coincidentally Isiah Berlin, the academic and British intelligence agent who had spent the previous weeks in Oxford was staying at the Palácio Hotel in Estoril at the same time. Settling down for what threatened to be a long wait Ursula was suddenly informed that they would be taken aboard a British ship SS *Androceta* on 10 January 1941 bound for Liverpool and granted a category 'C' endorsement requiring no internment on arrival.

Before leaving Switzerland, Ursula had asked Foote to send a message to Moscow instructing her GRU contact in England to meet her on 1st and 15th of every month at 15.00 hours GMT at Wake Arms in Epping. Exactly how Ursula could have known about this location and why it was important to tell Moscow begs questions. Professor Glees concludes that the address was given to her by Farrell in SIS so that her contacts with Moscow could be monitored. Ursula then passed on details of the rendezvous to Moscow to ensure that they avoided the location at all costs and also to warn them that she was being manipulated by SIS. It would have been an unexpected bonus for Moscow to discover that one of their top agents was now getting cosy with British intelligence. There is no evidence that, once settled in England, Ursula ever travelled regularly to Epping.

Before leaving Lisbon it is clear from a letter she sent to her father in London that she expected to settle in Oxfordshire. Just how she knew that again suggests that it had been prearranged with Farrell.

The *Androceta* docked in Liverpool on 4 February 1941 at which point Ursula was questioned by immigration officers. In reply she was very vague about her movements, and her testimony revealed some highly suspicious contradictions but there was no follow-up investigation. She and her two children were allowed to enter the country. The local police were given her description, destination and the part of the train she was travelling in and instructed to 'keep a close eye' on her.[37] There was no more specific surveillance put in place. When one keen young MI5 officer made inquiries of Special Branch about Ursula's background, he was quickly told that there was nothing to see. At this time MI5 surveillance of subversive movements in Britain was carried out by a staff of only seven in B Division. The section responsible for monitoring communists consisted solely of Roger Hollis, whom Ursula had known in Shanghai, his assistant Miss H. Creedy and Miss W. Ogilvie.[38]

Remarkably, given the wartime restrictions in place, Ursula and the children found hotel accommodation in Liverpool and took a train to Oxford the next day. MI5 informed the chief constable of Oxford to expect her arrival in the city and on 24 February, he reported back that Ursula was living at 97 Kingston Road along with her sister Barbara, whose husband Duncan Burnett Macrae Taylor was a trainee wireless operator in the RAF. Ursula moved again on 25 March to the rectory at Glympton, near Woodstock and then in April took up residence in a small furnished bungalow at 134 Oxford Road in the village of Kidlington just outside Oxford. Michael attended the local primary school in Kidlington. His knowledge of German, Chinese, Polish and French must have been a revelation to his teachers even at a time when refugees were not an unfamiliar presence in the country. The single woman with a slight foreign accent and two children was readily accepted by the community and neighbours, used now to the sight of refugee families, were only too happy to look after Nina when called upon. It is worth noting that MI5 had just moved the whole of its staff out of London to Blemheim because of the Blitz and the house into which Ursula moved was within easy cycling distance of where Roger Hollis had moved to.

Ursula's brother, Jürgen, had now moved into one of the modernist Lawn Road flats in Belsize Park in the London Borough of Camden. Amongst previous residents at Flat 7 was Arnold Deutsch born in Vienna but later a postdoctoral fellow in psychology at the University of London. He was also a professional recruiter for the Narodnyy komissariat vnutrennikh del (NKVD) Soviet intelligence tasked with cultivating 'young radical high-fliers from leading British universities before they entered the corridors of power'.[39] When Deutsch moved out his place was taken by Simon Davidovich Kremer also a recruiter of spies but this time for the GRU. Just along the corridor in Flat 4 were Ursula's sister Brigitte, who had recently been awarded a PhD by the University of Basle, and her husband Anthony Gordon Lewis.

Jürgen had arrived in England on 29 July 1936 and immediately set about coordinating the activities of the KPD in Britain. He found employment with the British government as an economic statistician specialising on Germany. He had become a highly respected academic with influential friends in the top echelons of British society including Lilian Bowes-Lyon, a cousin of Elizabeth Bowes-Lyon, who would become the wife of King George VI, and therefore was not best pleased when Ursula turned up on his doorstep. It threatened to bring extra unwanted surveillance of his and Brigitte's activities which were currently tolerated by the British authorities who might be less amenable if they knew the full extent of their espionage work. They would have been even less happy to learn that one of the GRU's ulterior motives for sending Ursula to England was so that she could take a leading role in illicit radio communications between British communist network and Moscow. In this way the GRU hoped to take control of the Comintern's intelligence apparatus in the country, of which Jürgen and Brigitte were a part.

Ursula waited. Arrangements for a clandestine meeting with a Soviet contact were established but nobody showed up. It was not at all clear to Ursula what she was supposed to be doing apart from waiting for a contact. Her husband was still in Switzerland unable to get a visa to return to Britain. Eventually in the early summer, she was contacted by a Soviet agent called Nikolai Vladimirovitch Aptekar who introduced himself as 'Sergei'.[40] She told Aptekar that she had purchased all the parts necessary to build a radio and was all ready to start transmissions to Moscow. According to her account, she then started transmitting messages twice a week by radio, travelling every fortnight or so to visit her father or her brother in London, who supplied her with valuable information. Aptekar gave her a sum of money and made arrangements for regular meetings whenever she was in blacked-out London. Microphotographed documents that could not be handled by radio were handed over to Sergei in person for courier transmission to Moscow…

Apart from what she was getting from her family, there is precious little information available about where Ursula was getting the intelligence from at this time. What is known is that she met Melita Stedman Norwood, a life-long Marxist and member of the British Communist Party (CPGB) who lived a seemingly normal life in Cheshunt, Hertfordshire, where her husband, Hilary, worked as head of science at Cheshunt Modern School and in the evenings as an air raid warden. Melita's sister, Gerty, and Ursula's father, Robert, had met at the Communist Group of the London School of Economics as far back as 1933 after Gerty's mother had helped Robert to bring his family to England through her position with the Quaker British Committee for the Relief of the Victims of Fascism.[41]

Melita had been talent-spotted in 1935 by one of the CPGB's founders, Andrew Rothstein, and recommended to the NKVD who approved her recruitment two years later. She had been involved with a spy ring operating inside the Woolwich Arsenal, whose three leading members were arrested in January 1938, but her connection to them was only uncovered many years later.[42] Having been stood down from active espionage after the Woolwich Arsenal episode, Moscow saw a chance to reactivate her and contrived for her to meet Ursula. The two of them seemed to hit it off straight away and subsequently became good friends as well as fellow conspirators.

Melita was working as a secretary at the British Non-Ferrous Metals Research Association (BN-FMRA), a research organisation linked to Britain's armaments industries. Later during the Second World War, she would have access to classified information on the Anglo-American atomic bomb project. In 1941, not only did she have access to BN-FMRA documents but also, she had access to documents from Metro-Vickers and ICI, two companies linked with British atomic research.

Someone else who was inadvertently providing intelligence to Moscow was the Labour politician Sir Stafford Cripps, a close friend of Robert Kuczynski and a member of Churchill's War Cabinet. He had only just returned from a two-year stint as British ambassador to Moscow. He talked freely to Kuczynski about the British approach to relations with Moscow all of which was passed along to Ursula.

An intercepted message from the Soviet Embassy in London to Moscow dated 31 July 1941 stated that Ursula was sending daily messages to Moscow at hourly intervals during the night and passing on additional intelligence using microphotographs, the size of full stops, attached to letters and sent to safehouses in neutral Spain or Portugal for collection by Soviet intelligence. For this she was being paid £58 a month.[43] The fact that after Operation Barbarossa when Germany attacked the Soviet Union the British, and the Soviets became allies made no difference to Ursula or the work she was carrying out.

Rudi Hamburger had been sent to Turkey but had got stranded in Teheran when Barbarossa was launched and was forced to stay there and serve the Comintern in whatever way they found for him. While Foote got his new orders in Switzerland to run spies in Germany and report back to Moscow from his location in Lausanne. Beurton, however, had slumped into despond. He was deeply unhappy in Switzerland and managed to alienate himself from Radó and other members of the Rote Drei. He desperately wanted to get passage back to England to be reunited with Ursula. All he seemed to come up against were brick walls until Farrell came to his rescue.

A dinner was held at the Lawn Road flat of Jürgen Kuczynski on 3 April 1941 where the guest of honour was a nuclear scientist who had been detained and held in a Canadian internment camp and only recently returned to Britain. This man, Klaus Emil Julius Fuchs, had been radicalised during the early 1930s as a student in Kiel in response to the growing tide of Nazism. Facing arrest for his membership of the KPD, he fled first to Berlin, then to Paris and finally, with the help of the Religious Society of Friends (Quakers), to Britain on 24 September 1933. Having already been awarded degrees in mathematics and science at Leipzig and Kiel, Fuchs was accepted as a graduate student at the University of Bristol where he completed a doctorate in theoretical physics. Already he had come to the attention of MI5 who categorised him as a 'notorious communist' even thought there was no evidence that he had been politically active since arriving in Britain.[44] From Bristol, Fuchs went on to take up a postgraduate position at Edinburgh University where he started work alongside fellow student Walter Kellerman under Professor Max Born. Fuchs was described by Born as 'weak in appearance but with a powerful brain, taciturn, with a veiled expression which disclosed nothing of his thoughts.' Born's daughter Irène saw something a little different saying that he looked as if he needed 'a warm coat and a good meal.'[45] Born advised him to avoid speaking in public so as not to attract attention to his German accent and also to refrain from all political activity while he was in Britain. Fuchs, however, had quietly strengthened ties with German communist friends in London especially Jürgen and had become one of thirty to forty long-time KPD members part of a tightly knit group.[46] The British authorities had initially put Fuchs in category C, given

'Refugee from Nazi oppression' status and granted exemption from internment with minimal restrictions on travel and movement but he was rounded up with others on 11 May 1940 and deported to Canada.

On his return, Fuchs was invited to join the atomic research team led by Rudolf Peierls, a German Jew who had left Germany in 1929 before moving to Cambridge four years later. In March 1940, Peierls and Otto Robert Frisch had published their ground-breaking two-part 'Memorandum on the Properties of a Radioactive Super-Bomb' which was the first technical description of how an atomic bomb might actually be built. Nils Bohr tried to persuade Fuchs to decline the invitation saying that success of the whole nuclear project would mean 'a new concentration of power in the hands of a few capitalists and nationalists.'[47] Fuchs, however, took the view that if the Germans were working on a nuclear bomb then he was justified in helping Britain to match it.

Peierls was told by the British security services that his new assistant's access to nuclear research must be restricted to only those aspects that he needed to know about to fulfil his allocated role. Indeed, Peierls himself had been singled out as a potential security risk but out of dire necessity they were allowed free access to all atomic research.[48]

Two other guests at Kuczynski's dinner party were Hans Kahle, who had been interned for a while with Fuchs and was now working as a military correspondent for *Time* and *Fortune* magazines, and Kremer who was again introduced as Alexander Johnson. Kremer recognised Fuchs as an important contact and arranged to keep in touch with him. When the Germans struck against the Soviet Union on 22 June 1941, Fuchs took the view that the Soviets, now being allies of Britain, should be given access to British research on atomic weapons. He would later say that he 'did not have the slightest doubt that Soviet foreign policy was correct and … was convinced that the Western allies were (doing their utmost) to see that the Soviet Union and Germany would completely exhaust themselves in their struggle to the death.'[49] However, as a sop to his conscience, he decided only to give the Soviets information about the work with which he was personally involved. He did not have security clearance to see top secret documents but that was immaterial since much of what was in those papers was the results of his and Peierls' research in the first place. Typically, the intelligence Fuchs passed to Kremer concerned calculations of nuclear fission and uranium diffusion, work being carried out at British Tube Alloys, which was the code for the atomic bomb research. He told Kremer that work had started on the building of a bomb in both Britain and the US when they met at a house near Hyde Park, not far from the Soviet

Embassy. Fuchs became an invaluable source for Soviet intelligence and was given the code name Otto.[50]

Kremer tried, in the short time they were together, to educate Fuchs in spycraft but Fuchs found this tiresome. Neither of the two men was particularly security minded. They would meet by taking the same bus, sitting apart then Fuchs would alight leaving behind a parcel that Kremer would pick up. Fuchs would also phone Kremer on his office number and one occasion even visited the Soviet Embassy to deliver a package. He was also a frequent visitor to the Lawn Road flats when he was in London. Despite MI5 surveillance of the flats and the Soviet Embassy whose phone were bugged, British intelligence made no move to intervene.[51]

Then Kremer was suddenly recalled to Moscow to take command of a tank brigade in the Far East. Given that Moscow, in their own files, made several clear references to the vital nature of the intelligence Fuchs was providing it must be assumed that he had now become too important to be handled by someone whose incompetence threatened to derail the whole operation. Fuchs needed a much more professional controller, one who was already involved with atomic espionage. Jürgen was called upon to arrange a meeting between Fuchs and Ursula.

Ursula and Fuchs first met in the late summer of 1942 in a café across from Snow Hill railway station in Birmingham. Fuchs had been nervous beforehand but Ursula found him to be 'calm, thoughtful, tactful and cultured'.[52] After this first meeting, Ursula arranged for all subsequent ones to take place in the quiet market town of Banbury. That in itself is suspicious. Quiet towns were alert to the presence of strangers, especially during a war. Ursula must have been well aware that MI5 had her under some level of surveillance and any meeting in Banbury would immediately alert the authorities to the identity of her fellow conspirator. A bustling environment would have been much more conducive to brief clandestine meetings and the discrete handing over of material. As Toby Esterhase said to George Smiley in John le Carré's *Smiley's People*, 'He has completely mistaken quiet for security ... Grigoriev is so conspicuous he's embarrassing.'[53] The choice of Banbury was either an indication of Ursula's incompetence or an sign that she knew they would be observed and didn't care.

After 18 June 1942, when Fuchs signed the Official Secrets Act he had been granted access to all 'matters of relevance' concerning Peierls' team and others in the Tube Alloys programme. At this time Fuchs would have been working on gaseous diffusion and he handed over all he knew on that topic. He also passed on what was the official British understanding that Germany was not making much progress on its own bomb and most unlikely to have one before the end of the war. This allowed the Soviets to hold back on excessive expenditure for their own research although Fuchs did also suggest that work towards a bomb in the US was progressing apace.[54]

Subsequent meetings took place in the woods near the Churchill family seat at Blenheim, the newly acquired wartime home of MI5. Ursula and Fuchs would bicycle there together.

> He would then pass over secrets, which she stuffed under her bicycle seat … The delivery system was breathtakingly simple, even naïve from an intelligence point of view. There was no dead-letter drop. The secrets were passed hand to hand, which would have been a gift for counterintelligence if it's agents had been watching.[55]

Ursula's account of the meetings was that they took place every few weeks, on a weekend morning. Ursula would catch a train to Banbury and leave a written message at a dead-letter box, with details of when and where to meet later that day, never the same place twice. Fuchs came on the afternoon train from Birmingham. 'It was more difficult to tail us in the open countryside,' she wrote and 'it would arouse less suspicion if we took a little walk together'.[56]

There are serious doubts about the accuracy of Ursula's account, however. When Fuchs has a 100-page book of blueprints to hand over, she had to travel to London to inform her handler that they would meet outside Oxford, and she then had to pedal out to the junction of the A34 and the A40 to hand over the formulae and drawings. It was 30 miles to Banbury and most of these excursions would have occurred in the windy and rainy English winter of 1942–1943 and Fuchs would not have been able to make regular forays to North Oxfordshire without drawing attention to himself just to inform Sonya when the next meeting should be. If Ursula had indeed been taking her bike to Oxford station at regular intervals, surely 'keeping an eye on her' would have quickly led to her being stopped, and interrogated about her business?

Neither does any of this explain why the British would have allowed the meetings to take place, if indeed they did know about them, because the material Fuchs passed on to the Soviets was of critical importance concerning the gaseous diffusion method of separating the uranium isotope U-235 and the mathematical methods then being deployed for evaluating the critical size and efficiency of an atomic bomb. Since the only account of the meetings in Banbury are those furnished by Ursula, they must be considered dubious at best and the arrangements for the transfer of intelligence between the two was done in ways that have yet to be explained.

Despite much of the research and development of atomic bomb being moved to the USA, Britain was still contributing a great deal of data on the corrosive nature of the fluoride gas on uranium metal. Klaus Fuchs was Ursula's most important source of intelligence but there were at least a dozen others providing 'a wealth of intelligence: military, political and scientific'. One particular source, an officer in the technical department of the RAF, codename James, provided details of military aircraft development.[57]

The period of contact between Ursula and Fuchs coincided almost exactly with Len's arrival, and idleness, before being enlisted in the RAF on 18 November 1943, as a trainee wireless operator. Carrying a passport identifying him as John William Miller, he had arrived by aircraft at Bournemouth Airport on 29 July 1942 having flown in from Lisbon. Farrell had facilitated his passage from Geneva through France, Spain and Portugal but he was held up at British immigration. His luggage was thoroughly searched and he was subjected to a rigorous interrogation. The discovery of a second, Bolivian passport, found in his suitcase, in the name of Luis Carlos Bilboa, did not help his cause. Despite serious concerns about why he had spent so long in Switzerland before applying for repatriation and an eager junior in F Division, Hugh Shillito, volunteering the suspicion that Beurton had been recruited by the Soviets, MI5 were unable to get authority from CPO to detain him. Subsequently, he was allowed to join Ursula in Oxford although arrangements were made to have his mail intercepted.

In the autumn of 1942, Ursula was forced to leave their bungalow in Kidlington and the family moved into 'Avenue Cottage' in the grounds of the house of Judge Neville Laski, a conservative and respectable non-Zionist, and his wife, Seraphina 'Sissie'. Soon after they moved in, Ursula asked Sissie for permission to erect an aerial leading from the roof of their cottage to one of the stables. It seems odd that questions were not raised about this but apparently Sissie saw no reason to deny her. By a strange coincidence, the Laski's son, Philip, had been in Lausanne in April 1941 at the same time as Ursula, staying with the Countess de Chelmisnka.

By now Ursula was creating a high level of radio transmission activity which one might have expected Britain's Radio Security Services to have picked up. She was a very experienced radio operator and fully understood that it would have been suicidal for her to transmit repeatedly from a single address in densely populated

England and expect not to be detected. Others certainly were on the case. The Försvaerts Radioanstalt (FRA) section of Swedish intelligence had intercepted and deciphered Soviet Embassy's traffic between Stockholm and Moscow referring to Simon Kremer described his meetings with 'the GRU spy runner Sonia, alias Ruth Kuczynski.'[58] Professor Glees asserts that either Ursula's claims about her multitude of transmissions were 'false, or if they were true, that there was a cover-up that must have gone beyond Hollis'.[59]

At some time towards the end of 1942, Detective Inspector Arthur Rolfe of the Oxford City Police made a visit made to Avenue Cottage and spoke to Mrs Laski, who claimed not to know much about the Beurtons but she did tell him about the aerial, which under the current wartime regulations was entirely unlawful. Apparently, Rolfe made no further inquiries about it.

Beurton, meanwhile, had joined up with the RAF, as he was obliged to do as a British citizen, and had moved back to live in Kidlington. One possible explanation for the complete lack of secrecy about the radio aerial at Avenue Cottage and the insouciance of the British authorities is that Ursula intended that MI5 would know about it and have her transmissions monitored. If indeed she was working with Farrell that would also explain the British attitude since the discovery of a wireless set would have required Ursula to be fined and forced to desist, with the equipment confiscated.

A highly plausible conclusion is that it was a distraction and a decoy. The real transmitter with the important intelligence was in Kidlington being operated by Beurton using a miniaturised transmitter that Ursula claimed had been given to her by Kremer. If Ursula did use the set in Summertown, it would probably have been to merely send unencrypted messages about the great British proletariat cheering on their gallant Soviet allies and calling for the opening of the second front. What little she probably communicated was listened to and found to be relatively harmless. It is highly likely that Dansey, with Farrell, was responsible for successfully infiltrating Foote into the Rote Drei and then helping to engineer Ursula's transfer to the UK, where SIS could extend its infiltration in, and surveillance of, communist espionage rings. Ursula was allowed to carry on broadcasting, so long as she did not reveal any secrets that might have been perilous to the war effort if they reached German eyes. With their agents such as Anthony Blunt inside MI5, it is clear that the Soviets would have been aware of MI5 involvement.

What SIS did not know about was the link between Ursula and Fuchs, however, and it was here that the real damage was done. One

GRU report attests to the fact that Fuchs, with the help of Ursula and Vladimir Barkovsky, head of scientific and technical intelligence in the Soviet Embassy was able to make copies of various keys at the Birmingham research centre. This gave him access secret documents the volume of which were, at times, 'almost too much for Ursula to cope with'.[60] In June 1943, Moscow issued 'shopping lists' of material they wanted which Ursula passed on to Fuchs. Ursula was now happily pregnant with Beurton's child and well-integrated in country life at Avenue Cottage. She was well-liked by her neighbours and took part in all the local activities. The children were attending local schools and Peter Beurton was born on 8 September 1943. Busy right up until the moment of Peter's birth, Ursula reported to Moscow on 4 September the outcomes of the highly secret military Québec Conference attended by representatives of Britain, Canada and the US. This included details of a proposed coordination of efforts to develop an atomic bomb. She had also learned from Fuchs that English scientists Peierls, Chadwick, Simon and Olifant had been sent to Washington.[61]

Rudi Hamburger, meanwhile, had been arrested in Tehran by American military police who handed him over to the British. He eventually admitted working for the Soviets and when Moscow found out about it they demanded that he be handed over to them. Upon arrival in Moscow he was arrested and held in detention. With no formal trial he was given a five-year prison sentence in the gulags ostensibly for spying against the Soviet Union. Despite the Americans waving a red flag over Rudi's spying activities, there is no indication in the record that British intelligence changed its approach to Ursula after Rudi's arrest which under normal circumstances, would have set alarm bells ringing.

In Canada on 19 August 1943, British Prime Minister Winston Churchill and US President Franklin D. Roosevelt signed the Québec Agreement, a secret arrangement to collaborate on building the atomic bomb. This vast industrial project, called the Manhattan Project, required the sort of finance and resources that Britain alone was quite unable to provide. British scientists would take part but as junior partners. The bulk of research would now take place in the US and Fuchs was one of several British-based scientists who crossed the Atlantic to work there. Sonya acted as courier for Fuchs and Melita Norwood, until both contacts were broken off at the end of 1943, with Fuchs sailing to the USA and Norwood giving birth soon after Ursula's Peter was born.

After Fuchs' departure for the USA and Len's eventual enlistment in the RAF, Ursula's espionage activities waned but she remained active.

She claimed that she maintained her contacts, and continued to use her wireless, even stating that she sent her son, Misha, and daughter, Nina, to boarding schools in Eastbourne and Epping. Apparently, the question of where the money came from to pay the school fees was never raised.

Jürgen had been approached in October 1944 by the Economic Warfare Division of the American Embassy with a request for detailed information on economic conditions inside German. Because of his technical expertise, they wanted to send him to France as a statistician with the US Army Air Force Survey team but first they asked for a vetting report from MI5, who saw no problem with that but warned the Americans about his membership of the KPD.[62] Nonetheless, the Americans made him a lieutenant colonel in the US Army and set him to work assessing the German armaments production and oil consumption. While this top secret intelligence was sent straight to Washington, thanks to Ursula it also ended up in the Kremlin.

In his new role, Jürgen was also approached by Joseph Gould, an OSS lieutenant who was recruiting German refugees for espionage missions inside Germany. He asked Jürgen if he knew of any suitable candidates. Ursula passed details of the plans to Moscow Centre, who gave her instructions to work with Gould but to exercise extreme caution. She took over from Jürgen communicating with Gould not directly but through a cutout, Erich Henschke. With Moscow's approval she recommended seven candidates who were accepted and given intensive training for the mission.

On 15 January 1945, Moscow sent a message to General Ivan Sklyarov at the Soviet Military Mission in the UK,

For your personal information. In the mountain country [Switzerland] Sonia was in contact with Albert [Radó] and his wife. The counterintelligence in your country knows about Albert's activities in the mountain country and his work for us. There are grounds to suppose that to some degree the counterintelligence may learn about Sonia's work during her stay in Albert's country.

In this connection:

1. Any personal contact with Sonia should be ceased and not to be resumed without our authorization.
2. To forbid Sonia to be engaged in our work. She should lead the life of a model mother, wife and housekeeper.

Report on the execution. Direktor.[63]

In May 1945 Ursula moved to a farmhouse, The Firs, in the Cotswold village of Great Rollright with Peter. The other children were at boarding school and Len was serving with the RAF in Germany. Then in the aftermath of Germany's defeat, new evidence emerged concerning Ursula's links with the Rote Drei. The Americans had found evidence that Rudi Hamburger had lived at 129 Rue de Lausanne, Geneva which is where Ursula and Len had lived. The FBI now asked MI5 to interview Ursula to see if she knew where Rudi was currently but MI5 'For a variety of reasons [did not] feel able to comply with this request', and wrote instead to Kim Philby, asking him to make enquiries in Switzerland about the Rue de Lausanne addresses. Philby responded that 'With regret,' he had 'no knowledge of the present whereabouts of Hamburger'.[64]

By the summer of 1946, Moscow Centre broke off contact with Ursula. Fuchs had returned from America to take up a post at the Atomic Energy Research Establishment at Harwell where scientists were designing a nuclear reactor to produce energy and had he come under suspicion after the defection of the cypher clerk Igor Gouzenko from the Soviet Embassy in Ottawa, Canada, on 5 September 1945. Gouzenko handed over a pile of documents on the Soviet espionage activities in the West exposing several spies and raising serious questions about the loyalty of a number of leading nuclear scientists, including Klaus Fuchs. When Philby passed this intelligence to Moscow, Fuchs was made aware of MI5 surveillance. Then in 1947, Alexander Foote was interrogated after giving himself up in Berlin. He explained his relationship with Ursula and the Rote Drei.

MI5 had no choice now but to confront Ursula directly. Letters to and from The Firs were intercepted and closely scrutinised; her bank statements were combed for evidence of suspicious money movements. Then on the afternoon of 13 September 1947, two men knocked on the door of The Firs and introduced themselves as Mr Saville and Mr Sneddon. In reality they were MI5 interrogators Michael Serpel and Jim Skardon. They were confronted by Ursula whom Skardon found to be 'a somewhat unimpressive type with frowsy unkempt hair, perceptibly greying, and of rather untidy appearance.' It is not difficult to imagine, Ursula in a kitchen apron, half-way through kneading a ball of dough, dusting off her floury hands and making a cup of tea for her guests. Hoping to catch her off-guard and give her a scare, Skardon wasted no time in accusing Ursula of being an agent of the Soviet Union and calmly declaring that they had come to arrest her. If he had been more aware of her background and experience dealing with hardship and danger in foreign lands, Skardon might have been more circumspect, but he had played his best card straight away. Ursula replied that she did not 'think she could cooperate', stating that she did not intend to tell lies and therefore preferred not to answer questions. This was a tacit admission, but Skardon and Serpel could get no further.[65] Ursula easily parried further questions, and they settled down to a long conversation to try and clear up what Skardon called a few anomalies. No arrest was made, however, and the two men left convinced that although she undoubtedly had communistic convictions, she was not currently engaged in espionage and had not been for some time. It was a particularly weak and submissive conclusion for two of MI5's top inquisitors.

Ursula was unsettled by the interview but saw no reason to panic. The children were now completely English. Daughter Nina was an ardent royalist who collected every newspaper cutting about the royal family and particularly admired Princess Elizabeth. Peter collected Dinky toys, while Michael was studying philosophy at Aberdeen University. After a lifetime of subterfuge and travel she felt completely at home and settled in England but Jürgen, who had by now gone back to Berlin, urged caution and suggested she join him in the Soviet occupied zone of Germany. Then a newspaper headline on 3 February 1950 changed everything. Under the headline, 'German atomic scientist arrested', she read the name of Klaus Fuchs.

Ursula wasted no time in arranging her flight, buying four US Army waterproof canvas kitbags with zip fasteners and packing them with as much as she could. Beurton, who had recently broken his leg in a motorcycle accident, could not join her but Nina and Peter, aged 13 and 6 respectively, were both minors and could travel on Ursula's passport.

They flew to Berlin via Hamburg on 27 February, two days before Fuchs' trial was due to begin but could not find Jürgen straight away. Without accommodation they went from one hotel to another looking for a place to stay and ended up in very dingy surroundings. Ursula wrote that 'The children slept together in one cold, damp bed, I in the other. It was early March. The room was only heated one day in three, with three or four pieces of coal. The ravages of war were still very evident in that part of town. Lots of pubs, lots of drunks and many bombed-out houses.'[66]

It was only in May 1950 that MI5 officers Graham, Reed and Marriott decided to conduct a further interview with Ursula. It took them until August to conclude that she was no longer in the country.

After a trial lasting less than ninety minutes, Fuchs was found guilty and sentenced to fourteen years' imprisonment. On Thursday, 13 July 1950, all Ursula's household effects that remained in England were sold by public auction, with Renate supervising and Len Beurton was nowhere to be found.

When Ursula sent her children to school, they were understandably ostracised for having little German and speaking only English. They were desperately unhappy after their idyllic life in England far away from the destruction of war. Ursula struggled to keep them clothed and fed having no income and little in the way of help from Jürgen who was forced out of his position as president of the German-Soviet Friendship Society in 1950 because of his middle-class Jewish background and became increasingly vulnerable to attack from within the ranks of the ruling Socialist Unity Party.[67]

There had come a turning point in her life as a spy, however. It may have been the sudden relief of no longer living with the constant threat of exposure with all that entailed. It may have been a sense that she now needed to devote herself to her children or it may have been that she was simply tired of subterfuge. Whatever the reason when the GRU came knocking on her door again she politely declined to go back to active duty. It was a perilous thing to do, the GRU did not like retired agents over whom they had little control.

She found work in the press department of the new East German government and Peter joined up with the family once he had finished his studies in Aberdeen but she was unable to evade the close scrutiny of the Stasi state police who kept her under constant surveillance. There is some evidence to suggest that SIS tried to persuade her to return to active spying by suggesting that the East German regime was about to embark on a major purge of Jewish communists, some of whom might be tempted to defect. A letter written by MI5 and sent to SIS stated that '[the Kuczynskis] are likely to possess valuable information about Russian espionage, and that it is worth going to considerable lengths to get them, and with them their information'.[68] Ursula was fired from her job in late 1953 for an alleged minor breach of security and began a career as a writer of books for children and young adults under the name of Ruth Werner. Then in 1955, Rudi emerged from his incarceration in Siberia. Ursula described him as 'Greying, slightly bowed, a brittle voice, and dazed, like a man emerging from a cellar into the light, a semi-stranger with a smile that hid a touch of melancholy.'[69]

Michael Hamburger, became one of Germany's leading Shakespeare scholars. For thirty years, he worked as dramaturge and director at the Deutsches Theater in Berlin. Nina Hamburger was a teacher. Peter Beurton, the youngest, became a distinguished biologist–philosopher at the Academy of Sciences in East Berlin.

In 1969, a second Order of the Red Banner followed the first, and Ursula was awarded the National Prize of East Germany, the Order of Karl Marx, the Patriotic Order of Merit and the Jubilee Medal. At the age of 84 she briefly visited Britain to publicise her memoirs while SIS turned a blind eye. She died in Berlin on 7 July 2000.

Chapter 3

RICHARD SORGE: THE TOKYO SPY

What amazed most of all was how one man's effort could achieve what whole armies not. One spy could decide the fate of thousands of people.[1]

Near the village of Sabunçu near to the Azerbaijan capital of Baku stands a bronze and granite monument dedicated to a man who was born there on 4 October 1895 and who James Bond author Ian Fleming would later call 'the most formidable spy in history'. The youngest of nine children, Rikhard Gustavovich Zorge, known in the West as Richard Sorge, was the son of a German father, Gustav, and Russian mother, Nina. Gustav, a man who had 'unmistakeable nationalist and imperialist sympathies' was an oil-drilling specialist who worked for the Deutsche Petroleum-Aktiengesellschaft the oil-fields on the edge of the Caspian Sea but when his contact was up the family moved from the heavily polluted Caucasus to the Lichterfelde region of Berlin when Richard was 2 years old.[2] He grew up there in a comfortable middle-class environment. Despite spending his first years in a blighted region that 'choked on its own effluent' and could have no recollection of his time there, Sorge retained a fanciful, nostalgic, emotional attachment to his Baku heritage.[3] When he started the *Oberrealschule*, he rebelled against the bourgeois sensibilities of his family and later characterised himself as 'a bad pupil refusing to submit to inflexible Prussian authoritarianism' but despite his wilful non-compliance with rules and regulations, he showed an intellectual capacity and athletic prowess that put him 'far above the rest of the class'.[4]

Adolescence found him absorbed in social and political developments in a fast-changing world but he remained fascinated by the Pan-German ideals of the *Jugendbewegung* youth movement that celebrated the great outdoors and the fabled German *volk*. He was caught up the patriotic fervour of 1914 that saw him enlist in the German army on 11 August. Posted to the Third Guards Field Artillery he got his first experience of slaughter on 11 November when his unit was called on to storm French and Belgian positions along the banks of the Yser in Flanders and was badly mauled by enemy machine guns. He saw a great many of his comrades fall on that day but he survived only to be wounded by shrapnel a few short months later. Convalescing at home in Berlin, he entered into a bleak landscape where the black market thrived in the face of food shortages. The corruption he saw there disgusted him after witnessing the sacrifice of his young comrades on the battle front. He began, for the first time, to question the validity of war and the motivations of the country's leaders who had brought this catastrophe on their people. However, he did not shy away when called to duty on the Eastern Front when he was well enough to return to action.

He was wounded again in 1916 but when he returned to the front a second time he found the mood among the troops significantly influenced by left-wing propaganda decrying the meaningless sacrifice of war. Sorge now began to seriously question the middle-class values he had grown up with and the patriotism that had driven him so willingly to war. When he suffered a third, much more serious, injury that saw him hospitalised for a lengthy spell in a field hospital at Königsberg his real political education began. Shrapnel had again been responsible for him losing three fingers and suffering two broken legs but at least this time the injury resulted in the award of the Iron Cross Second Class for bravery.

While chatting to Sorge as she tending to his terrible wounds, a young nurse noted that he expressed views that were somewhat critical of the war that had left him and so many other young men suffering such pain and mutilation to say nothing of the hundreds of thousands who had perished in the trenches. She, herself, was a radical socialist like her father who was a doctor in the same hospital and both together they befriended Sorge and began talking to him about left-wing politics and lent him books on the theories of socialism. This was not the first time that Sorge had been exposed to Marxist doctrine, his great uncle Friedrich Adolf Sorge had been an associate of Karl Marx and Friedrich Engels.

His legs were saved from amputation but left him with one leg shorter than the other and a physical disability that pained him periodically throughout his life. Being unfit for further active duty, he was left free to resume his studies first at Berlin University, then Kiel

University and finally at Hamburg University where he gained a PhD in political science in 1919.

After the success of the Bolshevik Revolution in Russia and the capitulation of the German army in 1918, there were turbulent days in Germany. The cities were haunted by hunger as the Allied naval blockade continued and an influenza epidemic felled many who had survived the trenches. Street battles raged between the far-left radical Spartacists and the far-right reactionary Freikorps. The country was on the brink of its own all-out communist revolution and civil war. Sorge had been drawn into the maelstrom whilst at Kiel where he had joined the Independent Social Democratic Party determined to fight the evils of society that had brought the country to the edge of chaos. It was the naval mutiny in that city that had first catalysed the left-wing uprising. Eager to support the communist insurgents not only ideologically put in practice Sorge secretly went around the docks preaching insurrection to the sailors. He helped to collect weapons which he and others took to Berlin but they were halted at the station and detained by police. Reactionary forces were gaining the upper hand. When Rosa Luxemburg and Karl Liebknecht, the Spartacist leaders were brutally murdered by fascist thugs the revolution was over. Sorge was released and sent back to Kiel.

In early 1921, he was a political editorial writer for a communist newspaper in the Ruhr. The Communist Party at that time was under close scrutiny from government officials, and Sorge became an important liaison, carrying messages between Berlin and the party in Frankfurt am Main. Between his comings and goings, he developed a close relationship with the Marxist professor of economics Dr Kurt Gerlach and, more importantly, Gerlach's wife Christiane who became infatuated with this handsome, brooding young man with 'clear, sharp eyes [in which] lay infinite distance, and loneliness [that] everybody could feel'.[5]

Sorge began working as an assistant to Dr Gerlach, but then decided to go to work in the Aachen coalmines to experience the working conditions there. He soon started inculcating the miners with revolutionary Marxist ideology, which may have been his primary motivation for going down the mines in the first place. This did not go down well with either the mine owners or the local authorities who were always on the lookout for agitators who threatened to stir up trouble and disrupt production. When it seemed to the authorities that his attempts at radicalisation of the workforce were rather more effective than the usual rabble-rousing rhetoric of the disgruntled, they had Sorge fired and driven from the town. This was not before the relationship between him and Christiane had reached the point where Dr Gerlach bowed to the inevitable and rather than suffer the ignominy of the cuckold, he agreed to a quick divorce so that the couple could marry in Solingen. This they did in May 1921, just a year before Dr Gerlach fell ill and died from diabetes.

In 1923, Sorge met the Soviet scholar David Riazanov who had come to Germany looking for original documents connected to Karl Marx. Sorge's great uncle Friedrich was in possession of several such documents. When Riazanov called on Sorge, he was impressed by his intellect and commitment to the communist cause and, upon returning to Moscow, mentioned his encounter to a number of high-ranking NKVD intelligence officers. In the following year Sorge joined the KPD and when he later moved to Frankfurt in 1924 he worked as a research associate at the Marxist Institute of Social Research. While attending a secret KPD conference in Frankfurt as a bodyguard for the Soviet delegation, he was approached by some of its senior members and invited to visit Moscow where he was recruited by the Comintern. He took out Soviet citizenship but retained his German passport.

At first Christiane had been enthusiastic about a move to Moscow and made plans to follow Sorge after he had been spirited away but when she joined up with him a year later, disillusionment soon set in. Neither spoke Russian and they were forced to mix socially with predominantly German expats which Christiane found suffocating and intolerable. While Sorge was having a fine time wining and dining with the Comintern elite and learning to speak the language, she was left at home feeling increasingly isolated. Living the high life as something of a celebrity in Moscow, Sorge found himself succumbing to the temptations afforded him by his status in the capital of what was not only a political but a sexual revolution where free love and sexual liberation were, if not exactly encouraged then at least tolerated. Christiane, however, was not someone who would put up with Sorge's heavy drinking and philandering finally leaving him in late 1926. Returning to Germany, she eventually sued for divorce in 1932 and emigrated to the United States under her maiden name of Sandler.

Sorge seemed as little disturbed by Christiane's departure as he had been by the desperately bleak post-revolutionary atmosphere in Moscow and threw himself into the role he was carving out for himself as a career Comintern activist. First, he created a reputation as an intellectual by both writing and lecturing on the class struggle in Germany. Then he pestered bosses at the Department of Propaganda to let him move into a more active role as a secret agent. It was an image of himself that he had nurtured ever since his days at university.

The romance of lonely heroism appealed strongly to him but he was going to have to learn the ropes before he would be let off the leash.

He was given a series of assignments to test his mettle. First to Frankfurt and then to Stockholm to organise local communist parties and bring them under the wing of the Comintern but neither of them required much of him in the way of initiative or imagination. He also spent three months in England in 1929 travelling on a false passport and reporting on the miners' strike while liaising with a Soviet spy inside SIS believed to be Charles Ellis. Sorge objected to this dual role on the grounds of security. An agent in a foreign land mixing with known communists risked coming to the attention of the police which in turn threatened to compromise their intelligence sources.[6] When he got back to Moscow he made his feelings known in as forceful a way as was prudent to do so. His bosses in the Comintern had other things on their minds, however. Comintern chairman Nikolai Bukharin was swept out of power and had to plead with Stalin for his life. This left Sorge in a very precarious position, but he was saved by Berzin who instructed him to sever all ties with the Comintern to give the impression that he was being sidelined from the espionage community then had him secretly recruited to the Fourth Department, the Red Army Main Intelligence Directorate. Berzin at the time was putting resources into establishing networks in the Far East, notably in Shanghai, Harbin, Mukden and Canton. These had been thought of as fertile ground for sowing the seeds of communism and undermining the colonies of the Western Powers but recent events had seen many communist leaders there executed as China slumped into civil war. Berzin desperately needed to know which side was likeliest to win and it would be the role of his agents there to ascertain the popular support and military strength of the two sides. He called for intelligence on:

a) specific coverage, with figures, of the work of the military plants;
b) provision of raw materials and fuel;
c) the condition of the railways and maritime transport;
d) construction of warehouses, bases, equipment of shipment ports;
e) the organization and condition of the air defence system;
f) the condition of the Japanese countryside and the agrarian question.[7]

First Sorge went to Berlin with Alexander Ulanovsky, who would be his chief in Shanghai, to create new identities as cover for their mission. Ulanovsky took on the guise of a Czech businessman called Kirschner going out to China as a representative of the German arms manufacturer Schelder-Consortium. This was totally in contravention of the terms imposed upon Germany under the Treaty of Versailles but these were circumvented by creating false export documents.[8] Sorge, meanwhile, working under his real identity, touted himself as an expert on Chinese social, political and economic affairs and advertised his availability as a freelance correspondent. He got a positive response from the *Deutsche Getreide Zeitung* reporting on agricultural matters. He also arranged with an influential consortium of German businesses with interests in China, to write a report on the development of the Chinese banking system. For this mission he would have the code name 'Ramsay' later changed to 'Vix'. The two men, along with a third member of the team, radio operator Sepp Weingarten, travelled to Marseilles, boarded a ship of the Messageries Maritimes line on 7 December 1929 and set sail for Shanghai, via Malta, Aden, Bombay, and Hong Kong, arriving there on 10 January 1930.

Shanghai was an international metropolis of some 2.5 million people many of whom were British and American. This city, often referred to as 'the whore of the Orient', was a burgeoning commercial economic dynamo and feeding ground trading a wide range of commodities through its factories and port and where the world's largest banks had premises.[9] Operating almost as an independent entity beyond the control of the Chinese government, Shanghai was famous for its 'vibrant' night life, gambling, prostitution and opium dens all under the jurisdiction of an indigenous police force run by the British who had to contend with rival gangsters and triad warlords as well as a multitude of foreign and Chinese spies. Situated on the southern estuary of the Yangtze River, the city had grown from a small fishing village to become one of five cities open to foreign trade and influence after the First Opium War. There were effectively several different Shanghais. The Shanghai of the Chinese had its roots deep in history where it had long been an important trading centre. The Shanghai of the Anglo-Americans was the business centre, and the Shanghai of the French was the preferred residential sector for the wealthy and the Europeans but was also home to the infamous Green Gang who ran the Shanghai underworld. Foreigners required no residence permit and had only to register at their respective consulates.

By 1930, Shanghai was also Asia's espionage capital through which passed many of the great Soviet 'illegals' of the age, Arnold Deutsch, Theodore Maly, Alexander Radó, Otto Katz, Leopold Trepper, Ignace Poretsky, Walter Krivitsky, Ruth Werner and Wilhelm Pieck. Illegals were covert espionage operatives with no links to official government agencies such as embassies. This city, the 'lair or the gathering ground of the spies of the world ... a town that collected the sharks and human debris of the universe' offered unparalleled opportunities for secret work.[10]

Rather late to the table, the NKVD had a hard time trying to catch up with their European counterparts in the Far East. Very few Soviet agents could speak, read or write any of the indigenous languages which made it extremely difficult to develop a network of non-Russian speaking informants. What little they picked up at Moscow language schools was far removed from the real language of the street. At best they could speak no more than a crude pidgin form of Chinese and understood very little of what was going on around them. Consequently, such informant network as they established were made up of Russian speakers which inevitably exposed them to tainted intelligence since many informants were reporting to various political entities and intelligence bureaus. Furthermore, once on station and almost 7,000 miles from Moscow, Soviet agents tended to show scant regard for their training or mission goals and 'acted as if they were a bird freed from a cage and eagerly dived into the vices of the Far East.'[11]

Ulanovsky and Sorge had been sent to Shanghai at short notice to replace the incumbent Alexander Gurvich and establish a new 'clean' network allowing the old one to wither on the vine. Before arriving in China in 1928, Gurvich had learned the espionage trade working for the Soviets in New York as an employee of the Radio Corporation of America (RCA) where he learned to operate long-range transmitters. He had built the Shanghai network from scratch with few resources under cover of a German trading company financed by Moscow. He was given no prior warning about the arrival of Ulanovsky and Sorge which made for an uneasy transition. He bitterly resented being usurped and did his best to disrupt it. Sorge effectively ignored Gurvich and left Ulanovsky to deal with him while he settled down to do what he did best which was socialising, drinking and womanising on a much more sophisticated level that he had ever been able to do before as he familiarised himself with the casinos and night clubs of Shanghai.

When Germany's covert collaboration with the Soviet Union on military research and development began to founder in 1930 due to a growing realisation that the Soviets were getting more out of it than the Germans were, Berlin had made overtures to Tokyo for a modest level of military cooperation. At the same time negotiations were underway for the import of Chinese raw materials such as molybdenum and wolfram, required for the production of hardened steel and German military advisers had been sent to help modernise the Chinese army.

It was this cadre that Sorge's credentials allowed him to penetrate. He effortlessly befriended these men, far from home in a city ripe with temptation as he trawled for information in the bars and brothels of the city where loose talk and gossip gave him an insight into both Chinese and German military capabilities and ambitions.

Not all of Gurvich's network was deactivated. Two notable exceptions that were kept on station were Max Clausen and Ray Bennett. The Russian-born Raisa 'Ray' Bennett, née Epstein, had been Soviet military intelligence's primary asset on the west coast of America before being called to Moscow in 1932 where she taught English to agents being trained for deployment in the Far East. A chance encounter with GRU chief Jan Berzin saw her recruited to Red Army intelligence. Berzin sent her to Shanghai in 1929 to work for Gurvich using the codename 'Josephine'. There she learned how to code and decode messages while running a language school as cover. Max Clausen had been Gurvich's radio man since 1928 and remained a vital part of the China operation until 1933.

One of Sorge's first contacts was the famous American journalist Agnes Smedley who wrote for *Frankfurter Zeitung* covering anti-British imperialism in India and anti-colonialism in China. She had arrived in Harbin, a Chinese city with strong Russian connections at the end of 1928. She found the city swarming with destitute and starving peasants about whom she reported back to Berzin. Moving on, Smedley went to Mukden, Dalian and then Peking where she attended secret meetings to plan strikes and demonstrations all the time sending copious reports back to Moscow about the appalling conditions of workers. She was an avid photographer and made a huge collection of prints of subjects such as child workers who had been sold into slavery by their destitute parents. These children worked twelve-hour days in exchange for two meals of millet gruel and a nightly spot in barracks-like rooms that afforded them little protection from the elements.[12] When she reached Nanking in March 1929, she witnessed leftist workers and intellectuals being dragged from their beds and tortured or beheaded in the streets. Two months later she was in Shanghai, a city of 'unrelenting misery' where rickshaws still jousted with American luxury cars.[13] With its substantial population of industrial workers, this was where the Chinese Communist Party had been born and where Berzin saw the best chance of rekindling the spirit of revolution in China. Having settled into the foreign YMCA on Bubbling Well Road, Sorge called on Smedley at her home in the French Concession with a letter of introduction from someone he referred to simply as a mutual acquaintance in Berlin.[14] He asked Smedley to help him to establish an intelligence network in the city. She readily agreed but it is likely that Sorge encouraged her to believe that he was working on behalf of the Comintern, which Smedley approved of, rather than the NKVD which she might have been less willing to risk her life for. Her role included acting as a mail drop and liaison, offering her home for meetings, paying agents and providing information about such things as the increasing American influence and investment in China.

Before long, Sorge's charms started to work on Smedley who told a friend that she had found a 'rare, rare person' who could give her everything she wanted and more. Completely smitten by Sorge's 'cold blue eyes, thick brown hair, and sensuous mouth' and despite his arrogance and fiery temper, she was frequently seen roaring through the streets of Shanghai on the back of Sorge's motorcycle.[15] By 1930 Smedley was writing to a friend Karin Michaelis saying that she was 'deeply involved in a relationship with a new man'.[16] On 28 May 1930, she told another fiend Florence Lennon, 'I am sort of married [but] I do not know how long it will last … these days will be the most beautiful of my life'.[17]

Sorge had been specifically ordered to keep clear of Chinese Communist Party members who might be known to the police, so he needed to establish his own network which he did using Smedley's contacts who were not party members. The British authorities in Shanghai, however, were keeping a close eye on Smedley, as were American, German, French, and nationalist Chinese officials. She knew this and took it as a great compliment but realised also that even though she felt that the British, in particular, overestimated her importance, the consequences for communist activists of any stripe could be fatal.

In June 1930, Sorge assumed full control of his network, which included informants in Canton, when Ulanovsky was forced to flee to Hong Kong having been blackmailed by one of his informants, Rafail Kurgan. Sorge now had a group of informants and mixed easily in the upper social circles of the city, soon becoming a favourite at parties and other gatherings. At consulate affairs, he was able to rub shoulders with Chiang Kai-shek's German advisers, through whom he picked up intelligence about Chinese military matters. There were also German merchants, scholars, military advisers to the Nanking government, and other officials who were linked to the German Consulate General but he still had plenty of free time to spend with Smedley and his friend Gerhardt Eisler, the German communist who had become the Comintern's chief representative in China. Despite Smedley providing him with intelligence through her own contacts, Sorge would later say that women were 'absolutely unfit for espionage work [having] no understanding of political or other affairs' although he admitted that she had 'a brilliant mind' and was more like a man in many ways.[18] It is perhaps surprising therefore to note that Chinese women played a prominent role in Sorge's Shanghai network whom he described as having 'fitted into our network extremely well'.[19] Smedley was far from useless in making contacts for Sorge providing economic data and military information, but he was becoming increasingly concerned that too many of them were Chinese recruits who could come under scrutiny for frequent contact with Westerners.

Just as Sorge was settling in to reap the benefits of his work an incident occurred near Mudken on the night of 18 September 1931 that would have catastrophic consequences before the decade was out. An explosion on the South Manchuria Railway saw fighting erupt between Chinese and Japanese forces resulting in the Japanese occupation first of Mukden followed quickly by their occupation of the whole of Manchuria. By the start of 1932, Chinese forces had also been driven out of Shanghai after a brutal battle.

Sorge recognised this as a foretaste of what was to come and reported that Japan seemed determined to extend its role and pose a serious threat to China. At the time, Moscow did not have any intelligence network in Japan but now it was clear that they would have to give much more attention to the defence of its vast eastern border regions and discover what Japan's ultimate ambitions were. Sorge's response was to immerse himself in a study of Japanese history, culture and foreign policy. He was also especially interested in acquiring a Japanese source and this time it was Ginichi Kito, a Japanese member of the CPUSA who was the catalyst bringing Hotsumi Ozaki into the network but Smedley remained the main contact for both sources.[20]

Hotsumi Ozaki was a respected journalist, fluent in English, German and Chinese as well as Japanese. When they met Sorge introduced himself as an American journalist called Johnson but Ozaki doubted that he was any of those things. Nevertheless, on the strength of Smedley's recommendation, he agreed to work with Sorge, believing him to be affiliated with the International Red Aid, the same Comintern auxiliary for which Ozaki believed Agnes worked.

Ozaki was born in Tokyo in 1901. After graduating from Tokyo Imperial University, he joined the *Asahi Shimbun* newspaper publishers. In 1928, he became a correspondent in Shanghai soon getting a strong journalistic reputation specialising in Chinese issues. He had excellent contacts in the Japanese official and business community and would later become Sorge's most important collaborator in Japan. Chalmers Johnson argued in his book *Instance of Treason: Ozaki Hotsumi and the Sorge Spy Ring* that they were the most intellectually overqualified spies in modern history.[21] Alongside Ozaki, Sorge also recruited Mizuno Shigeru and Kawai Teikichi. The affable and easy-going Ozaki educated Sorge about Japanese culture and the Japanese mind. They quickly bonded both as spies, drinking buddies and womanisers cruising the raucous and indulgent night club circuit of the city.

When Smedley returned from some months in the Philippines in the spring of 1931, the relationship with Sorge came to an abrupt end. Two Chinese Comintern members had been arrested by the police leaving a young son to fend for himself. Smedley asked her friend Ursula Kuczynski to take him in but Sorge persuaded her not to do so fearing that it would bring unwanted police attention on them all.

Almost before it began, however, the Sorge-Ozaki partnership was also sundered when Ozaki was recalled to Tokyo by his employer, the newspaper *Asahi Shimbun* in February 1932. Soon afterwards Sorge was also withdrawn to Moscow but his next assignment would reunite him with Ozaki. Berzin congratulated Sorge on three successful years in Shanghai while he worked out how to make use of him next. Sorge meanwhile settled down to rekindle a relationship with Katya Maximova, a lover from the time of his first arrival in Moscow when she had been assigned to teach him Russian.

Berzin was keen to send Sorge back to the Far East and Sorge was happy to oblige but they both agreed that Japan was now the place where he could be most useful. Russia had painful and humiliating memories of a defeat to Japanese forces in the Russo-Japanese War of 1904–1905. Russia's conversion to communist control had done little to mend relations between the two countries since then and Japanese soldiers were once again striking a belligerent pose as they swept away Soviet influence in Manchuria and massed on the Soviet border. There was little the Soviets could do in the short term militarily if Japan chose to extend its influence. Therefore knowledge of Japanese capabilities and intentions was vital which meant that an intelligence capability in Tokyo was urgently needed. Specifically, Moscow wanted intelligence about the power dynamics between the Japanese government and the Japanese military. The conquest of Manchuria suggested that the army and the fierce anti-Soviet element within it would now have the upper hand and that might presage a more adventurist policy towards the Soviet Union. The sheer density of Japan's population and the deep resentment felt against Western Powers that had colonised much of the Eastern

Pacific region pointed to a 'break-out' expansionist foreign policy but the question was in which direction would it go. Even if it was China upon which the Japanese fixed their gaze, that would have consequences for Moscow too.

Berzin finally decided that Sorge would go to Tokyo and set up an intelligence network but before he left at some time in July, Katya and he were married. Actually, neither was the marrying kind and the marriage was more of a transaction to ensure that as the wife of a Red Army officer, Katya would receive his salary while he was on foreign duty. Sorge went first to Berlin to freshen up his German credentials and renew his German passport. He had established something of a reputation as an expert on Chinese agriculture with his articles published in the *Deutsche Getreide Zeitung* which now got him a contact to write articles for the most influential strategic journal in Germany *Zeitschrift für Geopolitic* and the Dutch magazine *Algemeen Handelsblad* on Japanese agriculture. Sorge had done enough research to impress the journal's owner, Karl Haushofer sufficiently with his appreciation of Nazi ideology that in return he got a letter of introduction to the German ambassadors to both Japan and the US. Sorge then went to see the editor of another newspaper, the *Tägliche Rundschau*, who also agreed to publish articles on China and through him was recommended to look up Lieutenant Colonel Eugen Ott who had been instrumental in establishing military relations between Germany and Japan in 1930 and was now serving as liaison with the Japanese military. After an uncomfortable few weeks in the lion's den of Nazi Germany now starting to feel the icy grip of terror, Sorge sailed for New York and crossed the Continent to the west coast.

Here he met up again with Ray Bennett who had been recalled to Moscow in poor health and then after a period of rehabilitation had been sent back to the US with orders to establish a residency recruiting Japanese sailors and monitoring cargoes being exported to Japan. Another aspect of her mission was to find a radio operator to go to Japan and act as a translator for Sorge. She came up with Yotoku Miyagi, an artist who also ran a restaurant called the *Fukuro* (Owl) in the Little Tokyo district of West Los Angeles. Miyagi was born in Okinawa but had emigrated to the US where he joined the CPUSA. Although a committed communist, Miyagi at first refused to consider the idea but eventually agreed and was given a crash training course in radio by Bennett.

Sorge arrived in Yokohama on 6 September 1933. As an 'illegal' without diplomatic cover, he would need all his skills and more to survive in the charged atmosphere of a country only just emerging from feudalism but still firmly under authoritarian control of an illiberal regime and its confident ambitious military. The relatively few Westerners were treated with suspicion everywhere and closely observed by the police. Sorge knew that in order to pass scrutiny in Tokyo he would need extra special cover and this, he calculated could be achieved by forging links with the German Embassy in much the same way he had done in Shanghai. If he could get accepted by the Germans that would make it a lot easier to move about the city freely without raising concerns. There was a growing relationship between the German and Japanese governments and a sense that each could benefit from closer ties so the general mood was that Germans in Japan would not be harassed or intimidated by the police.[22]

Sorge set about establishing his network. Branko 'Vukie' Vukelić was a Croatian who had fled to Paris to avoid persecution for his communist sympathies and it was there in 1932 that the 28-year-old multi-lingual Vukelić had been recruited by Soviet intelligence for deployment in the Far East. He was far from being the most eager conscript believing himself to be quite unsuited for spying, but he was persuaded by assurances that it was nothing like the fictional accounts of magazines and novels. Given the codename 'Bernhardt', his cover would be as a correspondent for the French magazine *Vu* which featured reports from around the world, and also for the Yugoslav newspaper *Politika*. Before leaving he was given training in the photographing of documents and the creation of microfilms. He and his wife Edith sailed from Marseilles and arrived in Yokohama on 11 February 1933. His first meeting with Sorge, whom he knew as 'Schmidt' was not until October 1933 at the Meguro Hotel. Sorge was reading a book when Vukelić approached him and asked if he yet reached page 128. Sorge replied that actually he had got as far as page 171 and their bona fides were established. By this time Vukelić was ill, homesick and broke and tried to disguise his predicament with false bonhomie but the old hand Sorge could hardly believe that Moscow would send him someone who did not look at all like 'a serious type' and made no effort to hide his feelings.[23]

Vukelić, codename 'Gigolo', had been specifically warned to stay away from the Soviet Embassy in Tokyo but the money Moscow had given him to survive on had proved to be significantly less than he needed. Feeling abandoned in a strange and foreign land, it was only the fees for his newspaper articles and money Edith earned as a gymnastics instructor that stood between them and destitution. However, he had made important contacts within the French and

British communities in Tokyo and he would be important to Sorge's network for his photographic skills.

Miyagi arrived in Yokohama on 24 October with no clear idea of what he had let himself in for and nervously waited to be contacted. Vukelić placed an advertisement in the *Japan Advertiser* asking for anyone willing to sell any Ukiyo-e prints or books about the art form written in English. It was the signal Miyagi had been instructed to look out for. He duly replied and met Vukelić who introduced him to Sorge. Sorge reassured the clearly reluctant Miyagi by explaining that their mission was to do everything possible to avoid war between Japan and the Soviet Union. Miyagi was seriously regretting ever agreeing to his adventure and urged Sorge to find someone to replace him as soon as possible.

Sorge had no intention of doing so and in the meantime, instructed Miyagi, given the codename 'Joe', to make contact with Ozaki who was in Tokyo working for the *Asahi Shimbun* and bring him into the network. He would be vital for penetrating the inner sanctums of Japanese society to which no Westerner could ever hope to gain access. Ozaki was naturally suspicious of unsolicited contacts but when Miyagi mentioned a man called 'Johnson' he understood and agreed to a meeting with the man he had known in Shanghai but he did not know Sorge's true identity until 1936. When he readily agreed to provide Sorge with his assessments of Japan's political and military policies, Ozaki was effectively making himself a traitor to his country and it is not entirely clear why he should have endangered himself and his family in such a way. It's true that he was a committed communists and had been since his student days in Tokyo Imperial University when he witnessed the arrest and execution of many communist leaders in Japan and later he had been appalled by Japan's military adventurism in Manchuria. He was also acutely aware of the international hostility towards the home of communism, the Soviet Union. Sorge played on these sentiments but was careful to maintain the fiction that he was working for the Comintern and all through his involvement with Sorge, Ozaki, codename 'Otto', was unaware that he was actually passing intelligence to the GRU.

Sorge had used Bruno Wendt as a radio operator in Shanghai and he was currently with him in Tokyo but would later be replaced by Max Clausen, who had also worked for Sorge in Shanghai. When the German journalist Günther Stein joined them, the hard core of the network was in place. Stein, codename 'Gustav', was a naturalised British subject sent by Moscow to Tokyo where he made his house available to hide the radio transmitter. Sorge now set about establishing himself as a fixture at the German Club, the Silver Slipper, Rheingold and Fledermaus bars, the Florida dance hall, and, on a rather more respectable level, the German Chamber of Commerce and embassy receptions. He quickly won for himself a reputation as a 'sparkling conversationalist' and something of an 'eccentric, hard-drinking, fast-living bachelor'.[24]

One of the most valuable of his wide-reaching network of contacts and sources turned out to be the German military attaché Eugen Ott, who would later be appointed as ambassador in 1939. Ott, referred to by the Soviets as 'Anna', took to Sorge straight away when they met in September 1934. He was a dyed in the wool Prussian military man and admired Sorge's war record, not to mention his charm and adversarial worth on the chess board. The relationship between the two men even survived Sorge's seduction of Ott's wife, Helma, to which Ott turned a blind eye, the marriage having already broken down. When Ott undertook a tour of Manchuria he got permission to take Sorge with him resulting in a voluminous file of Japan's reconstruction of the region compiled by Sorge which he presented to Ott. At the same time Sorge was getting Ozaki's analysis of the Manchurian Incident which, he said was likely to lead to all-out war between Japan and China. All of this was put in a report that Ott forwarded to his superiors in Berlin mentioning that much of it had come from Sorge. It would have been quite a shock for them had they known that an identical report was put on Berzin's desk in Moscow at the same time as it hit theirs. Ott, whose enthusiasm for closer German-Japanese cooperation was substantially greater than other members of the diplomatic corps in Tokyo, then went on to create a study group to investigate Japanese army resources and potential deployment towards China and it was no surprise when Sorge was invited to join it.[25] He was also given access to negotiations taking place for the exchanges of technical, tactical and strategic data between Japan and Germany as well as an annual exchange of naval intelligence about the Soviet Union. This was a vital breakthrough for Sorge who had been particularly ordered by Moscow to uncover any evidence of a move away from talk to action in terms of Japanese military deployment along the Soviet border.

During his first year in the country, Sorge had tirelessly applied his keen intellect to a meticulous study and analysis of Japanese culture, history and current affairs with the help of Ozaki. He was particularly fascinated by Japanese religion, rituals and art not to mention the graceful and delicate women but the very different way of life from that he had known, over time, created within him a sense of isolation which increasingly burdened him especially after his accident in 1939.

His ability to entertain many of the German Embassy staff with his bonhomie made them feel a little less alienated in a strange city. Talking to them of home over a few glasses of saki, he quickly gained their confidence and they responded with unfiltered gossip about what was going on in Berlin. With a solid reputation as the 'best-informed' German journalist in Japan, he was regularly seen accompanying the German Ambassador Herbert von Dirksen and his military and naval attachés on official business. He even went so far as to join the Nazi Party (membership No. 2751466). It was not necessary to play the party angle too much, however, since the German Foreign Office, of which the diplomats were a part, was notoriously sceptical, even hostile to Nazi ideology. He was now effectively operating as an unofficial agent of the *Deutsche Nachrichtenbüro* (the official central press agency of the Reich, DNB) and keeping up a regular correspondence with its head Hugo von Ritgen. He was establishing a firm foundation on which to build his espionage ring.

In July 1935, Sorge was recalled to Moscow at short notice. Rather than go overland, he sailed to San Francisco which made it easy to convince Ott and other embassy staff that he was going to the US for a holiday. He crossed America and the Atlantic arriving in Moscow where he was reunited with Katya. When he looked for Berzin he found that he had been replaced by General Semyon Petrovich Uritsky but knew better than to inquire why. Fortunately for him, Uritsky showed great appreciation of Sorge's work in Tokyo. Asked for his appraisal of the network, Sorge suggested that maybe it was time to get a new radio man and proposed Max Clausen as a suitable replacement. Clausen was a plain stocky man with a sly grin and an ingratiating manner whose wife Anna, not without reason, thought that Sorge had been a bad influence on her husband while they had worked together in Shanghai.[26] Clausen had been in Moscow since his recall in 1933 training under Gurevich in the development and use of new portable radio transmitters and receivers at the new radio operator school on the Lenin Hills. With a new identity, Goldberg, his passport now showed him to be of German-Hungarian nationality.

Sorge gave no indication to his colleagues that he had been affected by the atmosphere of fear that pervaded every corner of Moscow and he made no mention of the number of his old comrades who had disappeared but to friends he showed signs of despair that the country he was risking his life for was slipping into a reign of terror. When he returned to Tokyo it was with a mixture of relief at leaving Moscow where he had begun to feel vulnerable and a reluctance to return to a role that no longer seemed as noble and virtuous as it once had. On

Leopold Trepper as a young man

Ursula Kuczynski

Ursula Kuczynski and Len Buerton

Ursula, Kuczynski, Rudi Hamburger and baby Misha

Shanghai in the 1930s

Richard Sorge

Richard Sorge in 1915

Clara Street, Benwell where William Fisher was born

Wiliam Fisher (top left) with his brother Henry and their parents

Willie Fisher with his wife Evelyn, circa 1927

Rudolf Abel in FBI custody 1957

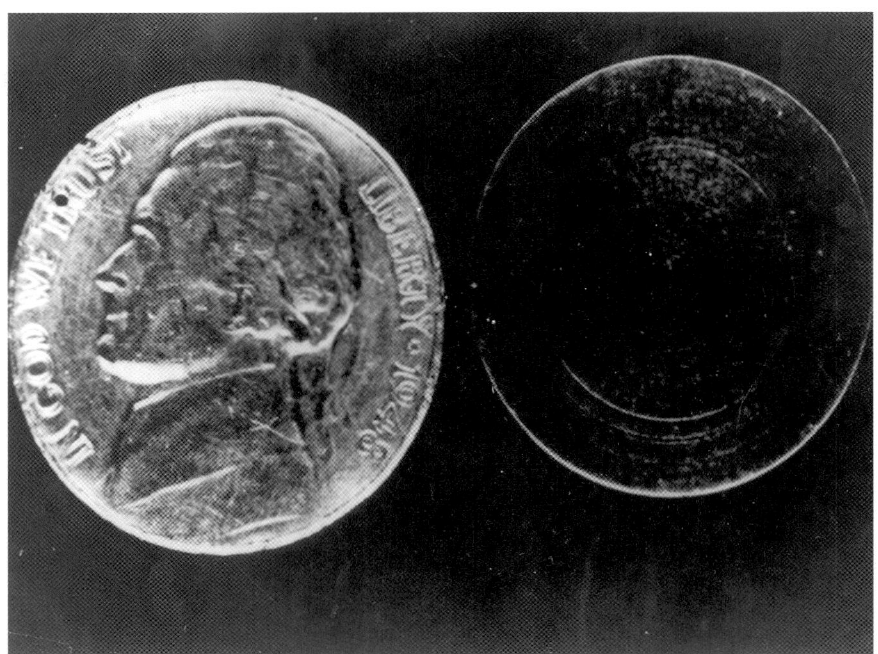

Abel's hollow nickel found by the Brooklyn newspaper boy

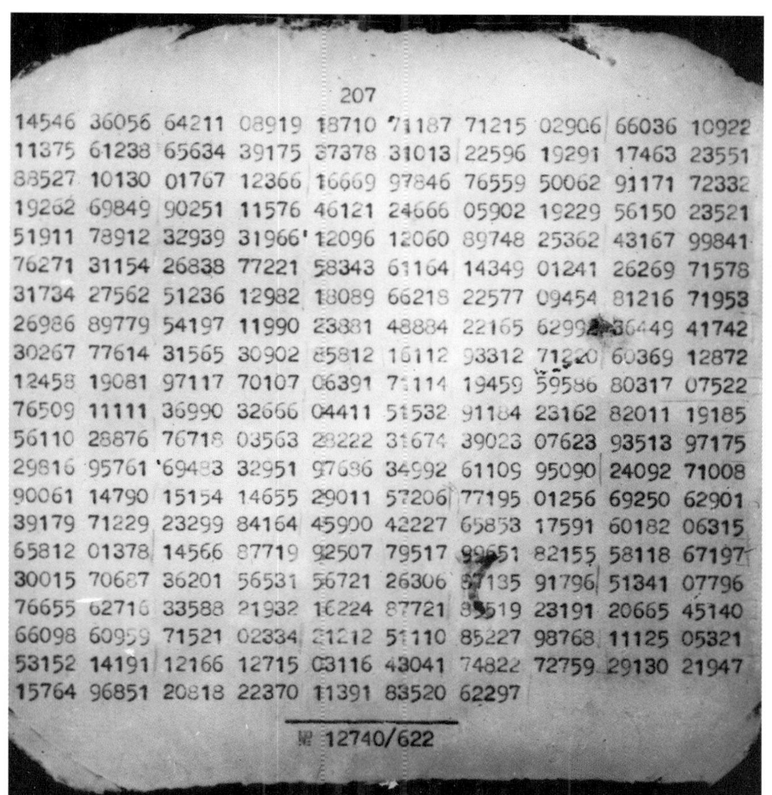

Contents of the hollow nickel

Kim Philby

Litzi Philby

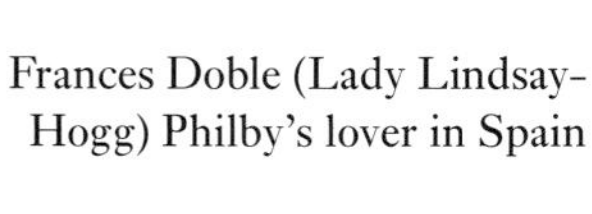

Frances Doble (Lady Lindsay-
Hogg) Philby's lover in Spain

his return journey through the US, Sorge met up with an old friend, an NKVD recruiter Hede Massing in San Francisco. Away from Moscow, Sorge was less inclined to put on a brave face and Massing found him 'transformed' from a charming, romantic and idealistic companion into a hard-bitten, cold and worried man.[27]

Clausen spent the next year setting up radio networks all across the Volga Republic and then, using the codename 'Fritz' met up again with Sorge in Tokyo in December 1935. Sorge, who thought traders and merchants to be dull, unimaginative people who could never be suspected of anything as sophisticated or challenging as espionage, suggested that Clausen should pass himself off as a businessman for cover. Clausen duly established M. Clausen Shokai producing copying machines, and was able to secure contracts with the Japanese army, large industrial companies and universities.

By this time, the network was generating considerable volumes of documentation in addition to the information sent via radio. About thirty microfilm cartridges were being created a month to be couriered to Moscow plus a large volume of written material. Sorge was in desperate need of more couriers so Clausen's wife Anna and then Vukelić's wife Edith were pressed into action as couriers to contacts such as Agnes Smedley at the Palace Hotel or the bookstore on Bubbling Well Road in Shanghai. On top of this an incident occurred on 26 February 1936 that stretched the network's capabilities to the limit.

Japanese troops of the First Division abruptly and without warning seized control of strategic points in Tokyo and murder squads began a purge of ministers in the government of Admiral Okada Keisuke deemed to be 'liberal influences'. Desperate to understand how serious the situation was becoming and what the implications were for them, German diplomats turned to Sorge because of what they saw as his unrivalled knowledge of the Japanese mind. Sorge went to see for himself onto the streets where rebels were held at bay by loyal soldiers and marines. Miyagi translated the rebels' manifesto and talked to anyone he could find who might have an insight. Together they concluded that the rebels would fail but that the army would emerge from the incident with enhanced power and that would mean a stoking of the fires of military expansion in China. Ozaki concluded that the root cause of the rebellion was the grinding poverty in regions from which many of the rebels had been conscripted but there was no suggestion that they had communist sympathies. He predicted that extreme right-wing elements of the military would become stronger and adopt a more anti-Soviet stance. Sorge put this all together and created a report which again went to both Berlin and Moscow. Moscow also had the benefit of reports written by von Dirksen, labelled 'superficial' by Sorge, and Ott which along with Sorge's file were microfilmed and couriered to Moscow via Shanghai.[28] The rebellion was duly crushed, and Japanese military spending was massively increased.

News reached Sorge from Moscow that Katya was pregnant but a few weeks later he learned that she had miscarried or possibly arranged a termination. Sorge's mood darkened even further and his letters to Katya at this time speak of loneliness. 'I'm tormented by the thoughts that I am getting old', he wrote, and went on to say 'it is hard here, really hard'.[29]

Political developments clouded the atmosphere in the German Embassy in Tokyo when it became apparent that secret negotiations had been taking place between Joachim von Ribbentrop, who was by now the unofficial but *de facto* German foreign minister and Hiroshi Ōshima the Japanese military attaché in Berlin proposing a bilateral treaty between their two countries. Neither Ott nor von Dirksen had been informed and once again Ott needed to send a telegram to the German Foreign Office in Berlin to find out what was going on but it was so secret that he could not ask anyone in his embassy to help so he turned once again to Sorge telling him that he 'must swear not to tell anybody about the matter'.[30] By involving Sorge, Ott had exposed him to the German army codes that he had used to code and decode telegrams at this point. This in itself is extraordinary testimony to the extent to which Sorge had been able to trick the Germans into trusting him. He even had his own room in the German Embassy where he had official recognition as a part-time employee of the German News Agency which by now was effectively part of German military intelligence. This afforded him a modest salary and a petrol ration but most of all it gave him unrestricted day and night access to other sections of the embassy. It is clear that Sorge had lower status in the GRU than he enjoyed in Berlin where his intelligence reports were eagerly anticipated and given much credence.

When Sorge became fully aware of the secret protocols that underlay what became the Anti-Comintern Pact, signed on 25 November 1936 by Germany and Japan, he was able to warn Moscow that the Soviet Union was explicitly mentioned in the text. The secret part of the pact, which was agreed but not made public, stated that should either country be subjected to an unprovoked attack by the Soviet Union, the other would consider safeguarding 'their common interests'. The unstated but clearly implied threat to the Soviet Union significantly increased the possibility that they might at some point find themselves facing belligerents on two fronts thousands of miles apart. The need for intelligence about Japanese ambitions was greater than ever and still growing. The importance of Ozaki in Sorge's network cannot be overstated.

Fortunately for Sorge, Ozaki's stock within the political elite in Tokyo was rising. He was appointed special adviser to Akira Kazami, cabinet secretary to Prime Minister Prince Fumimaro Konoye, with a brief to keep abreast of the situation in China. Ozaki's experience of Chinese affairs was soon called on. What seemed to be a minor incident on 7 July 1937 proved to be the spark that ignited the whole tinder box of Sino-Japanese relations.

A brief skirmish occurred at the Marco Polo Bridge over a misunderstanding concerning a Japanese soldier who was thought to have gone missing. He was found but not before Japanese and Chinese soldiers had exchanged fire. Reinforcements were hurriedly called in by both sides and before sense could prevail the incident had escalated into a pitched battle. Ozaki told both Sorge and Kazami that even if the incident was eventually contained the underlying tensions meant that similar incidents would crop up and the inevitable result would be all-out war between China and Japan. Sorge reported this to Ott and von Dirksen who laughed it off but Moscow took it rather more seriously and concluded that the risk of war between the Soviet Union and Japan had receded somewhat, if only temporarily.

Living thousands of miles from Moscow, Sorge had the advantage of unhindered access to foreign newspapers and diplomatic gossip. As a result, he was well aware of the show trials that were taking place back home and knew that his old boss Jan Berzin had disappeared. Perhaps because of this and fearing that, as a protégé of Berzin he was at risk, he had resisted calls for him to return to Moscow but his letters to Katya show how much he was missing her. Still his riotous existence in Tokyo continued. Always top of the list of invitees to German Embassy social functions, his drinking and outrageous flirting with both married and single women was accepted with a shrug and a 'you know what Sorge is like' nonchalance but the pressure of deception and long alienation from his spiritual home of Moscow was starting to take its toll.

In the early hours of Friday, 13 May 1938, he was roaring past the American Embassy in Tokyo on his motorcycle after a heavy drinking session with the journalist Prince Albrecht von Urach when he crashed into a wall and his face crunched into the handlebars. With all his front teeth smashed and deep gashes in his forehead and jaw, Sorge was taken to St Luke's Hospital which had been built by the Episcopal

Church of America. He was able to tell the staff there to send for Clausen immediately. When he came Sorge took intelligence reports out of his coat pocket and passed them to Clausen. Divested of these documents Sorge then slipped into unconsciousness. Clausen then went straight to Sorge's house and removed any incriminating documents and a diary. After a couple of days Sorge was able to receive visitors and there were many. His current girlfriend, Miyake Hanako found him with his head swathed in bandages, jaw wired up and his left arm in a sling. As well as Clausen, German Embassy staff including Helma Ott and Erwin Scholl made regular visits. Scholl was a military attaché and a close friend who had served with Sorge in the same student battalion in Flanders in 1914.

Sorge had now to rely completely on Clausen for coding and decoding his messages. It was an extra burden that Clausen did not appreciate and, on top of running his business, the stress caused his health to suffer. For a couple of months, St Luke's served as a clearing house for Soviet intelligence. When he was well enough to be discharged, Sorge stayed at Ott's residence. Ott was in Berlin receiving instructions prior to his appointment as ambassador but Helma took good care of him.

The accident left Sorge a changed man. In a letter to Katya he told her that he was no longer 'beautiful' and looked like 'a battered robber-knight'. Others told of how his features took on a fierce almost demonic appearance and he became subject to emotional imbalance and psychological disturbances.

Ozaki's analysis of the Marco Polo Bridge incident was accurate. Japan mobilised four infantry divisions and fighting erupted at Langfang after which Japanese laid siege to Chinese forces in Tongzhou. On 29 July they launched an attack against Beijing. China was totally unprepared for war unlike Japan which had marshalled huge resources in preparation for a *seisen* (holy war) led by the emperor with almost total public support. Within a year Japanese forces were in control of many Chinese cities and by March 1938 the Japanese controlled most of northern China.

Moscow could not get enough intelligence about the Japanese especially after the NKVD commander in the Far East, General Genrikh Samuilovich Lyushkov, fearing that he was being lined up for arrest and a show trial, defected on 13 June 1938 giving the Japanese detailed information about Soviet troop deployments on the border. In so doing, he highlighted the serious internal divisions that existed within the Soviet defence and political establishment over their foreign policy.[31] When the Soviets learned that German intelligence officers had been sent to debrief Lyushkov, Sorge was ordered to make 'maximum effort' to get hold of any report that was sent back to Berlin. This time it was Scholl, who had total confidence in Sorge, who gave him access to the secret report the German Embassy sent back to Berlin. It included the NKVD's own assessment of Red Army forces in the border regions that emphasised their low morale.[32]

There was every likelihood, Scholl told Sorge, that a Japanese-German military action was being considered to exploit weaknesses in the Soviet defences revealed by Lyushkov. Given this information, Moscow was able to reinforce those border areas. Encouraged by Berlin, Japan provoked border clashes with the Red Army at Lake Khasan at the end of July ramping up the tension. The Soviets used Sorge's intelligence to launch a massive counterattack backed with tanks, air support, and artillery that resulted in a Soviet victory. Japan asked for peace and accepted Moscow's terms.

The elevation of Ott to the ambassadorship, however, meant that he had much less time to spend with Sorge. His difficulties were compounded by the fact that the Japanese authorities were also beginning to impose tighter controls on the movement of foreigners. Coupled with the deterioration of his mental composure, Sorge was becoming depressed by not being able to freewheel like he had been used to doing. Restrictions frustrated him at a time when Moscow was increasing its demands. He asked Moscow to pull him out after his accident pleading exhaustion but he must have known that there was nobody remotely qualified to replace him and Moscow was totally disinterested in its agents' personal discomfort.

By July 1938 Ozaki had moved even closer to the levers of power and was appointed as *naikaku shokutaku* (consultant) to the Japanese cabinet giving him access to all sorts of classified documents throwing light on the direction of Japanese policy. In November of that year he became a member of a new informal advisory group set up by Prime Minister Fumimaro Konoe. The rise of Ozaki in Japanese political circles increased the importance and relevance of intelligence that he was feeding to Sorge and inevitably elevated Sorge's status within the German Embassy who relied on his advice more and more. A diplomat, Wolfgang Galinsky, would later recall that Sorge was 'completely at home' in the embassy.[33]

The Imperial Japanese Army had attacked Soviet forces at Nomonhan in the Mongolian plains (Khalkhin Gol) on 11 May 1939 and that turned into a prolonged engagement. Sorge sent one of his most recent recruits, Odai Yoshinobu, to the region. Odai had only just left the Japanese army after three years' service and proved to be an invaluable source. Given the codename 'Miki' he was able to report with authority on troop morale, strength and deployment. Ozaki told Sorge that he did not believe that the encounter was a precursor to an all-out attack and so Sorge reported to Moscow that the Japanese were anxious to deescalate and contain the conflict.[34] The Soviets, however, chose to launch a devastating counterattack led by Marshal Zhukov employing over 1,000 tanks that routed and humiliated the Japanese forces made up predominantly of infantry.

Sorge tried to capitalise on that by stressing to Ott how powerful the Soviet forces were and that the Red Army should not be underestimated. When Ott relayed this to Berlin, it was also met with disbelief. They had their own low opinion of Soviet military might and would not be swayed by diplomatic gossip.

Two important consequence of Khalkhin Gol were that the Japanese army suffered a loss of prestige at home, which Sorge was able to report to Moscow, and surveillance on foreigners in Japan was significantly stepped up. Japanese paranoia regarding espionage had reached a peak, with anti-spy posters plastered all around the city. The *Tokko* (Special High Police Bureau) agent Sergeant Saito Harutsuguo was assigned to trail and investigate Sorge. He kept careful track of Sorge's acquaintances, made friends with his housekeeper, and followed Sorge on his nightly trawl through the bars and night clubs.

Moscow was clearly getting frustrated with Sorge complaining and criticising at every turn. He had annoyed his superiors as early as 1937 by making excuses and refusing to return home when ordered to do so. Not only did Sorge have to live his life under constant threat from exposure in Japan but he was now clouded by suspicion and rapidly becoming *persona non grata* in Moscow. There was obviously much more pressure from the Kremlin for the GRU to provide up-to-the-minute intelligence about Japan and it was all coming down on Sorge's shoulders. His intelligence was 'deteriorating', they said and he was bluntly ordered to 'do more ... as a matter of priority' and 'exert utmost effort'.[35]

Berlin was equally interested in Japanese war production but for different reasons. They dearly wanted to coax Japan into action against British interests in the Far East and wanted to know what its military capabilities were. It was military attaché Colonel Gerhard Matzky, who would later become chief of intelligence division of German General Staff, who was tasked with investigating how Japanese industry was being converted to a wartime economy. Matzky was another one who held Sorge in high esteem and invited him to contribute his knowledge. Sorge was given almost unrestricted access to German Embassy files and secretly photographed many of them in a room provided for his personal use in the embassy building.

Relations between Germany and Japan were rocked by the signing of the Molotov-Ribbentrop Pact at a time when ferocious clashes were taking place on the Soviet-Japanese border. This virtual demolition of the Anti-Comintern Pact for which the Japanese were given no warning showed a callous lack of consideration but the Japanese were somewhat mollified in November 1939 by the signing of the Agreement for Cultural Cooperation between Japan and Germany. Then after the spectacular German successes of May and June 1940 in northern Europe, Japan made it clear that they were now open to formal negotiations towards a closer alliance with Germany. After all, the Fall of France and the humiliation of British forces at Dunkirk had opened up undreamed of opportunities for Japanese adventurism against European colonial assets in the Far East. When von Ribbentrop sent a special envoy, Heinrich Stahmer, to hold talks with the Japanese foreign minister, Sorge was privy to them. Stahmer had met Sorge on a previous visit and had been favourably impressed with him so much so that he had seconded him as an adviser behind the scenes at the talks. Copies of Stahmer's daily reports going back to Berlin soon found their way to Moscow. Long before the Tripartite Pact was signed between Italy, Germany and Japan on 27 September 1940, Moscow knew that they were being excluded despite the existence of the Molotov-Ribbentrop Pact. It was an uncomfortable reminder that the 'New Order' the fascist powers were planning did not give the Soviets a seat at the table.

It is credit to Sorge's professionalism that he was still providing his masters with vital intelligence when he was growing increasingly desperate to leave Japan. Foreigners were harassed in the street by the *Kempeitai* (military police) which increased the risk of being caught in possession of incriminating material and the police definition of incriminating was very wide indeed. Fourteen suspected British agents were arrested across several cities on 27 July 1940 accused of being part of a British espionage ring. Two days later, one of those arrested, Melville James Cox committed suicide by leaping from an open window at the headquarters of the *Kempeitai* while undergoing police interrogation.[36]

Edith Vukelić had divorced Branko in 1939 but had remained as part of Sorge's network by making her house available for Clausen's transmitter. Now she asked for and was given permission to leave taking her son Paul to Hong Kong then on to Australia. Ironically Clausen's business was actually showing significant profits which had the effect of diluting his enthusiasm for communism. He had a big house and he drove around in a Mercedes motor car. As his enthusiasm for espionage had waned so his involvement with his business had grown and he had built up an impressive list of customers. It was no surprise that he took umbrage at the suggestion that profits from his business should be channelled into funding Sorge's network. Encouraged by Anna, he preferred to reinforce his cover as a successful businessman by spending the money on maintaining an appropriately comfortable lifestyle for himself and socialising with other wealthy Germans. That had the inevitable consequence of weakening his commitment to Sorge's network. His loyalty to the cause was further eroded by Sorge's obvious disdain for him despite now relying on him for handling his messages. Unlike others like Stein who amused Sorge with intellectual conversation, Clausen was dull and boring which did not so much annoy Sorge as simply make him dismissive of his radio man. Clausen's mental and physical condition began to deteriorate to the point where he started drinking heavily to cope with the stress of his secret life. His wife Anna, who did not share her husband's devotion to communism, begged him to ask Sorge to give him a rest hoping that would lead to a complete break with the spy ring but Clausen could not do that. He reached breaking point in the spring of 1940 when he suffered a serious heart attack requiring three months convalescence under German medical care.

After the Luftwaffe's failure to crush Fighter Command in the Battle of Britain, Hitler had turned to what was always going to be his main target. Sorge began getting information about preparations for Operation Barbarossa from Colonel Alfred Kretschmer who had replaced Matzky as senior military attaché in Tokyo. Kretschmer like Sorge had been wounded in the First World War and that was the common ground on which they quickly built a close working relationship. His orders were to persuade the Japanese that the movement of German troops to the Soviet border was no more than a precaution against Red Army forces that were massing on the other side but he knew that it was much more than that and that is what he told Sorge.

Only ten days after Hitler had signed Directive Number 21 authorising an attack on the Soviet Union Sorge told Moscow on 28 December 1940 that as many as eighty German divisions were on, or in the process of moving up to, the Soviet border. Envoys reaching the Tokyo Embassy from Berlin told of a new reserve army of forty divisions had been created in the Leipzig area. Sorge reported that the word from Berlin was that the Germans were waiting for the least provocation from Moscow to launch an attack. There was a mood of extreme confidence that, after its ignominious defeat in Finland, the Red Army would take twenty years for 'to become a modern army like that of Germany'. On 1 March 1941, Sorge reported that a further twenty German divisions had been moved from France to the Soviet border.[37]

Stalin was clearly getting fed up with endless warnings of a German attack emanating from Tokyo and instructed Filipp I Golikov, Sorge's new boss in the GRU, to quieten him down. When Sorge's monthly cheque from Moscow was cut in half in February 1941, Sorge was livid and told Golikov that it was 'tantamount to destroying [the whole Tokyo] apparatus'.[38]

Ott was instructed to restore German-Japanese relations to their former closeness and persuade the Japanese to do the same with the Soviets and turn their attention instead to the 'Pearl' of the British Empire, Singapore. When approached with this idea, however, the Japanese demurred and chose to wait until they had hard evidence that Britain was finished off by a German invasion and occupation of its mainland. Naturally they wanted Singapore but it would be a whole lot easier to capture it if the heart of the British Empire was decked out in swastikas. Sorge told Ott that, in his opinion, Japan would not attack Singapore as long as it was receiving raw materials from the United States.

Despite their reticence to push its army further south, the Japanese were getting desperate and casting covetous eyes towards the oil, rubber and tin production areas of Southeast Asia. They had a million men squaring up to the Chinese who showed no signs of capitulating and their war industries were starting to run short of raw materials. In the vastness of the Chinese hinterland, Japanese forces were getting the first taste of what the Germans would also experience on the Russian steppes; an enemy resorting to guerrilla warfare that tied down huge numbers of troops with no clear path to eliminating them. On the domestic front, Prince Konoye was bending to the will of the military faction that was growing ever stronger. All semblance of democracy was cast aside as opposition to the military was crushed.

In early March, an exasperated Ott told Sorge that von Ribbentrop was again piling pressure on the embassy to urge Japan into attacking Singapore which he had been doing for the last two months without any signs of success. Sorge, who understood the Japanese mind as well as any Westerner at the time, sympathised and told Ott that they would never agree to provide the 'horse' upon which the 'knight' Hitler would ride to battle. There were clear limits beyond which the Japanese would simply not go just to accommodate the Germans and Sorge advised Ott to make that as clear as he could. Ott would get the chance to do that in person having been recalled to Berlin for consultations. What Sorge said was essentially true but he emphasised it to Ott as much as he could in order to nurture the sense of resentment that Ott was feeling towards the Japanese. No opportunity to drive a wedge between Berlin and Tokyo was ignored.

At the same time, Japan and the Soviet Union 'guided by a desire to strengthen peaceful and friendly relations between the two countries' signed a neutrality pact on 13 April 1941 agreeing to respect the 'territorial integrity and inviolability of Manchukuo (Manchuria) [and] the territorial integrity and inviolability of the Mongolian People's Republic'.[39] Stalin believed this to be a major achievement for him and celebrated by seeing off the Japanese delegation at the railway station in person, something he hardly ever did. The pact seemed to offer some assurance against a Japanese attack. Ott confided to Sorge that Berlin had reacted badly to the news and Sorge was able to report this to Moscow. Ozaki told him that the Japanese were pleased with having stabilised their northern flank and had turned their attention to the south. However, he doubted that they would be bound by the pact if circumstances indicated that there would be advantage to be gained by breaking it. This was reinforced by gossip picked up from the German Embassy saying that if the Germans attacked the Soviet Union the Japanese would not be expected to stand idly by.

Prince Urach, one of Sorge's old drinking pals, was now working for the German Foreign Ministry as a press officer and he too told Sorge that von Ribbentrop was doing all he could to stir the Japanese into action by encouraging them to build up their forces in Manchuria. The implications of this, as far as Sorge could see, was that if the Germans wanted to increase tensions on the Soviet eastern borders it was to distract them while they were probably planning action of their own in the West. At the same time Kretschmer showed Sorge a letter he had received from Matzky in which he predicted war between Germany and the Soviet Union.

The Japanese navy, in particular, opposed going to war with the Soviet Union arguing that the proximity of the Soviet aircraft on its eastern border could imperil Japanese industry if hostilities broke out. Far better, they said, to press further south towards the raw material treasure in the Philippines which was becoming 'a matter of life and death' for Japan. The simple truth was that there was no possibility of Japan waging war on two fronts, especially given the build-up of Soviet forces on the Manchurian border. It was not overlooked however, that any attack on Singapore risked a confrontation with the powerful US Navy.

By early May it was Sorge distinct impression that 'the possibility of war at any moment [was] very high'. Envoys and couriers from Berlin, whom Sorge had no trouble befriending on arrival, told him over a few drinks in his favourite night spots that German generals were confidently predicting that the Red Army would be 'destroyed in the course of a few weeks'.[40] By mid-May, Sorge was telling Moscow that war between Germany and the Soviet Union was already a certainty. Paul Wenneker, Ott's naval attaché who had sources within the Japanese navy, told Ott that the Japanese would remain neutral in any German-Soviet war, at least to start with because they were not yet prepared for it. Sorge made sure that Moscow got a cory of Wenneker's telegram to Berlin.

Sorge continued to warn that all non-essential staff and envoys at the German Embassy had been told to return to Berlin by the end of May. On 13 June, Sorge saw a copy of a telegram due to be sent to Berlin saying, 'if a German-Soviet war breaks out, it will take the Japanese about six weeks to begin offensive operations against the Soviet Far East … but the Germans consider that it will take more time because this conflict will be both on land and on sea.'[41]

The Japanese had their own intelligence sources in Europe and were well aware of the German military build-up on the Soviet border, but they doubted that it was Hitler's intention to launch an invasion. More likely it was a bluff and a threat to bring pressure on Moscow to increase the flow of raw materials to feed into their military-industrial programme. Even after Hitler had met Ambassador Hiroshi Ōshima in June 1941 and personally told him about plans for Operation Barbarossa, the Japanese remained sceptical.

During Ott's absence, Sorge had acquired a new drinking companions in the guise of Colonel Josef Meisinger the 'Butcher of Warsaw' who was now police attaché to the German Embassy and *de facto* the senior representative of Germany's Gestapo in Japan. He also served as the liaison between the Gestapo and the Japanese intelligence services. Meisinger had a fearsome reputation. When his boss, Walter Schellenberg read the file of Meisinger's activities in occupied Poland he called him 'utterly bestial and corrupt'. Even Himmler had been so appalled that he ordered Meisinger to be shot but Heydrich knew that Meisinger was exactly the sort of man he wanted on his own staff and managed to spirit him away from Berlin before any action could be taken against him.[42]

Tokyo was as far away from Berlin as Heydrich could send him so that is where he ended up with instructions to investigate Comintern activity there. Before leaving, Schellenberg took advantage of Meisinger's appointment to follow up on an issue that had been troubling him. He was aware that Sorge was passing high-value intelligence to von Ritgen but also knew that questions were being asked about his political past in Germany. The DNB was anxious to clear up any issues and remove suspicion from their top agent in Japan so von Ritgen had asked Schellenberg to take a look at Sorge so that he could get Sorge's critics off his back. Schellenberg drew Sorge's files which showed some left-wing activity in his early years which meant that he was unable to satisfy von Ritgen without taking a closer look.

Schellenberg asked Meisinger to conduct an unofficial investigation and report back but he asked the wrong man. Meisinger was a bully and a man without any sophistication on guile. He actually found Sorge to be a man after his own heart when it came to drinking and womanising and that might have coloured his reports which were entirely favourable. He saw no reason to challenge the prevailing opinion of Sorge in Berlin which was that he was providing valuable intelligence about the Japanese. He had, however, stirred up some reaction when he, somewhat ham-fistedly, started asking questions all around the city about Sorge which aroused the curiosity of the Japanese police. They wanted to know why this Gestapo man who had just arrived was taking such an interest in Sorge and wondered if he had been sent specifically to investigate him. That made them think that maybe they should take a closer look at Sorge too not least because of his increasingly erratic behaviour, hard drinking and mood swings which was also beginning to disturb the German Embassy staff. Even Ott was starting to regret his close relationship with Sorge and, unsuccessfully, tried to persuade him to return to Berlin. It was, at best, a half-hearted attempt since privately he knew that he had become so reliant on Sorge for advice and information, especially about US-Japanese negotiations, at a time when tensions were mounting daily that he hardly knew what he would do without him and he, unwisely, continued to keep Sorge informed about reports he was getting from Berlin.

At the end of May, he told Sorge that there were significant indications that a German attack against the Soviet Union would take place towards the end of June. Scholl chipped in by confidentially telling him that the attack would begin on 15 June. There were, he said, 170 to 190 divisions on the Soviet border including armoured and mechanised divisions. The main focus of the attack would be towards

Moscow and Leningrad followed by the Ukraine. Crucially, Scholl said that the attack would be launched without an ultimatum. It was no longer speculation but fact, Sorge told Moscow.

In the Kremlin, Stalin was getting reports of an imminent attack from various sources, some estimates put the number at close to 100, but he appeared to believe it was disinformation deliberately put out by the British amongst others. Leopold Trepper had warned Moscow as early as May that 22 June was the appointed date. Harro Schulze-Boysen confirmed that date from his position in the Luftwaffe. As an example of what Stalin thought of these warnings, one report from Sorge at the end of May had met with a venomous response from the *Vozhd* who called Sorge 'a little shit who has set himself up with some small factories and brothels in Japan'.[43] On a copy of one of Sorge's warning messages dated 1 June someone had scribbled the word 'suspicious' and directed that it be put in the pile labelled 'provocations'. He was told in plain language and left in no doubt by Moscow that they did not believe him. Sorge tried one last time on 20 June to make Moscow take notice of his warnings. Ozaki had told him that the Japanese High Command, who were convinced of an imminent German attack, were discussing how to respond to it.

Two days later, at 04.00 hours on Sunday, 22 June, von Ribbentrop notified the Japanese ambassador in Berlin that Germany and the Soviet Union were in a state of war. When news reached Sorge, he lost all control. He started drinking and began cursing Hitler in the bar of the Imperial Hotel. He was drunk to the point of incapacity long before the day was out and in no state to respond when an urgent message came in from Moscow demanding to know what the Japanese response to the attack was. Suddenly, he was a vital source of intelligence.

Moscow had repeatedly warned Sorge that, despite his deep penetration of both German and Japanese high-level sources, his network was absolutely forbidden to meddle in any activity of a political nature or get involved with propaganda but that had changed. Ozaki suggested that he try to exploit his influential position as one of Prime Minister Konoye's closest advisers by persuading him that it was not in Japan's interests to join the Germans in a war against the Soviet Union and Moscow, with some reservations, agreed to let him try.

Ozaki learned that Japan had chosen to expand into Southeast Asia but as a secondary issue would reinforce its position on the Soviet border as a contingency measure in case the progress of the German attack opened up an opportunity to take advantage of a seriously weakened Soviet Union. Ott confirmed to Sorge that this was also the

German understanding of the Japanese position and all of this was put in a despatch to Moscow on 12 July which said, 'If the Red Army suffers defeat then there is no doubt that the Japanese will join the war, and if there is no defeat, then they will maintain neutrality.'[44] The report went directly to Stalin who was now inclined to take more notice of Sorge's opinions. Every last resource was needed to stem the German onslaught that was forcing the Red Army back towards Moscow and that meant relocating troops from the east but the question was just how much threat did the Japanese pose and how much of his forces dare he strip from the Manchurian border?

The other great issue that was occupying the minds of Germany was the progress of Japan-US negotiations. The risk that these two nations might improve their relations was deeply troubling. Through Ozaki, Sorge was aware that during talks in Washington the US was trying to coax Japan into withdrawing from the Tripartite Pact. This would benefit the Soviets since Japan on its own would be unlikely to attack the Soviet Union. If the talks broke down that would also benefit the Soviets because it would probably mean a Japanese advance to the south. Sorge doubted that it would be a case of the Soviet Union benefiting either way because the US would only strike a deal with Japan if Japanese forces were withdrawn from Manchuria and that would leave a million men available for an attack against the Soviet Union. His analysis was eagerly devoured by both Berlin and Moscow.

Ozaki had picked up snippets of information about the Roosevelt-Konoye negotiations and passed the information on to Sorge along with the results of the Council in the Imperial Presence of 2 July 1941, which had finally decided to move Japanese forces to the south against British, US and Dutch assets. This directly contradicted the impression that Ott had formed after talks with meeting with the Japanese Foreign Minister Yōsuke Matsuoka which was that Japan would yield to German persuasion. 'Everything indicates that Japan will enter the war against Russia', he reported to Berlin on 9 July. Sorge was inclined to place more reliance on Ozaki and, on 23 August, he told Moscow that 'Many Japanese soldiers are being issued shorts especially for the tropics and from this it can be assumed that large numbers will be shipped to the south.'[45] By 14 September he was reporting that even Ott was now convinced that a Japanese attack against the Soviet Union was 'out of the question' but that '[Japanese] armed forces will stay in Manchuria for a possible offensive [in the] Spring'.[46] This information was taken very seriously by Stalin who was also getting reports from army listening posts along the Manchurian border that seemed to confirm a reduction in Japanese mobilisation there. This emboldened him to order large numbers of Red Army troops to be relocated from Siberia to the take part in the defence of Moscow.

The historian Nigel Askey, however, is of the opinion that these Far Eastern divisions were instrumental in halting the German at the gates of Moscow is not substantiated by the evidence. Only fourteen divisions were transferred west between August and December 1941 and these were spread out from opposite Finland to southern Ukraine. These were the only divisions that could possibly have been influenced by any information from Sorge's spy ring.[47]

The Washington political reporter John O'Donnell, claimed to have seen an undisclosed confession from Sorge, which was kept by the US department of the army according to which Sorge had reported to Moscow in October 1941 that Japan had plans to attack Pearl Harbor within sixty days. The Kremlin is believed to have passed this information on to Washington.

It is known that the Japanese Cabinet, at its Imperial Conference on 6 September, decided to complete preparations for war by the end of October but agreed to continue to hope for a diplomatic solution before then. After mid-September 1941 when Sorge had reported that there was no likelihood of an immediate Japanese invasion of the Soviet Union the focus of his reports to Moscow shifted to negotiations between Japan and the US, which were deteriorating when the US imposed economic sanctions on Japan after its occupation of southern French Indochina. Ozaki was able to pass onto Sorge information gleaned from the Japanese Cabinet about the progress of negotiations and the intensifying conflict within the Japanese ruling class over policies toward the Soviet Union and the US. Sorge's report of 14 September had been optimistic about the possibility of an agreement.

Then on 16 October, the Konoe Cabinet resigned and General Hideki Tojo was appointed Konoe's successor as prime minister. He was instructed by the Japanese emperor to smooth diplomatic relations for the time being and not risk any sort of crisis. Sorge had drafted a telegram for Clausen to transmit to Moscow earlier in the month and Clausen failed to send this one also. It was later found during a search of Sorge's house after his arrest. It read,

According to information acquired from various Japanese authorities, if Japan does not receive some sort of satisfactory response from the U.S. side by the 15th or 16th of this month to Japan's request to start negotiations, the Japanese government will either resign or be fundamentally reorganized. Whether the Japanese government resigns or is reorganized, it will mean that war with the United States will break out in the near future, either this month or next month.[48]

Sorge clearly very accurately predicted that the conflict in principle between Japan and the US was imminent, but no evidence has been uncovered to show that he had identified Pearl Harbor as the intended target of an unprovoked attack.

Ever since Khalkhin Gol, the Japanese secret police had been relentlessly tracking suspected communists and both they and the German, although quite separately, were very sure that a Soviet espionage ring was operating in Japan. The Japanese had a number of counterintelligence organisations. The army had the *Kempeitai* secret police whose primary mission was to enforce discipline. Internal security was carried out by its civilian counterpart the *Tokubetsu Kōtō Keisatsu* (Special Higher Police, *Tokkō*) a policing and counterespionage organisation. They had discovered illegal radio traffic but their direction-finding equipment was not sophisticated enough to locate the source and certainly could not decipher the messages. As international tensions increased the Japanese police got new powers to investigate foreigners and the courts were given authority to impose stiff penalties for espionage. The government fomented periodic campaigns of hysteria to warn the public about the dangers of spies. Sorge cut out all contact with Ozaki and Miyagi during the weeks when these were at their height.

Sorge's outward nonchalant demeanour changed little but, privately, he was becoming convinced that he was now under close surveillance by the Japanese police. Ozaki was also experiencing acute anxiety telling Kawai Teikichi that he was starting to feel trapped 'like a rat in a bag'.[49] Sorge's behaviour became increasingly erratic, driving at high speeds in his car while intoxicated. On one occasion, unaware that he had punctured one of its tyres, he crashed a German diplomatic car into a lamppost. He experienced wild fits of temper punctuated by periods of remorse.

The two men had good reason to be worried. In November 1939, the *Tokkō* had arrested Ritsu Ito, one of Ozaki's assistants, and held him for interrogation for almost a year before releasing him. Despite suspicions that Ito was now a police informer, Ozaki took him back onto his team. The two men, compatible in temperament, intellect and an appetite for debauch, had been close friends for many years and it is likely that the reintroduction of Ritsu was the first tiny wedge that opened cracks in Sorge's security.

The next breakthrough for the police was the arrest of Kitabatashi Tomo for her connection with the CPUSA. Her name had been given to them by Ritsu and under questioning, she gave up the name of Miyagi whom she had known in Los Angeles and who had also been a member of the CPUSA. For security reasons, Miyagi should never had gone anywhere near people like Ritsu who were part of the Tokyo communist groups but in reality it was impossible to run an espionage ring without recourse to using local communists as sources and informants.

At first light on the morning of 10 October 1941, officers of the *Tokkō* burst into Miyagi's lodgings in Roppongi and hauled him off to Tsujiki police station. After two days of intense interrogation and taking advantage of a lapse in his captors' vigilance, Miyagi threw himself out of window hoping that the fall would kill him. He was not high enough however and succeeded only in breaking his leg. There was no further resistance to questioning. The police had not really suspected Miyagi of having anything to do with serious espionage, all they were investigating was the distribution of communist leaflets, so when he told them about his connection to Sorge and Ozaki it came as a great surprise. It was beyond their jurisdiction so they called in the prosecutor Yoshikawa Mitsusada.

Sorge, meanwhile was incapacitated by a fever and was bedridden for days. He was visited by Ott, who had always valued Sorge as a companion with whom he could discuss sensitive political issue freely and unburden himself of opinions that might have got him into trouble in more orthodox company. It was relaxing to be privately indiscrete. He brought Sorge a bottle of brandy to comfort him in his sick bed. On the same day, the police picked up two more members of Sorge's network who worked for Miyagi, Kuzumi Fusako and Akiyama Koji. Two days later it was Ozaki's door the police knocked on.

He was taken to the nearby Meguro police station where he was rapidly disabused of any notion that he might resist. The police soon convinced him that they knew all about the Sorge network, although they had only vague suspicions of what it actually consisted of. By the end of the day he was ready to make a statement. When Clausen met Sorge the next day, he was more than usually worried because he had not seen Miyagi for a few days. Fearing that his network had finally run out of time, Sorge, already weak and struggling to recover from his fever, ordered Clausen to radio Moscow requesting permission for them to return to Moscow or be reassigned possibly to Germany. Clausen, however, was in no hurry to leave Tokyo. Ideally he preferred to see Sorge leave the city so that he could have done with espionage altogether and get on with running his business but he was not the sort of man who could argue with Sorge face-to-face. Behind his back, however, he chose to ignore Sorge's instruction and the message was never sent.

Had Sorge known that Ozaki was giving a full account of his part in the network he might have been rather more circumspect and taken a little more care but, by all accounts, he appeared to be concerned but not particularly anxious. For his part, Yoshikawa was not willing to risk a diplomatic incident by arresting someone with such powerful friends in the German Embassy until he had firm proof of Sorge's perfidy. If he showed his hand too soon, Sorge might take refuge there and they would have the devil of a job getting him out.

By 17 October, it was no longer possible to believe that all was well. Sorge had been unable to contact Miyagi or Ozaki. He had lunch with Clausen at the Minoru restaurant both soothing their nerves with copious amounts of alcohol then went to the cinema to watch an American movie. Later they went back to the Minoru where they were joined by Vukelić and discussed ways and means of getting out of Japan preferably a cargo ship heading for Germany. The likelihood of that happening was seriously compromised by the heavy police surveillance that all three men were now under.

Before dawn on 18 October an early visitor to Sorge's house from the German Embassy arrived and left unaware of a heavy police presence all around. When Sergeant Saito rang Sorge's doorbell just after 06.30 hours Sorge appeared washed and shaved, despite his heavy drinking of the day before, but still in his pyjamas. Saito made out that he was making enquiries about Sorge's recent motor car accident but as Sorge stepped back to let him enter, more police appeared and pinned Sorge to the wall. Covered in an overcoat that had been produced Sorge was then bundled into a police car and taken to the nearby Toriizaka police station where he was told he was being detained under suspicion of conducting espionage. Clausen was arrested at the same time. Having been acutely aware of the increasing danger it is odd that he had made no attempt to hide his radio equipment and code books. The police dragged Vukelić from his bed and he too was taken in for questioning.

Sorge was taken to a fortress called the Tokyo Detention House where he was allocated cell 11 on wing 5. He would remain there for the next three years. When he heard, Ott was astounded and thought Sorge's arrest was a case of Japanese spy hysteria. Who did they think he was spying for, he wanted to know. When it was suggested that it had been the Soviets, Ott saw his career, and possibly more, coming to an abrupt end. All German Embassy staff were ordered not to speak of Sorge's arrest.

Mitsusada began his interrogation of Sorge on 19 October under intense pressure from both his own political masters, who feared a diplomatic incident if Sorge's arrest proved to be unwarranted, and from Ott who was demanding to speak to Sorge. All of Mitsusada's accusations of spying met with a blunt denial at first but, after three days without sleep and faced with Clausen's confession, Sorge admitted his role in espionage. In doing so he buried his head in his arms across the table and collapsed in tears. To his interrogators he now looked 'a pathetic figure, physically and emotionally drained'.[50]

There was a brief meeting between Sorge and Ott who still could not bring himself to accept that Sorge was guilty of spying. He had been so close to Sorge for all that time and never had an inkling of his perfidy. After Ott had asked about his health and treatment both of which Sorge described as satisfactory, no more was said and Ott left the prison. Von Ribbentrop called for Sorge's extradition to Germany, but the Japanese refused to consider it.

The consequences for embassy staff were profound. Meisinger, who had been ordered to investigate Sorge but instead had spent so many hours trawling the bars of Tokyo with him looked a complete fool. Ott was relieved of his post but was allowed to stay away from Berlin. He sat the war out in Peking. In September 1942, Katya was arrested by the NKVD, charges with being a German spy and deported to the gulag where she died in the following year.

Sorge was eventually brought to trial in September 1943 in the Tokyo District Criminal Court and found guilty on four counts of spying and plotting to overthrow the Japanese emperor. His sentence of death was appealed but Sorge's lawyers were a day late in presenting it and the appeal was thrown out. Ozaki was tried, convicted and sentenced to death also. According to Japanese custom they would only be informed of their execution date on the morning of that day. The two men spent ten months waking every day wondering if it would be their last. Finally on the morning of 7 November 1944, the prison governor and a chaplain came to Sorge's cell. He was taken to a small room where his arms and legs were bound. At 10.20 hours a noose was put around his neck and a trapdoor snapped open. Sixteen minutes later he was pronounced dead. In the same room, Ozaki had suffered a similar fate only thirty minutes earlier.

Clausen and Vukelić were tried and given life sentences. Clausen served his sentence in Sugamo but, because of the constant bombing raids, he was then transferred to a penitentiary in Sendai Prefecture. Both he and his wife were released by US forces on 9 October 1945. Vukelić died of acute pneumonia in Abashiri prison during the first winter of his sentence.

Chapter 4

WILLY FISHER:
THE GEORDIE SPY

He always seemed to me an exceptionally interesting and in many ways a really remarkable person. This quiet, unhurried and somewhat elderly man never attracted attention by his appearance and easily lost himself in any crowd. At a party he never attracted undue attention, while at the same time impressing everyone by his attentiveness and courtesy. His intelligent and penetrating gaze never stopped for long on any particular object but always noticed everything of real interest. His self-control and tenacity always impressed me.[1]

On 25 June 1957, a man, claiming to be Emil Goldfus was being held at the alien detention facility in McAllen, Texas just a few miles from the Mexican border but unlike all the others incarcerated there, he had not just crossed the border. He was indeed being detained on a charge of entering the country illegally but he had been flown down from New York. At first, he refused to answer any questions but relented and told his captor that his name was Rudolf Ivanovich Abel, a Soviet citizen. He admitted to having entered the USA illegally from Canada on a forged passport nine years previously in 1948. However, he was not Rudolf Abel either. Abel had been a Latvian sailor and member of the Soviet Red Guard but rather than being in Texas, he was lying in the German Cemetery in Moscow.

The man who called himself Goldfus then Abel was in fact William 'Willy' August Fisher who certainly had Russian connections, but he had been born in 'Geordieland' at 140 Clara Street in the Benwell district of Newcastle-upon-Tyne in North-East England on 11 July 1903. Clara Street was one of the long rows of steeply sloping terraced

116

houses running down towards the banks of the River Tyne between Adelaide Terrace and Scotswood Road. His parents, the German Russian Genrikh (Heinrich Matthäus) Matveyevich Fischer and Lyubov Vasilievna (Zhidova), a midwife, had arrived from Russia three years earlier.

Genrikh had been born the son of German immigrants working on the estate of a Russian prince in the province of Yoroslavl. When the family moved to St Petersburg in 1887, Genrikh took up employment as a metalworker in a German-run factory. There, inspired by revolutionary fervour, he met Lenin several times and became a labour organiser and activist. This brought him to the attention of the tsarist police who arrested him in 1894 after which he was sentenced to three years' exile in the Archangel region of northern Russia. When he was released, he was denied Russian nationality because of his German background. He was denied the right to live in any major Russian industrial region where he might return to his revolutionary activities and was told that he must decide between deportation to Germany or exile to another country.

Germany meant military service so Genrikh chose to take his new wife to the bustling shipbuilding city of Newcastle in 1900 where his skills as a metalworker would guarantee him work and the booming industrial landscape would give him ample opportunity to continue his political activity. Anglicising his name to Henry Fisher, he found work immediately as an iron turner at the Armstrong Elswick Work and an opportunity to spread his revolutionary message through the Newcastle Socialist Institution on Leazes Park Road but he found the local brand of socialism unacceptably meek and mild in compared to that which he had been used to in Russia.

In 1906, he was appointed secretary to the Newcastle cell of the Social Democratic Federation of Great Britain which is when he came into contact with Latvian revolutionaries. On their behalf, he began smuggling copies of the revolutionary newspaper *Iskva* (the *Spark*) onto Russian ships that docked at Newcastle and nearby Blyth and Sunderland before heading out to the Baltic ports. In his memoirs, Genrikh writes that 'the whole family' would go abord ships such as the *Smolensk* and socialise with the Russian crews.[2] That was far from the least of his involvement in the Russian Revolution of 1905–1907. Ships came in from Hamburg and Antwerp carrying crates of Brownings, Mausers and rifles which were offloaded and repacked in smaller packages. These would be stored in warehouses along the Tyne before being loaded onto the Baltic-bound vessels.

When the family moved to 24 Eleanor Street in Cullercoats in 1908, Willy and his young brother Henry, growing up in a decidedly radical home environment, attended Whitley Bay High School and Monkseaton High School. In what would become a life dedicated to espionage, Willy, in particular, enjoyed his first taste of involvement with his father's subversive activities helping out with distribution of anti-war leaflets to factories and shipyards on the Tyne almost as a fully-fledged member of the movement. He was also acutely aware of animosity levelled at his family during the First World War for their German background. Genrikh, and to a lesser extent Lyubov, still felt themselves to be more German than Russian and retained a strong cultural relationship to the land of their fathers. Willy got a taste of chauvinism and injustice that coloured his worldview when his father was fired from his job where he had worked for thirteen years simply because of his German background.

The Bolshevik Revolution of October 1917 was celebrated in the Fisher household but when British government put its diplomatic weight behind the 'white' Russian counter-revolutionaries and British troops set sail for Vladivostok to help them it was clear that there would be a backlash against communist activists in Britain. Despite this, Genrikh, with Willy's enthusiastic support joined other left-wing sympathisers and started a local branch of the 'Hands Off Russia' campaign with funds supplied by Moscow during which he gave propaganda speeches to meetings.

Having excelled at mathematics, Willy left school and was taken on as an apprentice draughtsman at Swan Hunter shipyards before enrolling for night classes at Rutherford College and being accepted for entrance to London University in 1920 which he was unable to attend due to financial constraints. Frustrated by the hostility the family had endured and encouraged by reports from friends in Russia now that the Bolsheviks were in charge, Genrikh took the whole family back to Russia in 1921. Willy had been issued a British passport on 21 July 1920. They took up residence in the Kremlin itself while they looked for more permanent quarters. Genrikh thought that this would get Lenin's attention and secure him an important job in government but as the weeks passed it was clear that the leader had no plans for him.

Willy and Henry were granted Russian citizenship and Willy, who spoke English and German fluently but Russian somewhat haltingly and with a noticeable accent, joined the Komsomol, the Vsesoyuznyy leninskiy kommunisticheskiy soyuz molodyozhi (Communist Party youth organisation). He attended a special school for English-speaking students and was soon working as an interpreter in the Executive

Committee of the Communist International (Comintern) but in his spare time developed a fascination for the emergent science of radio communications which he studied at night school. He remembered this part of his life as an intense and formative time where he engaged with 'Old Bolsheviks [and] revolutionaries [who had] an aura of mystery and adventure surrounding them'.[3] His father, however, was disappointed to find that his absence during the years of revolution had left him with low political status and he did not get the sort of position in the government administration he felt he was entitled to. In 1924, Willy entered the Indian department at the Institute of Oriental Studies in Moscow but he finished only one course before he was called up for military service where he served initially in a Red Army radiotelegraph battalion.

At the end of his military service in 1926 there were a number of factors that brought him to the attention of the edinënnoe gosudárstvennoe politícheskoe upravlénie (Joint State Political Directorate, OGPU). His special attributes of competence in foreign languages and expertise in radio alongside his possession of a British passport made him of particular interest to the Foreign Department. This attention was not immediately welcomed by Willy who would much rather have devoted himself to a career in radio technology. During his life, Willy would work under several different aliases but he will be referred to throughout the rest of the chapter simply as Fisher.

Whilst contemplating his future, Fisher had made the acquaintance of a younger 'blonde and petite' music student, Yelena (Elya) Stepanova Lebedeva who was training to be a harpist at the Moscow Conservatoire.[4] It was soon clear that they had much in common, attending concerts and visiting art galleries. Fisher himself was a musician playing classical guitar and the two also duetted on piano. Both enjoyed quiet country walks and the company of friends. Neither seemed at all interested in material wealth. They married on 22 April 1927 and Fisher thought it was time for regular employment, so he took up the offer to join OGPU. The focus of this agency at that time was twofold; to prevent the emigration to foreign powers of people who might pose a threat to the Soviet state and to induce those who had already left to return and so weaken counter-revolutionary movements with power bases outside the Soviet Union. To achieve its aims, OGPU employed a range of strategies both 'hard' and 'soft'. Fisher was by no means given to violence and so underwent intense training in coercive techniques. The core skills of his repertoire were recruitment, assessment and handling of agents. He learned how to organise the security of clandestine meetings, how to recognise and evade surveillance, how to employ 'dead-drop' locations for the passing on of intelligence, how to utilise cutouts to reduce the risk of contamination of networks, surveillance techniques of potential targets, the use of codes and secret writing, burglary and techniques of lock-breaking and most important of all and the one aspect of training that interested him the most, radio communications. He learned quickly and he learned well. It was at this time that Fisher struck up a friendship with a fellow OGPU recruit called Rudolf Abel whose identity he adopted thirty years later.[5] After completing his training, Fisher's first assignment involved placing 'illegal' residents of foreign countries.

Given this experience, his languages and British passport, this inevitably led to Fisher himself becoming an 'illegal' when he travelled to France to meet up with his new boss, Alexander Orlov. They travelled together to England, where Fisher utilised his love of and skill in painting to pass himself off as an artist, but according to his friend Kirill Khenkin with whom he worked at OGPU and who would later write about him, Fisher thought Orlov to 'behave stupidly as a clandestine operator'.[6] Having trained as a lawyer, Orlov, born Leiba Leyzerovich Feldbin was, at the time, head of the Paris *rezidentura* and now using the working name Lev Lazarevich Nikolsky.

Despite Fisher's less than glowing assessment of him, Orlov would go on to play a significant role in Soviet intelligence operations by transforming Soviet policy in the running of spies. He moved reliance for intelligence gathering away from diplomats, who had freedom of movement and association in foreign countries but, little opportunity for clandestine work, to 'illegals' such as trade delegates and it was he who took on responsibility for establishing these spying networks. Travelling all across Europe, he made arrangements with the heads of the legal *rezidenturas* to establish support networks and secure communications systems.

He would later spend time in the USA and England laying the foundations for deep cover espionage networks. It was he who recognised that the class system in Britain offered a unique opportunity to recruit 'sleeper' agents from the bright young men who belong to the upper class, especially sons of political leaders, high government officials and influential members of Parliament who would themselves inevitably rise to hold high office in government. Given the general disillusionment with capitalism and the severe social and economic consequences of the Great Depression, many of these young men would become converted to the promises of communism to right the world's wrongs. Naturally they had little understanding of, nor were they encouraged to investigate, the gross violations of human rights being perpetrated by the Stalin regime inside the Soviet Union. One of those employed by Orlov as a 'talent-spotter' was Arnold Deutsch who selected talented, idealistic and disenchanted students and persuaded them to disengage with any communist groups they might have joined and bide their time until they could be of greater use to the Soviets. Their dalliance with left-swing politics would be overlooked by their future masters as temporary youthful, misguided enthusiasm.

Orlov was later given special responsibilities during the Spanish Civil War including the transfer of the whole of Spain's gold reserves to Moscow as payment for Soviet military support for the nationalist government. When rumours of embezzlement of part of the shipment began swirling around leading Soviets involved in the operation were executed. In 1938, fearing that he would become a victim of Stalin's purges Orlov fled with his family to Canada and found asylum in the USA.

After a short spell in England, Fisher returned to Moscow. During the following year on 29 October 1929 Yelena gave birth to a daughter, christened with the English name Evelyn (Evelina). It would be the couple's only child. Fisher was now primed for an assignment of his own and renewed his British passport on 6 August 1931. Travelling on his new passport, and working with the codename Frank, he took his family to Oslo where he set up in business trading in radio components and running a radio repair workshop. This gave him excellent cover for establishing his own radio communications set-up with Moscow and identifying local radio enthusiasts with communist sympathies who might be recruited as part of a Scandinavian espionage network. It proved to be something of an idyllic time for Fisher and Elya and baby Evelina far from the overbearing atmosphere and privations of Moscow. Fisher was free to travel all across Scandinavia establishing his networks.

Khenkin would later say that, during this time, Fisher made use of his British passport to make several trips to England with Orlov to make contact with the Soviet-born physicist Peter Kapitsa who was working with Ernest Rutherford in the Cavendish Laboratory at Cambridge University. His specialisms were high-magnetic field research and low-temperature physics. When Kapitsa later travelled to Moscow in 1934 to attend a scientific conference, the Soviet authorities denied him an exit visa. He would go on to play a significant part in the development of the Soviet atomic bomb. Apart from Khenkin's assertion, there is little hard evidence to say that Fisher had any part to play in persuading Kapitsa to make the journey to Moscow knowing that he would be refused permission to return to England.

By the end of 1934, Moscow was getting a bit jittery about leaving Fisher to enjoy his new lifestyle. They saw a risk that he might be 'corrupted' by Western values, something that Stalin worried about constantly. Fisher was recalled to Moscow, debriefed and relieved of active espionage duties. For a time he was sidelined into an administrative role while his new boss Genrikh Yagoda decided what to do about him. Fisher was cautious. He had learned all about Bolshevik politics from his father. He understood how paranoia, jealousy and envy were rampant in the ruthlessly ambitious ruling cliques and he plotted his way through Moscow's treacherous landscape. He did not make a fuss when he was assigned as an instructor for intelligence probationers but conscientiously applied himself to the task and tried to attract as little attention to himself as possible. He found himself once again working alongside his old friend Rudolf Abel.

Fisher's daughter, Evelyn, recalled Abel as a calm, cheerful man. Born in Riga on 23 September 1900, he suffered in the Stalinist purges when his brother, Voldemar, who worked as head of the political department of the shipping company, was accused of participating in the Latvian counter-revolutionary conspiracy of 1937. For espionage and sabotage Voldemar was sentenced to death, and Rudolph was fired. He would be recalled to service in 1941 to carry out special tasks in the Caucasus where he won the Order of the Red Banner and two Orders of the Red Star. In 1946 as a lieutenant colonel, Abel was again fired. He died suddenly in 1955 just two years before Willy Fisher took on his identity.

Among Willy's trainees was the American Kitty Harris who had been radicalised as a youth factory worker in Winnipeg before moving to Chicago where she joined the CPUSA. In 1927, she joined the Communist Party of the USSR and visited Moscow where she was recruited by OGPU and sent to Shanghai. After a couple of years she returned to the US then spent time in Berlin before going to Moscow in 1935 for special training in radio operation, photography, and cryptography.

She proved to be inattentive, forgetful and generally hopeless but Fisher was patient with her and slowly she improved her concentration and efficiency, Fisher's approach paid off when Harris proved to be a nimble operator of Morse code keys and acquired some proficiency in radio assembly. Operation, however, was another matter. It was clear that she had no grasp of even elementary mathematics so Fisher made sure that she was given special remedial classes. Still her personnel file recorded her as getting 'muddled when dealing with technical aspects'. Her final assessment records that 'any more technical training would be a waste of time and that she should only be used as a radio operator in an emergency.[7] Nevertheless, it is clear from subsequent encounters between the two that Fisher, despite his failure to instil even basic radio skills into Harris, retained a fond personal attachment to her.[8] Harris would go on to play a role in the running of Donald Maclean in the years before the Second World War and then went on to act as a courier for the agent Lev Vasilevsky during Soviet penetration of the Manhattan Project.

When Orlov defected in 1938 it put Willy in a very precarious position. Many were executed in the purges for much less serious 'crimes' than having worked alongside, and been something of a protégé of, a defector. Somehow he escaped the firing squad but he was dismissed from the NKVD on 31 December 1938 after which he worked for some time in the All-Union Chamber of Commerce as a patent technician and later as an engineer at an aerospace manufacturing plant.

After the German invasion of June 1941, the acute shortage of radio experts saw Fisher and Abel recalled to the service. Little is known about Fisher's service at that time but records show that on 7 November 1941 he was in the post of head of the communications department involved in ensuring the security of the parade, which took place on Red Square. With the rank of lieutenant, he later became chief of the radio communication section Otdelnaya Brigada of the NKVD in Pavel Sudoplatov's 4th Special Tasks Directorate. This was a unit principally responsible for intelligence operations against Germany. Its tasks included organising guerrilla warfare and establishing illegal networks in the German-occupied territories as well as *maskirovka*, deception operations designed to feed disinformation of a plausible character to the German forces to trick them into making poor military decisions.[9] In the following year he was put in charge of transmitting controlled material as part of the highly successful *maskirovka* deception operations, Operation Monastery and later Operation Berezino.[10]

Operation Berezino illustrates just how effective the deception was. The German 36th Security Regiment of the 286th Security Division led by Lieutenant Colonel Heinrich Gerhard Scherhorn had been destroyed and he was captured by the Soviets on 9 July 1944 near Minsk. Scherhorn had been one of a group of 1,800 Germans surrounded near the Berezino river. The Germans were aware that such a group had been isolated in that region and had some intelligence to suggest that it was still holding out. Soviet counterintelligence knew about this situation from radio intercepts and started passing misinformation through a fictitious ragtag band of underground monarchy sympathisers, codename Prestol (Throne), to create a fiction. The besieged Germans were determined to make it back to their own lines, the story went, but they were running short of ammunition and had many wounded who required immediate medical aid. What the Germans did not know, and did not find out, was that all but 200 had been killed and the rest, including Scherhorn, taken captive.

Colonel Worgitzky, chief of intelligence for German Army Group Centre, after much deliberation decided that there was a high probability that the information was reliable and that steps should be taken to relieve Scherhorn's group by dropping supplies and sending in radio operators to establish communications. The man chosen to make contact with Scherhorn's fictitious force was Otto Skorzeny who described what happened in his memoirs. A plan, codename *Freischütz* (magic shooter), had four groups, each of five men, with wireless transmitting set, parachute rations for four weeks, tents, etc., and Russian machine-pistols, all disguised as Red Army soldiers. Meticulous preparations included the men being given the vile Russian machorka cigarettes and having their heads shaved. Some would be dropped near Borisov and Cervenj, east of Minsk, while others were to be dropped near Djerzinsk and Viteika and make a concentric approach to Minsk.

On the night of 15 September 1944, three German radio operators landed at specified coordinates but were quickly captured and coerced into taking part in the 'radio games' by sending back false information. On 27 October two more parachutists, one doctor Jeschki and Harry Vivor followed but, like the previous men, they were immediately taken captive. When, under Soviet control, they reported back, the correct password was given and also the secret codeword indicating that the speaker was not being held by the Soviets. Scherhorn, himself, was forced to take part in the subterfuge by speaking a few words personally. The group now numbered some 2,500 men, Scherhorn said, with several hundred wounded.

Despite regular communications with Scherhorn's men, Army Group Centre was still not entirely convinced but could not risk abandoning forces that appeared to be a thorn in the Soviet flesh. Radio messages continued pleading for help. They continued to drop supplies, men and equipment at designated site and even sent an engineer to scout for a suitable landing zone so that evacuation of wounded could begin but Scherhorn was becoming ever more distant from a constantly retreating German army and fuel was in desperately short supply. Skorzeny was no fool and suspected foul play so he sent other agents not connected to *Freischütz* to try and verify the existence of Scherhorn's group. Unfortunately for him, all eight men were caught and forced to become part of the subterfuge.

All this time, Scherhorn was reporting that his men were moving westward engaging the rear units of the Red Army, conducting sabotage, taking prisoners, and collecting intelligence. All this was reinforced by an intricate web of other misinformation such as newspaper reports and fake agent messages all under the control of Abel.

On 23 March, Hitler announced that members of Scherhorn's officer corps, who were actually far from Berezino in Soviet captivity, were to be promoted. Scherhorn, himself, was awarded the Knight's Cross and promoted to colonel. It was Hitler's way of abandoning the men because very soon afterwards all contact was broken off. Between September 1944 and May 1945, the Germans flew thirty-nine missions in support of Scherhorn and lost a total of twenty-two agents. Besides that, they dropped into Soviet hands several tons of cargoes with medicines and warm clothes along with 2,258,330 roubles.[11] Fisher did not come out of the war unscathed, however. Poor diet while on field duty and the stress of operating behind German lines had resulted in stomach ulcers that would affect him for the rest of his life.

After the Second World War the Kremlin found it convenient to identify the USA as a direct threat to the survival of the Soviet Union in much the same way as Western countries did with them. The political dynamic shifted with the advent of the Cold War that saw the uneasy alliance between the Western Powers and the Soviet Union begin to unravel heralding the beginning of geopolitical rivalry between them. The development of weapons of mass destruction brought both sides to a realisation that all-out war would end in 'mutually assured destruction' (MAD). As a result, intelligence services on both sides came to prominence in this new reality as a way of gaining advantage and neutralising the opposition. The USA created the Central Intelligence Agency (CIA) and the Soviets responded by merging the GRU and the Ministry of State Security (Ministerstvo Gosudarstvennoi Bezopasnosti, MGB) into the Committee of Information (Komitet Informatsii, KI).

Sudoplatov only just survived the shake-up of leadership in the Soviet intelligence agencies which was a relief to Fisher who had become closely associated with him but Fisher now had a new boss, Aleksandr Mikhailovich Korotkov. If Fisher thought that the relaxation of state control that had been essential to conduct the war would continue, he was seriously mistaken. Stalin lost no time in re-establishing iron control through his security organs making his point clear by instigating a wave of arrests and executions.

It was not inconceivable that escalating international tensions could see withdrawal of diplomatic residencies and both sides saw the vital importance of 'illegals' if that was to come to pass. This elevated the status of Fisher's agency and his own given the vast experience of running illegals he had gained during the war. Neither was it overlooked that Fisher was a vastly cultured and intelligent man with many skills, not all of which were underhand. He was a trained engineer with a basic understanding of nuclear physics which he had studied to some extent. He was also a musician and someone well able to hold his own in intellectual conversations and polite company. The fact that he spoke faultless English without an accent was the clinching characteristic that made him a perfect choice to operate as an undercover agent inside the USA. He was even invited for a private conversation with Minister of Foreign Affairs Vyacheslav Molotov to discuss his suitability for the work. That went so well that Molotov later hosted a dinner for the whole Fisher family.

The idea was for Fisher to enter the USA and take over the organisation of existing network that had been stealing secrets of the American atomic bomb programme and establish a new up-to-date radio communications system. His family would remain in the Soviet Union as an insurance policy against defection. The job had originally been reserved for André Deutsch before his untimely death demanded a new candidate. Fisher underwent a comprehensive training programme on American history, geography, economics and culture. Soon he was ready for deployment. He travelled to Warsaw where he ditched his Soviet passport and picked up a new one in the name of Andrei Yugesovich Kayotis.

Kayotis had been born in Lithuania in 1895 but had become a naturalised American citizen. Unmarried and living in Detroit, in 1947 he had travelled to Europe to visit his homeland which was now under Soviet control. It was a sentimental journey for Kayotis to see his homeland one last time because he was now in poor health. The Soviet Embassy in Copenhagen issued him with travel permits but withheld his passport until he returned but he never did come back to reclaim it. His health deteriorated while in Lithuania and he died in hospital there.

As Kayotis, Fisher boarded the *Sythia*, crossed the Atlantic and landed in Québec on 14 November 1948 before crossing legally into the USA a few days later. In New York he made contact with a

Soviet 'illegal' Iosif Romualdovich Grigulevich, who took his Kayotis passport and swapped it for one in the name of Emil Goldfus. He also gave Fisher $1,000 in cash. Soviet intelligence had made a habit of scouring files of old US newspapers studying obituary notices to for the purpose of creating false identities (legends) for future agents. Emil Goldfus had been born of German immigrant parents in living at 120 East 87th Street in New York but had died aged 2 months and 7 days on 9 October 9 1903. By 1948, there were no close living relatives of Emil. To complete the legend, Grigulevich gave Fisher a copy of Emil's birth certificate, a bogus draft card and a forged tax return. His story would be that he had spent his childhood in New York before moving to Detroit, Grand Rapids and returning to New York just a year before, in 1947.[12]

Fisher's first few months were taken up with travel to acclimatise himself to American culture while trying to maintain a low profile and not attract any attention to himself for any reason. He went to the west coast to report on shipments of military arms leaving Long Beach bound for Chiang Kai-shek's nationalist forces in the Chinese Civil War against Mao Zedong's communists. In early 1950 he had returned to New York and rented an apartment in a four-storey red brick building at 216 West 99th Street using his Goldfus identity. In the city he 'melted into the crowd looking for all the world like an old-world … charming, sad … disinherited European intellectual' currently self-employed as a photographer.[13]

He set about establishing a record that would stand up to scrutiny. He opened an account at the 96th Street branch of the East River Savings Bank making small monthly deposits and occasional withdrawals. He was polite and amiable with his neighbours and local shopkeepers but as Goldfus he made no friends. He did, however, mix socially with others such as Morris Cohen and his wife Lona Teresa, née Petka, a couple in their mid-thirties whom Fisher knew to have been dedicated communists for many years. To the Cohen's however, he was known as Milton (Milt), a wealthy English businessman whom they entertained in their apartment at 178 East 71st Street.

Morris Cohen was born in Harlem to a Jewish immigrant family. He had gone to Spain in 1937 to fight with the predominantly communist-populated Canadian Mackenzie–Papineau Battalion as part of the XV International Brigade. While there he had been recruited by the Soviet agent Amadeo Sabatini and returned to the US as Israel Altman to conceal the fact from immigration officials that he had been to Spain. Once inside the country he took up his true identity again as

Cohen working for a time with the Amtorg Trading Company a sort of Soviet trade delegation with diplomatic credentials then took up a teaching post. Lona was the daughter of Polish immigrants. During the Second World War, both Morris and Lona had been part of the Soviet 'Volunteer' espionage ring acting as couriers for atomic spies such as Theodor Alvin (Ted) Hall and the Rosenbergs but since 1945, they had been stood down when a number of Soviet spy rings were compromised.

Fisher had been authorised to reactivate the Cohens and their contacts but the Soviet networks in America were again under threat after the Venona counterintelligence programme had uncovered evidence of their espionage activities. Decryptions of intercepted Soviet radio traffic had revealed the identity of Klaus Fuchs as a Soviet spy and Senator Joseph McCarthy's witch hunt of suspected communists all across the American landscape had created a febrile atmosphere. The arrests of David Greenglass followed in June 1950 and of Julius Rosenberg a month later.

Suddenly neither of the Cohen's could be found. They had cashed in their savings bond on 16 July, the day of Rosenberg's arrest, fled the country leaving most of their belongings behind them, gone to Mexico and were now in Lublin, Poland where they continued to work for Soviet intelligence later going to the Far East. Then in 1954, they turned up living at 45 Cranley Drive in Ruislip in England posing as antiquarian book dealers under the names of Peter and Helen Kroger. They would be arrested by British security officials on 7 January 1961 for their part in Portland spy ring. Convicted of espionage, they were sentenced to ten years in prison but after eight they were exchanged for the British spy Gerald Brooke.

In March 1950, Valery Mikhailovich Makaev had arrived in New York to take up a post teaching music at New York University. His secondary role, however, was to act as case officer to the British Secret Intelligence Service officer and Soviet mole Kim Philby, at that time first secretary to the British Embassy in Washington working under the codename 'Stanley' and using Guy Burgess as courier and cutout. The unstable and alcoholic Burgess, who cruised neighbourhood in pursuit of homosexual encounters, was a clear security risk. Makaev and Fisher were aware of each other, but they did not interfere with each other's work.

When the Rosenbergs went to the electric chair on 19 June 1953 without making any confession, Fisher could relax a little. He moved into an apartment at Riverside Drive on West 74th Street where he set up a short-wave radio receiver attached to a tape recorder through which he received his orders from Moscow. Continuously aware of his vulnerability, he moved again to Brooklyn taking up residence in a boarding house in Hicks Street. Seeking to enhance his cover as an artist he also rented a studio at the Ovington Studios at 246 Fulton Street close to Brooklyn Heights. Fisher's life took on a somewhat different aspect at this time. He began socialising with other writers and artists who rented space in the building. He showed interest in their work and invited others to criticise his own. While many of these artists had left-wing sympathies, Fisher never made any move to recruit them as agents. It was as if he was deliberately attempting to live a 'normal' life alongside his espionage role possibly as a safety valve for the many years of stress he had endured and as compensation for the warmth of family life that he must have missed terribly. He was, for a moment, allowing himself to express his real persona. It was a risk, however, to cast off the protective cloak of anonymity and become involved with people who might find themselves caught up in McCarthy's broadly cast net searching for 'subversives'.

His fellow tenants were used to mixing with other artists and were sympathetic to different character traits of creative and complicated people but Fisher, somehow, didn't quite fit. Danny Schwartz thought him 'too cultivated, too intelligent, too worldly' for a man who purported to be a retired small businessman. His 'subtle, wry humour' and wide range of interests puzzled him. Jules Feiffer thought he had the look of a man who 'had been on the bum (a vagrant)'.[14]

When later questioned about Fisher's time at Fulton Street, one of his artist neighbours thought that in time, he could have been 'a very good painter'. Fisher himself said that 'I would have progressed more in my painting career if I had had more time to give to it'. His work consisted mostly of sketches made in run-down neighbourhoods of New York City showing 'lonely, older men standing, sitting or huddled over. Some were playing chess or checkers in a small park; others talked quietly, almost sadly, on the street.'[15]

Recognising his own shortcomings as an artist, Fisher showed great eagerness to learn from people like Burt Silverman who was ever willing to give him advice. Fisher also took up the guitar again, studying the classical works of Segovia. He mixed freely with his fellow artists and while he could hold his own in discussions on wide range of subjects, he lacked spontaneity and tended to listen more than speak.

Little is known about Fisher's espionage activity during these years but he was sufficiently occupied with it to warrant Moscow sending him an assistant, someone who had been training for the role since 1948.

Reino Häyhänen had been born on 14 May 1920 in the village of Kaskisaari, some 40 kilometres from St Petersburg and close to the Finnish border. His impoverished family was descended from Finnish immigrants but he rose above this modest background to join the Komsomol and later to be recruited by the Narodnyy komissariat vnutrennikh del, (People's Commissariat for Internal Affairs, NKVD). Having been brought up bi-lingual, Häyhänen, became an interpreter assigned to the Karelian Isthmus during the Finnish-Russian War of 1939–1940 interrogating prisoners of war. During the Second World War, he trained undercover agents to operate inside Finland and rose to the rank of lieutenant, senior grade. He remained in Finland after the end of the war creating a network of informants to spy on suspected pro-capitalist members of the intelligentsia.

In 1948, he was called to Moscow by the Pervoye glavnoye upravleniye (foreign operations division of the KGB) which had now taken over the NKVD, to receive special training in photographing documents and coding of messages. Moscow had a special mission for him which required him first of all to create an elaborate 'legend' for himself. After a year living in the Estonian capital Tallinn studying English and further developing his espionage skills, he was given the cover name Eugene Nicoli Maki. The real Eugene Maki had been born in Enaville, Idaho on 30 May 1919 but had moved to Finland with his family in 1927. The PGU knew this because they had possession of his birth certificate.

Häyhänen was smuggled across the border into Finland in the boot of a car and lived for a while in southern Finland working in a factory. For two years he lived in Tampere and Turku in a variety of jobs. When he applied to the US Consulate in Helsinki for a US passport on 3 July 1951, he could produce his birth certificate showing that his mother Lillian Luoma Maki had been born in New York and his father was a Finnish immigrant August Maki, born in Oulu, Finland. Both were now dead he said. He swore that he had never served in the Finnish army nor ever voted in a Finnish election. He also provided affidavits from two witnesses who had been bribed to affirm that Häyhänen had lived in Finland since 1943.

With his US passport, he returned to Moscow, again in the boot of a car, leaving behind a second wife Hannah Kurikka whom he had married under the name of Maki despite already having a wife and son under the name of Häyhänen in the Soviet Union. Back in the Moscow he was sent on a crash refresher course on the creation of microdots (text or an image substantially reduced to the size of a full stop) a particular skill that he was never able to get to grips with. Something new to him was the use of hollowed-out items such as screws and coins that could be used to secrete messages in. In this short time he was also instructed in the use of 'drops' for the placing and retrieval of secret items and the security signals to be used between agents. Then he was ready to learn about his new assignment.

It was Vitali G. Pavlov, deputy chief of the PRU's American department who briefed Häyhänen for his mission and gave him the codename 'Vik'. He was being sent to New York to work as an assistant to an undercover agent he would know as 'Mark'. He would receive $5,000 and a further $400 every month as salary while his family back in the Soviet Union would get financial support from the state. To cap it all he was promoted to the rank of major.

The first 'drop' he would use to receive items from Mark was a hole in the wall on Jerome Avenue between 165th and 167th Streets. Another was a bridge over a footpath in Central Park near 95th Street, a third was in Fort Tryon Park under a lamppost. A subway station at 80th Street and Central Park Avenue in Manhattan was where a vertical line of blue chalk would signal that there was something in a drop to collect. A second line would indicate that the item had been retrieved.

Häyhänen went back to Finland, became Maki again then travelled through Sweden to Enfdland where he boarded the *Queen Mary*. Pavlov meanwhile had returned to New York with his wife Raissa Vassilievna Svirina, rented an apartment on Upper West Side of Manhattan and had taken up his post as first secretary of the Soviet Embassy. Häyhänen stepped onto the pier at New York on 20 October 1952 and cleared immigration. After a couple of days finding somewhere to live at 816 43rd Street in Brooklyn, he went to the Tavern-on-the-Green restaurant which was in the park on 79th Street and placed a white drawing pin in the restaurant sign. He was telling Moscow that he had arrived safely. Moscow's acknowledgement of this confirmation was sent by radio to Fisher for him to forward to Häyhänen who would decode it. Fisher wrote down the coded message and converted it into a microphotograph which he then arranged to pass on to Häyhänen. Given what we know of Fisher's character and that of Häyhänen it seems probable that the message was handed over to Häyhänen but he did not decode it until four years had passed and he was in FBI custody. It congratulated Häyhänen on his safe arrival and described arrangements for the transfer of funds to him invest in a local business.

The story of how the FBI got hold of the message is as follows. On the evening of Monday, 22 June 1953, a boy delivering a copy of the 'Brooklyn Eagle' to an apartment at 3403 Foster Avenue in Brooklyn dropped a coin on the floor and it split apart. Inside it was a tiny photograph that looked like a series of numbers. The boy kept it and told his friends one of whom was the daughter of a detective of the New York City Police Department. The detective happened to mention it to someone he knew in the FBI. The agent was intrigued and contacted the paper boy who handed over the coin and its contents.

The face of the coin was a 1948 Jefferson nickel. In the 'R' of the word 'TRUST', there was a tiny hole apparently drilled there so that a fine needle or other small instrument could be inserted to force the nickel open. The reverse side had been made from another nickel – one minted sometime during the period of 1942 to 1945. It was composed of copper-silver alloy, there being a shortage of nickel during the Second World War. When it was closely examined, the microphotograph showed ten columns of typewritten numbers. There was five digits in each number and twenty-one numbers in most columns. The FBI immediately suspected that they had found a coded espionage message, and they made every effort to try and find out where it had come from but all to no avail. Neither could they decipher the coded message.

Months of determined probing by the FBI's scientists and investigative staff had led merely to one blind alley after another. Yet, the relentless search to identify the person who had brought the hollow nickel to New York, as well as the person for whom the coded message was intended, continued. It would not be solved until four years later.

Meanwhile, on the 21st of every month, Häyhänen took the BMT subway to Prospect Park station and went to the Lincoln Road exit. He hung around for a few minutes and then returned home. It was some months before he was contacted by Mikhail N. Sivrin whom he knew from his training days in Moscow and who was now an official with the Soviet delegation to the United Nations in New York. This contact was authorised by Moscow but, in fact, was highly insecure. It was quite against all protocols for 'legals' such as Sivrin to have anything to do with 'illegals' such as Häyhänen. It was either showing contempt for the effectiveness of Hoover's FBI to detect them or an admission that Häyhänen required careful monitoring. His proclivity for hard drinking allied to poor self-image, already well known from his time in Finland, had not improved since his relocation which begs the question of why he was thought to be such a good fit for the mission in the first place. Maybe Moscow hoped that he might settle down when his second wife Hannah joined him in New York in February

1953 but that did not happen. They moved into a furnished apartment in a dreary neighbourhood at 176 South 4th Street which depressed Hannah and led to domestic rows. A move to 932 Madison Street was a step further down the social ladder and Häyhänen's drinking got worse.

The first meeting between Häyhänen and Fisher took place in the summer of 1953 in the men's smoking room of Keith's RKO theatre in Flushing, New York. Thereafter, Häyhänen was assigned to missions in Salida, Colorado, and Quincy, Massachusetts. Later the two men went together to Poughkeepsie, New York to locate a suitable site for a short-wave radio transmitter. Häyhänen performed other basic duties such as monitored 'drops' and passing on material to contacts. He was also occasionally required to hand over sums of cash to various people, something that he was not always scrupulous about. Money that he was given to set up a business usually ended up in the till of the local liquor store.

A large part of the problem for him was that he did not like America. He had a poor grasp of the language at the best of times and was completely flummoxed by New York slang. Neither he nor Hannah had any hope of integrating into American life. Häyhänen made no effort to start up a business or invest in an existing one as he had been instructed to do. Instead, he spent a lot of time seeking out and drinking with Finnish or Polish immigrants. Fisher did not approve of this at all. Häyhänen was an accident waiting to happen as far as he was concerned. He did his best to instil some discipline into Häyhänen's life and tried to instruct him how to carry out his orders. He also urged Häyhänen to mix more with Americans to improve his understanding of the language and local idioms. It came as a shock to Fisher when he learned that Häyhänen did not even understand Morse code. He could not understand at all why Moscow had sent him this 'bumbling misfit' who seemed to have no idea what he was supposed to be doing in America.[16]

Eventually, Fisher's persistence paid off and Häyhänen took out a lease on an empty store with a four-roomed apartment at 806 Bergen Street, a poor neighbourhood in Newark with the intention of opening a photographic shop and studio. Together they installed some photographic equipment in the store and Fisher tried to educate Häyhänen in the rudiments of photography especially the production of microdots which Häyhänen seemed to know nothing about. Fisher now made a mistake that was to come back and haunt him. In his eagerness to help Häyhänen to create a 'front' for his illicit photography he took him to his Ovington studio at Fulton Street on three occasions always late at night to collect some equipment. Given his low opinion of Häyhänen's reliability it was an egregious lapse of security to expose any detail of his own life or operations to Häyhänen's glare.

Fisher had done all he could, even going beyond what was prudent, to establish Häyhänen as an effective agent but he could only have felt trepidation when he was given permission to return to Moscow for a family visit which meant leaving Häyhänen without any support to keep him on the straight and narrow while he was away. There was no attempt to open the store for business. Fisher flew to Paris then he took a train to Vienna where he picked up a new passport from the Soviet Embassy. Days later he was reunited with his wife and daughter, now 23 years old, in Moscow.

It was almost inevitable that Häyhänen would regress. In Fisher's absence he started drinking heavily and arguing loudly at home with Hannah, who had also searched for solace in a bottle of vodka. On one occasion the police were called after reports of an affray. When they entered the store they found Häyhänen and Hannah both drunk and Häyhänen with a knife wound to his leg. Immigrants who hardly spoke English, got drunk and fought with each other was nothing new to the police and, after calling for medical help to treat the wound, they took no further action.

While Fisher was out of the country, Häyhänen continued his dissolute existence by purloining $5,000 that he was supposed to pay to the wife of Morton Sobell. Sobell had been imprisoned for his part in the Rosenberg spy ring. When Fisher returned he saw a marked deterioration in Häyhänen and decided that he was now a serious liability. Fisher told Moscow that something had to be done. Moscow agreed and sent word to Häyhänen that he had been promoted to lieutenant colonel and was being rewarded with a vacation in his homeland. Häyhänen was no fool, he knew what that meant. He knew perfectly well that he was completely hopeless as a spy. He was acutely aware that Fisher despised him. His marriage offered him no comfort and Moscow had cut off his supply of money. He did all he could to delay the trip but he was caught in a bind. Fisher procured for him a passport using a forged birth certificate in the name of Lauri Arnold Ermas who, allegedly, had been born in Portland Oregon. Reluctantly, Häyhänen booked a passage on the *Liberté* and left New York Harbor on 24 April 1957.

While he crossed the Atlantic, he had plenty of time to think. He decided that he would not go back to the Soviet Union to face whatever fate awaited him and so when he got as far as Paris, instead of following Fisher's instruction by phoning a given number to indicate that he had arrived, Häyhänen went to the US Embassy there, on 4 May, he identified himself as a KGB officer and said that he had important information to impart. As evidence to support his story, he showed a hollowed-out coin. When interviewed, he told a CIA officer that he wanted to defect. The CIA made arrangements to hand him over to the FBI and he was flown back to New York a week later.

Soon after Häyhänen had left New York, Fisher had taken a short trip to Daytona Beach, Florida and booked into the Plaza Hotel under the name of Martin Collins for a short vacation during which he did some seascape painting. By the time he returned to New York, which was then same day that Häyhänen arrived under FBI guard, he would have been told by Moscow that Häyhänen had disappeared. There are various explanations for why Fisher did not take immediate steps to leave the country. He may have assumed that Häyhänen had suspected that he would face a severe dressing down, or worse, in Moscow and had taken some time to drown his sorrows somewhere en route. Given Fisher's own experience of Moscow methods, he may also have feared that Häyhänen had been quietly disposed of. Whatever his thoughts, Fisher saw no reason to panic. He still had work to do, and he knew that Häyhänen was out of the country, he had seen him board the *Liberté* in New York Harbor.

He was cautious enough to check into a hotel rather than go back to his own apartment, however. He took room 839 at the Hotel Latham on 28th Street off Fifth Avenue registering as Martin Collins and stayed away from the Ovington building for a few days. When he eventually did visit Fulton Street, the building was under FBI surveillance. Häyhänen had only ever visited late at night but he gave the FBI enough details for them to identify the building from which Fisher had taken photographic equipment for Häyhänen's studio.

FBI agents had installed themselves in the Hotel Tourains facing the Ovington building. Special Agent Neil Heiner was on duty on the night of 23 May with binoculars trained on the building opposite when he saw a light go on and he identified a 'middle-aged, bald [man] with a fringe of grey hair wearing glasses'.[17]

The man put on a dark straw summer hat with a bright white band, turned out the light and left the building. He was followed by Special Agent Joseph C. McDonald to the BMT Borough Hall subway station and down the elevator onto the platform. McDonald followed Fisher onto a train and went with him as far as the City Hall stop when both alighted. Fisher walked up Broadway to the corner of Chambers Street and took a bus. McDonald followed in a taxi. When Fisher got off the bus, he managed to keep an eye on him as far as the corner of 28th Street and Fifth Avenue but lost him. Surveillance on the Ovington building was stepped up and three weeks later, it was Heiner again who spotted Fisher in the building wearing the same distinctive hat. This time, the man was followed by agent Fred Sowick who tailed him as far as the Hotel Latham. This was the man that Häyhänen had called Mark. FBI officers were installed in the room next to Abel's in the hotel.

Häyhänen's intelligence was the only thing the FBI had to go on but, although he was later to be the government's principal witness at the trial, Häyhänen, at that time, insisted that he would refuse to testify, although he was quite willing to cooperate in secret. The FBI realised that without Häyhänen's testimony they did not have a case against the man they had identified as Martin Collins so they contacted the Immigration and Naturalization Service (INS) and told them that they suspected the man they knew as Collins of not being who he claimed to be and was in fact an alien residing in the US illegally. The hope was that the INS would begin deportation proceedings against him on the grounds that he had failed to comply with the legal duty of aliens to notify the attorney general every January of their address in the United States.

On 20 June, the INS sent two of its officers, Schoenenberger and Kanzler, to New York armed with a warrant to investigate Collins' residency status and an order addressed to him directing him to show cause why he should not be deported. They were escorted to the Hotel Latham by FBI agents, who had no powers or authority in the operation but nevertheless, they requested permission of the INS agents to question Collins before the actual arrest was made with regard to suspected involvement in espionage.

Officers Gamber and Blasco who had no warrant either to arrest Collins or to search his room, entered room 839 at 07.00 hours on the morning of 21 June with instructions to telephone to their superior for further orders if Collins agreed to cooperate or, failing that, to call on the INS agents to execute their warrant for his arrest. Fisher was naked and told to put on some underwear and to sit on the bed, which he did. He was questioned by the FBI officers for about twenty minutes but although he answered some of their questions, Fisher would not admit to having been involved in any espionage. INS agents then entered the room, addressed him as 'colonel' and arrested him. It was a clear indication to Fisher when they addressed him as colonel that it was Häyhänen who had given him up.

INS agents, without requesting Fisher's consent, then undertook a search of the room and the adjoining bathroom which took about fifteen minutes. No weapon was found neither was there anything suggesting that their suspect was an alien, but they turned up a birth certificate in the name of Martin Collins. Fisher was then told to dress and pack such things as he wanted to take with him. Some things he chose to leave and others were put in the waste paper basket. When the packing was finished, Fisher asked and received permission to repack one of his suitcases. While he was doing so, Schoenenberger noticed him slipping some papers into the sleeve of his coat. Schoenenberger grabbed them and they were later presented as evidence at Fisher's trial. One of the items was a piece of graph paper containing a coded message.

The agents took Fisher to the lobby where he paid his bill and then they handcuffed him and took him to INS headquarters in New York. A search of the items Fisher had packed produced, a birth certificate, certifying the birth of Emil Goldfus in New York in 1902, an international certificate of vaccination, issued in New York to Martin Collins in 1957 and a bank book of the East River Savings Bank containing the account of Emil Goldfus.

Despite having no warrant to do so, the FBI agent Kehoe asked the hotel manager for permission to search Fisher's room which was legal now that it was officially unoccupied. The contents of the wastepaper basket included a hollow pencil containing microfilm and a block of wood containing a cipher pad. A few days later, a search of Fisher's studio and storeroom turned up a one-third-horsepower generator, a Hallicrafter short-wave radio and earphones, a Speedgraphic camera with assorted photographic equipment and supplies, metal dies and tools, numerous film containers and some clothing, a general map of Bear Mountain-Harriman section of Palisades Interstate Park and street maps of Queens, Brooklyn, Westchester and Putnam Counties, New York; other maps, of Chicago, Baltimore and Los Angeles, loose nails, film strips, cuff-link containers and odds and ends, a schedule of international mails, a clip pad with mathematical formulas, musical scores, a gramophone and records, art sketchbooks, scientific magazines and technical pamphlets, a bankbook, an oil painting of a refinery, a box of prophylactics, and artists' paintbrushes.[18]

The sheer volume of incriminating material found in the hotel and studio speaks volumes for how careless Fisher had become after his initial fatal error of letting Häyhänen know where his studio was. Even when there had been no confirmation of Häyhänen's arrival in Moscow, Fisher still did not take the obvious step of clearing out his studio or at least keeping well away from it. His years of freewheeling, carrying out his espionage duties with ease and enjoying the stimulation of a social network of artists in New York had lulled him into a false sense of security and dulled his survival instincts.

Fisher was then flown to the alien detention facility in McAllen, Texas in a special DC-3 aircraft accompanied by two Federal agents. He was questioned for days but would only say that he was a Russian citizen who had found a large sum of American money in a ruined blockhouse in Russia. With that he had bought forged American passport in Denmark then used it to entered the United States from Canada in 1948. The FBI suggested that he could earn $10,000 a year if he agreed to cooperate in a counterintelligence operation against his Soviet masters but Fisher declined the offer. While admitting that he was working for Soviet intelligence, he denied any involvement with espionage into atomic energy saying that his mission had been simply to obtain general information of a non-military nature from scientific magazines and newspapers.

After six weeks, Fisher was served with a criminal warrant for his arrest. An insurance lawyer, James B. Donovan was assigned to act as legal representative for Fisher. Donovan had been a top assistant to Supreme Court Justice Robert Jackson in prosecuting Nazi war criminals at the Second World War Nuremberg Trials. When Fisher was officially charged, the indictment included the following,

That from in or about 1948 ... Rudolf Ivanovich Abel, also known as 'Mark' [code name] and also known as Martin Collins and Emil R. Goldfus, unlawfully, wilfully and knowingly did conspire and agree with [Reino Häyhänen also known as 'Vic' ... and with Reino Häyhänen, Mikhail N. Sivrin, Vitali G. Pavlov and Aleksandr Mikhailovich Korotkov] to ... agree to communicate, deliver and transmit to ... the Union of Soviet Socialist Republics ... documents, writings, photographs, photographic negatives, plans, maps, models, notes, instruments, appliances and information relating to the national defense of the United States of America, and particularly information relating to arms, equipment and disposition of the United States Armed Forces, and information relating to the atomic energy program of the United States ... It was further a part of said conspiracy that the defendant ... would activate and attempt to activate as agents within the United States certain members of the Armed Forces who were in a position to acquire information relating to the national defense ... the defendant would use short-wave radios to receive instructions ... of the Union of Soviet Socialist Republics and to send information to the said government ... the defendant would fashion 'containers' from bolts, nails, coins, batteries, pencils, cuff links, earrings and the like ... suitable to secrete microfilm and microdot and other secret messages ... defendant and his co-conspirators would communicate with each other by enclosing messages in said 'containers' and depositing them … in pre-arranged 'drop' points in Prospect Park, Brooklyn, and in Fort Tryon Park, N.Y., and at other places … defendant would receive from the Soviet government … large sums of money to carry on their illegal activities … some of which money would be stored for future use by burying it in the ground … defendant and certain of his co-conspirators would, in the event of war between the United States and the Union of Soviet Socialist Republics, set up clandestine radio transmitting and receiving posts for the purpose of continuing to furnish … information relating to the national defense of the U.S., and would engage in acts of sabotage against the U.S.[19]

At first, having looked at all the evidence, Donovan told him 'it will be a miracle if I can save your life'.[20] But Fisher's prospects improved when it was discovered that the seizure of Fisher and all his effects at the Hotel Latham unquestionably violated the United States Constitution. No evidence seized in the Hotel Latham or in the Fulton Street studio could be used in any criminal prosecution. Added to this was the fact that Fisher had been secretly transported to an alien detention camp in Texas and held for forty-seven days, the first five incommunicado. Donovan was now confident that the government's case against Fisher would collapse but he was wrong.

On 7 August 1957, a grand jury in the Eastern District of New York found Fisher, whom the Americans now called Rudolf Ivanovich Abel, guilty of conspiring to violate the espionage laws of the United States. Specifically, by communicating information concerning the national defence of the United States to the Union of Soviet Socialist Republics and to receive and obtain material connected with the national defence of the United States for the purpose of transmitting such material to the Soviet government. On 15 November 1957 he was sentenced to a total of thirty years' imprisonment.

Lawyers for Fisher would later claim that all the items recover from him on the day of his arrest, having been seized without a search warrant, were obtained under false pretences and could not be used as evidence in a trial. They claimed that Fisher had been taken into custody so that pressure might be brought to bear upon him to confess his espionage and cooperate with the FBI. On 25 February 1960, an appeal court considered whether the Fourth and Fifth Amendments of the US Constitution were violated when agents searched and seized evidence from Abel while he was in custody pursuant to an INS warrant. In a 5:4 decision, Justice Felix Frankfurter concluded that Fisher had been properly arrested. While acknowledging both that the

INS delayed its arrest of Fisher and that the FBI searched his room immediately after INS agents' search, he did not consider this to be sufficient evidence of unreasonable 'bad faith' cooperation between the INS and FBI. He also held that the items seized by both the INS and the FBI were properly introduced into evidence at trial. The dissenting judges warned against allowing administrative officers such as INS agents to enter people's homes without warrants, especially when the invasion is a front for a criminal investigation. They argued that the FBI were clearly the moving force behind Fisher's arrest and the search of his hotel room, noting that the FBI made no effort during the investigation to obtain a search warrant despite having plenty of time to do so. They rejected the notion that the fruits of a deportation warrant may be used in a criminal trial and that an administrative search can never be reasonable under the Fourth Amendment.

Fisher appeared doomed to spend what would probably be the rest of his life in an American prison but the Cold War in which he had so long been a loyal foot soldier hotted up somewhat on 1 May 1960 and he once again found himself back on the chess board of international politics as a vital pawn. The nuclear arms race demanded that the leadership of both the US and the Soviet Union placed a priority on information about the other side's progress in the development of nuclear weapons. The US tried to get agreement for an 'open skies' agreement in which each country would be permitted to make overflights of the other to conduct mutual aerial inspections of nuclear facilities and launchpads. The Soviets rejected the offer out of hand so the US made arrangements to conduct illegal surveillance of their nuclear facilities.

The Lockheed Utility-2 (U-2) single engine high altitude spy plane, nicknamed Dragon Lady by the Americans and 'the Black Lady of Espionage' by the Soviets, was developed as part of this programme. It could fly at a ceiling of 70,000 feet which, it was believed, would put it beyond the capability of the Soviet Union to detect it. This was important because an unauthorised invasion of another country's airspace was considered an act of war. The U-2 was operated by the CIA with the first flight over Moscow and Leningrad taking place on 4 July 1956 and others continuing over the next four years.

Then on 1 May 1960, on the eve of the Paris Summit, CIA pilot Francis Gary Powers took off from Peshawar, in Pakistan, with the mission of flying across the Soviet Union over the Aral Sea and via Sverdlovsk, Kirov, Arkhangelsk, and Murmansk to Bodø military airfield in Norway. Soviet radar picked him up near the city of Sverdlovsk Oblast in the Ural Mountains and the aircraft was shot down by a Soviet surface-to-air missile. Powers ejected and parachuted safely to the ground, where he was captured and within a matter of hours was a prisoner under interrogation at Moscow's famed Lubianka prison. The aircraft crashed, but parts of it, including a camera, were recovered and placed on public display in Moscow as evidence of America's perfidy.

US officials claimed that the U-2 had been conducting a routine weather flight when it experienced a malfunction of its oxygen delivery system that had caused the pilot to black out and drift over Soviet air space. They did not get far with that excuse because on 7 May, the Soviets revealed that Powers was alive uninjured, and being held captive clearly having suffered no oxygen deprivation. US President Eisenhower refused to issue a formal apology to the Soviet Union claiming that in the absence of an 'open skies' agreement, such spy flights were a necessary element in maintaining national defence, and that he planned to continue them. He cited the 'Abel Case' as an example of how the Soviets were doing very much the same thing.

At Fisher's trial, Donovan had argued against the death penalty for Fisher on the grounds that 'It is possible that in the foreseeable future, an American of equivalent rank will be captured by the Soviet Union or an ally. At such time, an exchange of prisoners could be considered to be in the best interest of the United States.'[21] The American media now took up the banner and began calls for an exchange of Powers for 'Abel'. The *New York Daily News* argued that 'Abel' was of no longer had any value as a source of information and an exchange would be quite a natural thing.[22] In addition to that, the family of Gary Powers had their lawyers put strong pressure on Eisenhower to agree a swap. The Soviet leader Nikita Khrushchev called the U-2 incident an 'inadmissible provocation' and refused to consider the idea and walked out of the Big Four Summit meeting in Paris.

Oliver Powers, the father of Gary, wrote to Fisher, addressing 'Dear Colonel Abel', he asked that Fisher urge the Soviet government to reconsider. Donovan released the letter to the press but there were still two stumbling blocks to a deal. The Soviets had never admitted that Fisher was one of theirs and Powers had not yet stood trial. Fisher, himself, was totally opposed to any publicity believing that it would only harm his case for remission of his sentence. Sensing a good story, the press across America went all out to get Powers released from a Soviet jail.

Powers came to trial on 17 August 1960 at the Hall of Trade Unions in Moscow where many of the 1930s show trials had taken place. He was charged with being a spy under Article 2 of the Soviet Law on Criminal Responsibility for Crimes Against the State. With his family in the public gallery, Powers pleaded guilty and after three days was sentenced to three years in Vadim Prison and seven more of hard labour which, under the circumstances was relatively lenient.

While the families on both sides continued to petition for a swap, Fisher had dropped off the front pages but events on the other side of the Atlantic would revive press interest. Peter and Helen Kroger were arrested on 7 January 1961 as part of the round-up of the Portland spy ring. They were quickly identified as Lona and Morris Cohen. This was significant because the FBI had recovered a photograph from Fisher's room at the Hotel Latham marked 'Shirley and Morris' that had been strapped to $5,000 in cash with a rubber band. It was a picture of the Cohens and the cash was presumably money that Fisher was planning to give to them.

By the beginning of 1962 there was a willingness on both sides now to negotiate a deal for Fisher and Powers but the Americans clearly thought that Fisher was a much bigger 'fish' than Powers and wanted more, specifically, apart from Powers, they wanted the release of a student Frederick L. Pryor, who was detained in August 1961 in East Berlin for espionage, and Marvin Makinen, who was in prison in Kyiv.

Before the Berlin Wall was put in place, Pryor had been a researcher in East Berlin working on a doctorate thesis on trade behind the Iron Curtain. During his research he, apparently got access to material regarded as confidential and was arrested. The East German prosecutor had publicly announced he would demand the death penalty. Makinen was a student from the University of Pennsylvania and had also been arrested for spying on the ground that he had taken illegal photographs of military installations while touring Russia. He was currently serving eight years' imprisonment in Russia.

Donovan agreed to go to East Berlin to discuss the terms of a trade and flew into Tempelhof Airport on 2 February 1962. In a city that he had not seen since 1945, when he had been part of a team collecting evidence to present at the Nuremberg War Trials, he crossed over the wall taking a train from Zoo Station to Friedrichstrasse. He went to the Soviet Embassy and was introduced to Fisher's wife Yelena and his daughter Evelyn, who spoke perfect English. They talked for some hours with Donovan answering all their questions about Fisher then they were joined by Ivan Alexandrovich Schischkin, second secretary of the Soviet Embassy and all arrangements were made for the exchange although not without a great deal of discussion over the details.

It was bitterly cold on the Glienicke Bridge on the morning of 10 February. Spanning the Havel River and joining the Wannsee district of Berlin with Potsdam the bridge formed the border between West Berlin and East Germany. After the construction of the Berlin Wall in August 1961, it was the only checkpoint under full Soviet control. All other checkpoints were under East German control. Fisher arrived in a car filled with guards in civilian clothes just after 08.00 hours but was then surrounded by US military police who had replaced the West German guards at the Wannsee end. Donovan walked to the middle of the bridge and Schischkin met him there. They exchanged greetings and signalled to their respective ends from where a trio walked towards them from each side. Both Powers and Fisher were flanked by two guards. The two groups stood facing each other but Donovan would not allow the exchange until he had confirmation that Pryor had been released. He was due to be delivered at Friedrichstrasse. The arrangement was for Makinen to be released a month later. When the confirmation came through, Powers and Fisher crossed sides.

Fisher was welcomed in Moscow as Colonel Rudolf Abel and would be publicly referred to as such for the rest of his life. He became an agent of the Fifth Department of the First Chief Directorate (Foreign Intelligence) but he was not given a specific active role in intelligence. He was deployed to Hungary where he helped to train agents but he mostly settled down to a quiet life painting and drawing and going to concerts with his wife. He was briefly reunited with the Cohens after their release from imprisonment in England.

Retirement came in 1971 but by then Fisher's health was suffering after a lifetime of smoking cigarettes. He died of cancer of the lungs on 15 November that same year. Even in death the Soviet authorities refused to recognise his real name which infuriated Yelena to such an extent that she refused to condone a public funeral. He was buried privately in the Donskoi Cemetery but it was only after another year that the authorities agreed to the erection of a headstone bearing the name of Vilyam Genrikhovich Fisher.

The full story of Fisher's accomplishments as a spy will only be told if and when Soviet files of the Cold War period are opened for examination but the words written by a group of his comrades in a eulogy cannot be disputed when they credited him with 'exceptional patriotism, tenacity and steadfastness.' He was, they said, a man of 'high moral character' with 'great personal charm, modesty, simplicity, and a sympathetic nature'.[23]

Chapter 5

KIM PHILBY:
THE CAMBRIDGE SPY

The word most consistently used to describe Kim Philby was 'charm',
that intoxicating, beguiling, and occasionally lethal English quality.[1]

A tempest was brewing on the morning of 16 January 1963. It was
threatening to be one of those wild winter storms that hit Beirut four
or five times a year and lasted for days. The bar of the St Georges Hotel,
which dominated the seafront in St Georges Bay, was already filling
up. In the summer, it was a regular haunt of film stars like Brigitte
Bardot and Richard Burton as well as political leaders such as the Shah
of Iran and King Hussein of Jordan but in the winter, it was mostly
journalists and Cold War spies who gravitated there. About an hour
after noon, a regular came in and ordered the first of what would be
five or six of his regular tipple. Kim Philby needed them.

He had just taken a phone call at his flat in Rue Kantari from Peter
Lunn, SIS station chief at the British Embassy in Beirut ordering
Philby to come in and see him. In response to the phone call, Philby
considered a number of possible options, none of which involved going
to see Lunn. Exhibiting a capacity for self-control that novelist John
Banville called 'well-nigh inhuman', Philby spent a couple of hours
chatting nonchalantly to regulars such as CIA operative Bill Eveland,
journalists John Mecklin of *Time* magazine, Ralph Izzard of the *Daily
Mail* and Sam Brewer whom Philby had known both during their time
together during the Spanish Civil War and later in Washington.[2] Then
he told the others he would see them again the next day and returned
to his flat.

His wife Eleanor was neither surprised nor worried when Philby told her that he had to go and meet someone. Despite the rain that was now lashing down in torrents, Philby grabbed a raincoat, told his wife that he would be back in time for the party at the home of Embassy First Secretary Glen Balfour-Paul and walked out. An hour later Philby's 13-year-old son, Harry, answered the phone. 'Daddy says he will be a bit late,' he told his stepmother but by midnight, when Eleanor returned from the party, Philby had still not shown up.[3] The raging storm had made her nervous for Philby's safety and she called the British Embassy, where she thought Philby might have gone for his meeting. Lunn was knocking on her door minutes later asking all sorts of questions. What had Philby said? What had he taken with him? Had she really no idea at all where he was? None of the answers Lunn got gave him reason to suspect that, by this time, Philby was already on board the Soviet freighter *Dolmatova* that had been loading cargo, but which had suddenly weighed anchor, leaving half of its freight on the quayside and was now making smoke chugging through the rain and mist at best speed heading for the Black Sea and the nearest Soviet port.

MI5 had held files on Harry St John Bridger Philby since 1926. This 'small and stocky' British Arabist, explorer and colonial intelligence officer, also known as Jack Philby or Sheikh Abdullah, a 'little king in his desert places' as the writer John Le Carre described him, sold Cadillacs to the Arab sheiks and sold oil concessions to the Americans.[4] When St John married Dora Johnson in September 1910, his best man had been Bernard Law Montgomery who would later become the war leader Montgomery of Alamein. Dora was a resourceful and courageous woman and far from meek character that some accounts have depicted her to be. Although overshadowed by her husband's domineering presence, she blossomed and retained a measure of independence in his absence. Their first child, Harold Adrian Russel nicknamed 'Kim' by his father after a spy character in a Rudyard Kipling story, was born on 1 January 1912 in Ambala, Punjab in what was then the British Raj. At the time St John was a reluctant member of the Indian Civil Service much given to criticising what he saw as the shortcomings of British rule in India.

Kim Philby spent the first four years of his life in India playing with the local children, growing up speaking Hindi almost as his first language before moving to England with his mother when his father had been sent on a mission to organise an Arab revolt against the Ottoman Turks in Mesopotamia. Father and son would not be reunited until January 1919 when St John returned temporarily to settle Philby as a boarder at Aldro School in Eastbourne. Once back in England, the young Philby had been parked with his grandmother, May Philby at Camberley after his mother had quickly returned to India. When Philby was reunited with his parents in 1919, they appeared as almost total strangers to him.[5] The reunion with the domineering St John whose approval of his son would never be easily won must have been traumatic for young Philby because he developed a terrible stammer described by Malcolm Muggeridge as 'truly agonising, his lips moving convulsively and his hands clawing the air as he tried to get words out. It was more like some kind of fit than just a speech impediment'.[6] Despite this he made a universally positive impression on those who met him. Four years later, at the age of 11, Philby was summoned to see his father in Amman. There he was treated to a grand tour of the Middle East in the company of his father a man completely at home in the Arab world and 'on easy terms with everyone from King Abdullah to the bootblack'.[7] The visit included a thrilling flight with his father in a bomber aircraft that terrified a band of Bedouin horsemen.

After the end of the First World War St John became political officer of the Mesopotamian Expeditionary Force and succeeded T.E. Lawrence as chief British representative in Transjordan. He then became adviser to Abd al-ʿAzīz ibn Saʿūd, who would later become the first king of Saudi Arabia. In 1924, after sixteen years in the service of his country, St John finally lost all patience with the British government's policy towards King Abdullah and resigned. He abandoned Christianity and became a Muslim, took a second wife, and dressed as an Arab but never took his anti-British feeling quite as far as to give up his membership of the Athenaeum Club.

Philby won a scholarship to his father's *alma mater* Westminster School in Central London, where St John had been head boy and where, on 18 September 1924, Philby became one of the King's Scholars in College House, a sort of school within the school with its own traditions and rules. So pleased was his father that he took the 12-year-old Philby on a touring holiday in Andalucía where Philby kept a compendious diary in which he recorded the 'calm gravity and noble bearing of the Spaniard'.[8] It was the first of many visits that Philby would make to Spain. Time spent with his father was something that Philby had done very little of and these weeks that the two of them were together was a period of education and enlightenment about St John's politics. Irascible and profoundly independent, St John instilled into the son the necessity for him to find his own answers to life's questions, to reject conventional wisdom and the herd mentality. The proximity of such a passionate individual, so sure of his own judgement and someone who obviously carried considerable weight in the exotic world of Middle East politics must have had a profound influence on Philby at such an impressionable age.

Westminster at this time was not a typical school nor was it a particularly successful public school like Eton or Harrow. There was little or no bullying neither was there any great emphasis on sports and games. A school profoundly loyal to Britain's political values, it is somewhat incongruous to find the Assistant Master in Classics and Master of the King's Scholars, the Reverend Harry Kenneth Luce, to be a vociferous social radical and internationalist whose impact on the young Philby would establish a basis for influences he would come under later at Cambridge. In his book about Philby, Tim Milne a contemporary of his at Westminster says that he was a loner, neither popular not unpopular but he exhibited 'a kind of inner strength and self-reliance that made others respect him'.[9] Philby's academic record was, if anything, slightly below average for the school but by the end of his time there, he had done enough to get accepted to read history at Trinity College Cambridge in the autumn of 1929 when he was still only 17. This was an elite college, populated for the most part by progeny of the rich and powerful but during the 1930s, it would find itself harbouring a burgeoning communist movement under the guidance of Maurice Herbert Dobb.

Philby made few friends during his first year at Trinity. Milne had gone to Oxford but they kept in touch. Keeping very much to himself, Philby spent hours listening to Beethoven and reading Russian literature. The only other students who managed to strike up any meaningful relationship with him were two 'fierce warriors from the class struggle'. These were coal miners who had won scholarships to Cambridge through the Miners' Welfare Fund. Harry Dawes had spent ten years at the coal face before arriving at Trinity and he stubbornly refused to make any concessions by giving up his working-class cloth cap or by trying to moderate his broad proletarian accent. He and another miner-turned-undergraduate Jim Lees had suffered great hardship during the General Strike of 1926 and were more than willing to describe their suffering to anyone who wanted to listen. Lees was especially bitter in his criticism of what he saw as the moral turpitude exhibited by the Labour government under Ramsay MacDonald that, he felt, was betraying the workers by making political deals with the Tories instead of radically changing the system. While Dawes and Lees were both popular with other students, it was Lees who became particularly friendly with Philby whom he found to have a generous nature untainted by his obvious privileged background but someone who did not necessarily appear to show any particular sympathy for the working class.

During the summer holidays of 1930, Philby arranged to holiday with Milne. Philby had gone ahead to Budapest and was travelling back to France when his motorcycle broke down. Going by train to Nancy he met up with Milne and travelled to the Black Forest by train to collect Philby's motorcycle where it had been left for repair. From there they travelled at a leisurely pace to Budapest. Milne described Philby as 'a marvellous travelling companion, intensely interested in everything and impervious to discomforts and setbacks'. Philby was already a competent linguist with adequate German and a smattering of Hungarian.[10] The next summer Philby travelled alone to Yugoslavia where he developed a strong attachment to the lands and peoples of the eastern Austro-Hungarian Empire and planned to return there the following year.

The world was changing under the catastrophe of the Great Depression and the rise of fascism in Europe, however. Dawes had set up the Cambridge University Socialist Society (CUSS) as a platform for debate and was probably pleasantly surprised to see it gathering support from members of an altogether different social background to his own. Philby and other Cambridge students campaigned for Labour in the October 1931 general election, but CUSS meetings were disrupted by protestors. When the election came the Labour Party was badly beaten which had the effect of further radicalising many CUSS members and within weeks the first communist movements were born in London, Oxford and Cambridge universities but membership was really quite small. Students could be sent down if they were deemed to be agitators and, even if they remained, could find themselves ostracised from former friends. Notwithstanding the barriers and inspired by the overtly communist student David Guest, a tiny clique of communist came together including Donald Maclean and grew sufficiently confident to hold rallies and meetings. Philby observed from the sidelines without getting too involved but switched from the study of history to economics and came under the tutelage of the Marxist economist Maurice Dobb. It was probably at this time that Philby came to the attention of MI5. Some early references to young Philby's socialist involvement were included in his father's file (PF 40408) indicating that SIS also were interested particularly in his link with his father's activities.

He and Milne met up again this time in Paris in mid-July 1932 and together they travelled to the Black Forest but Kim's fascination with German politics took him to Berlin to witness the elections while Milne waited for him in Munich. When Philby returned to Munich, the two of them got firsthand experience of the mood in Germany by going to see a Nazi torchlight rally and even attended a gathering where they heard Hitler make one of his rousing speeches. Leaving Bavaria, they made it to Albania and spent many days walking around the country and eventually across the border into Yugoslavia.

Milne found Philby changed from their previous time together. He was now more serious and insisted on taking the cheapest lodgings and third-class rail travel wherever they went. He knew a great deal about the history and complex politics of the region even having a working knowledge of the Serbo-Croat language. Their whole journey during this long summer is described in great and fascinating detail in Milne's book about his friendship with Kim.

Back at university, Philby witnessed the 1932 National Hunger March as it passed through Cambridge during October. Many students became involved in organising meals for the marchers and finding church halls and other empty buildings where they could rest for the night. The sight of ragged but tough, proud and disciplined men was a rude awakening of a social conscience for many and a galvanising experience for those already moving towards adopting a strong socialist viewpoint. Cambridge University as a whole was becoming a place where almost the only subject of discussion was contemporary politics, but the majority of students remained unaffected and carried on much as before.

When the Christmas holidays came at the end of 1932, Philby found himself at a loose end with both his parents abroad. Lees arranged for him to go to Nottingham and stay with a coal-mining family. He came across to his hosts as polite and free of any embarrassment that someone of his class might feel in such an environment. For Philby it was a further education in the social and economic conditions experienced by the working classes.

After Hitler had been appointed as chancellor of Germany, Milne and Philby decided to go to Berlin during the Easter holidays of 1933 to see for themselves how Germany was changing. Again they witnessed another huge torchlight parade. It was an opportunity for Milne to assess Kim's politics. Milne was a student at Oxford and so really only saw Philby during the holidays so probably noticed changes in him more than someone who saw him on a more regular basis. Philby certainly exhibited left-wing sympathies, although he was careful not to voice his opinion too loudly in Berlin despite his horror at witnessing the beginning of antisemitic persecutions. Milne says that Philby even bought a twelve-volume set of the works of Lenin in German but it was the communist movement in Germany that interested him much more than what was going on in the Soviet Union. Even as early as March 1933, it was clear that the German communists were in for a hard time and that all communism movements outside the Soviet Union would struggle to survive.

In his book, *The Third Man*, E.H. Cookridge, apparently using the deputy director of counterespionage at Special Branch, Guy Maynard Liddell, as his source, reported that it was the communist Douglas 'Dave' Springhall who first introduced Philby to the Soviet diplomat Leonid Tolokonski early in 1933 at 3 Rosary Gardens, Kensington in London. Tolokonski persuaded Philby, who had left Cambridge with a good second-class degree in June, to go to Vienna, working as a courier to maintain communications between the outlawed leaders of the Austrian Communists and the members of the local Comintern.

With a £50 gift from his father, Philby bought an old motorcycle and took off once more for Vienna. On this his second visit to the city, he found it wracked by economic hardship. Upon arrival he made contact with two officials at the Soviet Embassy, Igor Vorobyov and Antonov-Ovseyenko, both of whom were NKVD agents.

He took lodgings at Latschkagasse 9, the house of a Polish minor civil servant, Israel Kohlman. Kohlman had a 'dark, vivacious' 23-year-old daughter Alice, who 'dressed like a gypsy' and whom everyone called Litzi. Philby could not fail to have been impressed with her 'effervescent zest for life'.[11] She had been briefly married to Karl Friedmann but was now divorced and had also been the mistress of Gábor Péter, a Hungarian communist activist.

It was almost inevitable that the young handsome, polite and charming Englishman and the lively, passionate, emancipated young woman living in such close proximity would become lovers but the involvement of each was unequal. For Philby it was significant as his first sexual relationship and had deeper emotional meaning for him than it had for Litzi. He allowed himself to be swept up to take part in Litzi's dangerous left-wing political activities which were on quite a different scale to those he had known in Cambridge. This was the real thing. The emotional experiences of witnessing street violence, bloodshed and fascist repression became inexorably intertwined with his sexual awakening. Ideas and concepts were morphing into stark, exhilarating reality. Someone who met him at the time called him 'a shaggy, bumbling Englishman overwhelmed by the passions swirling around him'.[12]

Philby and Litzi took a flat together in the working-class district of the city but events were moving fast and life for left-wing agitators was getting very dangerous. Government forces completely wrecked two blocks of workers' flats with shelling killing hundreds and publicly hanged nine left-wing leaders. Evidence of the power of fascist governments to brutally crush nascent left-wing movements and the apparent reluctance of democratic countries to take any interest convinced Philby that resistance to the growing Nazi threat could only come from the Soviet Union.

As members of the International Organization for Aid to Revolutionaries (IOAR), the couple helped activists in danger from the police, including refugees from Nazi Germany. Philby, whose British passport enabled him to travel as a courier to Prague and Budapest, became the treasurer of the branch. Litzi, meanwhile, was attracting more and more attention from the authorities for her political activism and was forced to go into hiding. To give her an avenue of escape, Litzi and Philby were married on 24 February 1924 thus making Litzi a British citizen. Philby wrote to his parents to tell them about his marriage but sought to reassure them that it would be dissolved once the political repression had subsided. Litzi would later say that it had been primarily a marriage of convenience although it was probably rather more than that for Philby.[13] Between 6 March and 15 April 1934, Litzi made three journeys into Czechoslovakia from Vienna on her British passport which she obtained two days after her marriage.[14] Nothing is known outside the Moscow archives what these trips were about, who arranged them or whom Litzi met but the implication, given her past involvement with communists such as Péter, is that they were facilitated by Soviet intelligence.

When introduced to her new daughter-in-law, Dora was cold and unwelcoming describing her as 'too strident and showy' as well as being Jewish, a communist, and a divorcée none of which endeared Litzi to her.[15] It is possible that the marriage was instigated by Moscow Centre in order to facilitate her entry into Britain in the same way as they had done with Edith Tudor-Hart and would later do with Ursula Kuczynski. However, as an openly communist Austrian-born Jew and someone who never made much effort to conceal her loyalties, she can have had little hope of ever being able to work undercover as an employee of the British establishment.

When Philby applied to join the Indian Civil Service, two Cambridge dons whom he approached for references drew attention to his unsuitable 'sense of political injustice' which left him no option but to withdraw the application and he looked instead to a career in journalism. He was appointed as a sub-editor of the Liberal monthly

Review of Reviews in late 1934 contributing feature articles under the name of Adrian Russel. It was an undistinguished job carried out in an undistinguished manner. The £4 a week this paid him was about the same as he was getting from the NKVD at the time.[16] His wife, meanwhile, had met up with Edith Tudor-Hart whom she had known in Vienna as Edith Suschitzky and through her joined the Austrian Communist Party cell in London. Neither of the Philbys were making much of an effort to disguise their left-wing sympathies which cannot have gone unnoticed by SIS.

There is every reason to believe that Philby would have had a file opened on him after his visit to the Continent in the same way that one had been opened on John Lehmann (KV 2/2253–2255), who also went to Vienna at this time on a similar mission. Lehmann was put under close surveillance both abroad and at home and it is likely that Philby was too. The fact that no SIS personal file on Philby had been uncovered suggests that it is being withheld for some reason or that it has been destroyed. What sundry references there are to Philby in PF 40408 cease in November 1934 showing that either they had been placed there accidentally and there was another file, not yet released, was opened at that time, or it was decided that he was not considered to be of interest to SIS after this time.

Edith Suschitzky had worked with Arnold Deutsch in the Vienna communist underground since at least 1926 and for part of that time, at least, had been in a personal relationship with him. In Vienna, she had been an 'immensely vivacious, amusing, curious, and gifted' anti-fascist activist and Montessori kindergarten teacher.[17] Her files (KV 2/4091–4093) show that she had first arrived in England in 1925 but had then been excluded in 1931 after her involvement in a Trafalgar Square demonstration in late October 1930. Bringing herself to the attention of the authorities in this way was an indication of her relative naivety as an agent at that time. Guy Liddell of Special Branch requested that enquires be made in Vienna about 'this woman'. SIS replied saying that '[Suschitzky] is stated to be a Social Democrat, but she has shown no political activity in Vienna. There is nothing on record to show that she has communist tendencies.'[18] After that she worked as a photographer for TASS, the Soviet news agency, before being imprisoned for a short time in Vienna in early 1933 for 'suspicious activity', then carried out minor courier roles for the NKVD. On 16 August 1933, in the British Embassy in Vienna she married another communist, a British doctor Alexander Ethan Tudor-Hart who, up until June of that year, had been a house surgeon working at St Mary Abbott's Hospital in Kensington. The couple had known each other since at least April 1931. There remain questions as to why the embassy allowed the marriage of two known communists to take place on their premises has never been satisfactorily answered. The implication is that the British had some ulterior motive for sanctioning a process that gave Suschitzky, now Tudor-Hart, automatic British citizenship.

Stories of espionage do not unroll in predictable ways. Even when records are made available to the public, they are frequently deficient, or incorrect and probably filtered before release to suggest a version of events that suited the nefarious purposes of the agencies involved. Ghost-written memoirs, such as Alexander Foote's *Handbook for Spies*, have been shown to be unreliable. It is because of this that a fog has been created around Tudor-Hart It is likely that she was 'a relatively insignificant contributor to the Soviet cause', but that she occupied a useful role as a consumer of MI5 attention and time to distract the surveillance organisation from more worthy subjects. Once she had been arrested as an agitator, her cover was completely blown. The NKVD knew that once she returned to Britain in 1934 her usefulness would have been minimal since she would have been subject to close and constant surveillance. The NKVD considered Litzi Philby a much more important agent even more so than her husband otherwise they would not have allowed the couple to remain together and prejudice any chance Philby had of penetrating British intelligence which Philby would later say was their long-term objective.

Tudor-Hart was clearly not an important piece in the narrative surrounding the recruitment of the 'Cambridge Spies' despite Anthony Blunt, the 'fifth man' quite mendaciously claiming that she was 'the grandmother of us all'. She was not completely inactive, however, becoming very intimate with Engelbert Broda, who, while working at the Cavendish Laboratory, provided highly important nuclear secrets that she passed on to Moscow Centre.

Despite Philby's setback when seeking a civil service career, Moscow laid out its plans for him. They instructed Edith Tudor-Hart to arrange a meeting between Philby and Arnold Deutsch, 'a handsome man with twinkling blue eyes and fair curly hair'.[19] Deutsch had travelled the world working for the Comintern as a recruiter and had, himself, been recruited by the NKVD in 1932. By 1934 he was enrolled at London University and living in the Lawn Road flats. Philby found him to be a man of 'considerable cultural background'. Deutsch, an 'illegal' NKVD officer working with forged papers and without diplomatic immunity, reported to Moscow that he considered Philby to be 'very timid and irresolute' because of the dominant character of his father, an ambitious tyrant who repressed all his son's desires. Nevertheless, he showed 'seriousness and honesty' and was ready 'to do anything' for the communist cause.[20]

Authorised to recruit Philby, Deutsch then set about instructing him in the rudiments of spycraft. He was to break of all contacts with known communists and establish a new political persona as a right-winger even going so far as to exhibit pro-Nazi-sympathies, in other words, a conventional member of the bourgeoisie. Unusually, Deutsch did not suggest that Phiby's relationship with Litzi should be terminated even though it had clearly been no more than an arranged marriage for the purpose of getting Litzi a British passport and now had only disadvantages given the rebranding of Philby as a fascist. It could only undermine the fiction that he was part of the Anglo-German movement which already had to survive questions over his Damascene conversion from socialism. Perhaps Moscow was not yet taking Philby sufficiently seriously as to worry about such anomalies.

Deutsch seemed much more interested in using Philby as a conduit for more recruits. He told Philby to think about all his friends and acquaintances and assess their potential as Soviet agents. Donald Maclean, Philby said was a strong possibility but Guy Burgess, whom he also suggested, did not inspire Moscow with confidence. A rather more active role for Philby was proposed when Deutsh introduced Philby to the head of Soviet 'illegal' intelligence in Britain, Alexander Orlov, in late December 1934 and after this time it was Orlov who ran Philby along with Burgess, who had been recruited with some scepticism, and Maclean. Philby was allocated the codename Synok (Sonny) presumably a reference to his famous father.

Philby and Litzi had already visited Spain in February 1934 ostensibly on holiday but Moscow was now anxious for the relationship to end or at least for the couple to move apart. Litzi was a constant reminder of Philby's communist past and a hindrance to building his new right-wing persona. Litzi, meanwhile, was very active. Records show that on 4 September 1934 she went to France and entered Spain on the following day. Ten days later she left a French port and six days after that she entered Austria where she remained for over a month. On 8 April 1935, she went to Holland for a week and then on 16 August she went again to Spain via France. On 3 April 1936, she entered Austria and a week later went on to Czechoslovakia, returning to Austria again two weeks after that. Between 25 May and 22 July 1936, she was in Paris.[21] There is no record of SIS having made any attempt to find out who her contacts had been in any of these instances.

By 1936, Philby had a new handler, an NKVD officer, Theodore Maly, who had arrived in Britain in 1932 under the name of Paul

Hardt. He had been tasked with setting up and running a spy ring. In 1936, now using the name Peters, Maly instructed Philby to join the Anglo-German Fellowship from where Maly knew British intelligence recruited agents. Wary of how touchy Moscow was about the fealty of its agents, Deutsch warned Philby to be careful and not go too far with this pro-Nazi persona.

It was small fry stuff reporting back on the antics of the Anglo-German Fellowship and Soviet involvement in the Spanish Civil War had given them a lot of other things to think about. Moscow had plenty of informants on the Republican side in Spain but few in Franco's camp. An upper-class Englishman with impeccable credentials and known right-wing sympathies might just be the man to rectify this. All that was needed was a cover story. On 15 February 1937, Philby crossed the border into Spain at Badajoz and registered with the British Consul in Seville as a freelance journalist, with arrangements to report on the civil war for *The London Central News* and the *London International News Service*, as well as from the *Evening Standard*. He also wrote, without accreditation for *The Times*. It was his objective to get a permanent post as a *Times* correspondent not a few of which, it was well understood, had been seconded to secret intelligence work. At the same time, he was collecting intelligence on the nationalists and reporting on troop movements, communications, morale, and the military support being provided to Franco's forces by Germany and Italy. All this was written in invisible ink, in letters to a 'Mlle Dupont' with a Paris address Philby discovered much later was the address of the Soviet Embassy. This was a serious breach of tradecraft and would have seen Philby before one of Franco's firing squads if one of the censors had picked it up.

Then came a half-baked plot dreamed up by Moscow for Philby to get close to Franco and assassinate him. Such a mission was very unlikely to succeed and would have been tantamount to suicide for Philby had he tried it. Why he should be thought a suitable candidate can only indicate that Maly and Moscow Centre held him in low esteem and had no more important plans for him. It was early days in the war and neither the trajectory of the war nor Philby's usefulness to them could be predicted. Maly, who was in Spain acting as executioner to Stalin's Trotskyite political 'enemies' there would, himself, face a Soviet firing squad a few months later.

Philby had several pro-Franco articles published in *The Times* that helped to enhance his image as a neo-fascist. Twice during this brief stay in Spain, on 2 March and again on 22 March, Philby went to Gibraltar for meetings with Burgess in the bar of the Rock Hotel where he received funds from Moscow. He was back in London by 25 April

1937 after a fairly fruitless three months in what Maly described as a depressed state. Litzi had moved to live in Paris on a semi-permanent basis. Ostensibly acting as a courier for Philby, it appears that she spent much of her time partying with her new Dutch lover. She wrote to her daughter saying, 'Never again in my life did I live in such grand style and toss money around that way … it was all great fun.'[22]

In his absence, friends of Philby had been pushing for his membership of the prestigious Athenaeum Club which was approved by the committee on 10 May 1937. Moscow still wanted Philby in Spain as close to Franco as possible but the question was how he could operate there under cover. The obvious answer was for him to get a permanent assignment as a correspondent with a reputable right-wing newspaper. Having impressed *The Times* with the odd freelance article he had provided them with, Maly suggested that he write another carefully scripted 2,500-word article for them analysing the conflict with a mild pro-Franco bias. It worked. By 24 May he was on the payroll.

Deutsch explained the new arrangements for communication once he was back on the peninsula. Twice a month, he was to cross the border from Bayonne to Narbonne where he would pass along both written and verbal reports to Alexander Orlov. On 14 June 1937, Philby was again crossing the Spanish border this time at Irun. Very soon it was not only Litzi who had a new lover. Philby had been introduced to the Canadian-born actress Frances 'Bunny' Doble ten years his senior who specialised in light romance and melodramas. Doble had married Sir Anthony Lindsay-Hogg, 2nd Baronet Hogg, of Rotherfield Hall in 1929 and despite them getting a divorce in 1934 she had retained the title of Lady Lindsay-Hogg. Philby had to make a good show of hiding any hint of left-wing views from Doble who was on friendly terms with the exiled King Alfonso of Spain and was a passionate supporter of the nationalist cause. It was perfect cover and an added reward for his deception was that Philby, through Doble, got privileged access to Franco's inner circle.

Gathering intelligence in a war zone was not without its risks, however. In late 1937, a Republican shell landed near the car he was sitting in with three fellow journalists. He alone survived the blast with only a minor head wound. Litzi recalled him causing a great stir in a Saragossa restaurant, his head heavily bandaged and his hands shaking. His own clothes had been blown of his back in the explosion and he was wearing 'an old pair of sandals, a woman's coat with a fur collar, pale blue, moth-eaten and too long'.[23] It had the effect of cementing his reputation as an intrepid war correspondent. Franco was grateful for the support Philby gave to the nationalists and on 2 March

1938, awarded him the Red Cross of Military Merit at the same time as conferring the same posthumously to Edward Neil, Dick Sheepshanks and Bradish Johnson who had died in the explosion. Philby responded with a favourable article in *The Times* boosting Franco's reputation.[24] What evidence there is of the sort of material Philby contributed to the NKVD is still firmly locked up in the Kremlin vaults but the British *chargé d'affaires* in Madrid, Geoffrey Thomson said that he 'seemed to know almost everything about German and Italian military assistance to Franco'.[25] At press conferences, Philby was the one who asked the pertinent questions and probed for more details about troop strengths and movements well beyond what his *Times* articles would require. It was widely assumed by other correspondents that Philby was collecting this information on behalf of SIS. In a piece of misdirection, Moscow went so far as to accuse him publicly of spreading 'falsehoods and propaganda' which *The Times* proudly rejected calling Philby completely 'trustworthy'.[26]

Events far from Spain in Moscow would impact on Philby's espionage career in 1937 when Stalin's paranoia spilled over into terror causing agent after agent to fall under suspicion as supporters of Leon Trotsky and his theory of World Revolution. A new Soviet task force was set up under Nikolai Yezhov, the Administration of Special Tasks (AST) the purpose of which was to take control of the NKVD and purge it of all those who had knowledge of the conspiracy to destroy Stalin's rivals. More than forty intelligence agents working abroad, including Deutsch, Maly and Orlov, were recalled to Moscow. The task of running Philby now fell on Gregory Grafpen but his recall in 1938 ended that relationship also.

There is evidence from refugee records, alien's tribunals, and death certificates that at some time during 1938, Litzi was able to arrange for her parents to be exfiltrated from Vienna to St Albans in Hertfordshire. It is beyond belief that she could have done this without significant assistance from somewhere, the implication being that it was SIS. This was similar to an arrangement made for Tudor-Hart to travel abroad and return to Dover on 27 August 1937, accompanied by her mother, Adele who was given permission to stay in the country for three months. Records show that Adele never left the country again and went to live in Bournemouth supported by what SIS called 'private means'. She had no restrictions placed on her as might have been expected of an alien and relative of a known communist. She died in London on 24 May 1980.

Philby went again to Spain but this time he used a courier to get his reports to Paris. Crossing the border at the black-market and espionage hubs of Hendaye or St Jean de Luz, he would pass his reports by hand. Other times he would meet Litzi in hotels in Biarritz or Perpignan, sometimes even Gibraltar, where he passed on information that she took back to her handler in Paris. Before long, however, in another indication that the Philbys were not thought too highly of in Moscow, Litzi's expensive lifestyle came in for criticism and she was ordered to abandon her apartment in Paris and return to Britain.

Philby's connection to Tudor-Hart threatened to cause him embarrassment and draw the attention of SIS when, in March 1938, she was questioned over a Leica camera she had purchased. The camera was discovered in a police raid on the home of Percy Glading, who was subsequently convicted of spying for the Soviet Union. Tudor-Hart simply denied any knowledge of the Woolwich Arsenal spy ring that Glading had been running and since the police could find no other evidence, she was released without charge. SIS would surely have been alerted to Philby's once removed connection to the incident.

With the Spanish Civil War having played itself out, there was a seismic shift in European diplomacy when the Nazi-Soviet Pact was announced on 24 August 1939 and the Continent was ruptured by Britain's declaration of war with Germany on 3 September 1939, two days after the German invasion of Poland. The demand for intelligence exploded. The GRU came under intense pressure from Stalin to come up with the goods and so the Philbys, for no other reason than that they had experience, were available and had not yet shown any signs of weakening their allegiance to Moscow, had become important assets. It was time to build on the reputation as a right-wing activist and war-hardened correspondent and Spain expert that Philby had built up during the Spanish war. Moscow had intended to deploy Philby to Berlin or Rome but that idea was dropped when it became known that Britain intended to send an Expeditionary Force (BEF) to France to bolster the defences along the Belgian border. St John was able to lend his weight to the important matter of kick-starting Philby's career when he applied for a position as a special war correspondent with *The Times* and went to France with the BEF on 9 October. This was around the same time, 27 September 1939, that SIS filled out a vetting-form for Philby. There is no evidence that they followed up on the evidence submitted by the NKVD defector Walter Krivitsky that he knew of 'a young Englishman, [whom he could not identify] a journalist of good family, an idealist and fanatical anti-Nazi' who had been active in Spain on behalf of the NKVD.[27]

Litzi was able to regain entry into the United Kingdom, arriving at the port of Newhaven on 2 January 1940. The Foreign Ministry apparently saw nothing wrong with approving Philby's request to allow his wife, a known communist, to regain entry to Britain just a few short months after the signing of the Nazi-Soviet Pact.

Tony Percy on his intelligence website *Coldspur* advanced the theory that Philby struck a deal with British intelligence whereby he and Litzi would renounce any sympathies for the Soviet Union and work for them.

This may explain why Litzi was able to operate freely within the country all during the war infiltrating communist organisations such as the Austrian Communist Party in exile under the pseudonym Litzi Feabre.

Donald Maclean had joined the Foreign Office and Guy Burgess had joined SIS working in Section D responsible for sabotage and subversion. Returning from France after the country's collapse and submission at Compiègne, Philby bumped into an old acquaintance called Hester Marsden-Smedley whose husband was also in Section D. Smedley had been a war correspondent in France. When Philby told her he was at a bit of a loose end, she offered to mention him to her husband. When MI5 did a background trace on Philby, it was rather perfunctory given the massive workload they had suddenly found themselves under after the Fall of France and the threat of a German invasion of the British mainland.

The vetting process seems to have concluded that Philby's association with the known communist recruiter Maurice Dobb at Cambridge had been no more than dalliance and any residual left-wing sympathies Philby might have carried over had completely evaporated after the Molotov-Ribbentrop Pact. They certainly seem to have had no hard evidence to the contrary. Neither did his marriage to a known communist impede his recruitment. Soon he found himself in a bit of a dead-end job teaching subversive propaganda to foreign exiles, a field in which Philby, on little evidence, was considered an expert, at Beaulieu Abbey near Southampton. It was far from the heart of British intelligence, but it was enough to reignite Moscow's interest in him and he was contacted by an envoy in December 1940.

In the summer of 1940, Philby had started a relationship with Aileen Furse, whom he had met through a mutual friend, Flora Solomon, the daughter of a Jewish-Russian gold tycoon. Philby had known Solomon, a family friend, since he was a child and had even tried to recruit her for the Comintern in 1937 when she declined saying she was 'too busy saving the persecuted Jews of Europe'.[28] Aileen had been an unhappy child, given to harming herself to attract attention and was working as a store detective at Marks and Spencer's Marble Arch store when she and Philby met. Solomon said of her that she 'belonged to that class, now out of fashion, called county. She was typically English, slim and attractive, fiercely patriotic, but awkward in her gestures and unsure of herself in company.'[29] She and Philby were immediately attracted to each other and were soon living together. Aileen changed her name by deed poll to Aileen Philby and the couple would go on to have three children before Philby divorced Litzi in 1946. They would be married a week later, on 24 September 1946, when Aileen was pregnant with their fourth child.

By the middle of 1941, Britain's urgent need for counterintelligence saw Section V of SIS crying out for more recruits. It had been created specifically to obtain intelligence about German and Italian activities in Spain and Portugal. The pressure of work on Section V (five), which included the distribution of Axis messages deciphered by Bletchley Park, was so intense that Dick White, the future director general of MI5 (not to be confused with Dick Brooman-White) questioned whether it could function effectively against enemy espionage efforts outside the security cordon placed around British territories. Criticism of SIS coming from MI5 was nothing new. The two bureaucracies had much in common in that they were both painfully unprepared for war and recruited almost exclusively from the military cadres of the British middle class but they 'hated each other bitterly' and expended a great deal of energy feuding with each other.[30] Neither could advertise for recruits and relied mostly on personal recommendation.

During his time in Section D, Philby had become friends with Tommy Harris who introduced him socially to other members of both MI5 and SIS whose expertise was Spain and Portugal and who called themselves 'the outfit'. One of its members was Dick Brooman-White, head of MI5's Iberian section who was open to the possibility of recommending Philby to the counterespionage section of SIS as someone with extensive knowledge of the region. Again it was St John who used his influence with an old family friend Valetine Vivian (Vee-Vee), who was head of Section V to promote Philby's candidacy. Any flirtation with communism, St John said, was all schoolboy nonsense and he was now quite a reformed character.[31] 'Lean and elegant with crinkled hair and a monocle', Vivian was one of those who thought that SIS needed to spread its net a little wider and bring in some more sophisticate recruits such as university dons, journalists and writers.[32]

If Vivian had received a transcript of a series of interviews that Jane Archer and Stephen Alley of MI5 had conducted with Walter Krivitsky, an NKVD defector in London during January 1940, he had either forgotten the details, thought them irrelevant to Philby or he deliberately ignored them. Krivitsky said that in early 1937, Theodore Maly had been sent instructions from Stalin himself to recruit an Englishman to assassinate Franco. Krivitsky told Archer that Maly had found the perfect candidate. The man he described had fitted Philby remarkably well.[33]

Philby found himself stationed at Glenalmond, a country house near St Albans, working for Felix Cowgill running a sub-section of twelve officers working in counterespionage both at home and in the Iberian Peninsula. Spain was an unknown factor in the war. Even if it did not come right out and side with the Nazis openly, the country was flooded with Germans and its ports could be used to refuel and restock the Atlantic and Mediterranean U-Boat packs. There was also the risk of Franco giving the Germans free rein to bring pressure to bear on the Straits of Gibraltar. It was not thought likely but it was certainly entertained as a possibility in the early years of war, that the Germans might even occupy Spain and Portugal.

Philby found himself with a not insignificant responsibility and he seemed to thrive on the challenge. His whole attitude of diligence, without the encumbrance of intellectual curiosity that might have sidetracked others, and a formidable memory saw him step up to the mark. Within months agents had penetrated both the Lisbon and Madrid Abwehr headquarters and identified numerous German agents in Spain. The amount of intelligence that came through his office, including transcripts of decrypted German communications from Bletchley Park, was huge but his painstaking methods of filing, analysis and distribution resulted in reports which were 'models of lucid, well-ordered prose and his briefings were excellent.'[34]

One of his successes and possibly his most important was the uncovering of the German Abwehr *Unternehmen Bodden* (Operation Bodden), set up with the aid of the Spanish government to gather military intelligence through a network of stations to the north and south of the Strait of Gibraltar tracking the movements of Allied warships and merchant vessels. By the autumn of 1941 it had grown into an effective source of intelligence. One station alone at Algeciras was sending more than twenty reports a day to Berlin. British intelligence, however, was intercepting and decoding these reports and learned that construction had started on buildings to house infrared technology to upgrade the surveillance capabilities.

It was part of Philby's brief to keep track of developments. His warnings to the Admiralty saw plans for an attack on the stations rejected for fear of a reprisal attack on Gibraltar but the British ambassador to Spain, Sir Samuel Hoare, insisted on a meeting with

Franco who denied that the network existed and claimed that the German personnel were providing technical assistance to Spanish coastal artillery batteries. Nevertheless, after a meeting with the head of the Abwehr, Admiral Wilhelm Canaris, in June, the generalissimo ordered the closure of the stations.

Philby had agents inside the Spanish Embassy in London and he made regular trips to the peninsula to maintain a hands-on approach even drawing up a list of names for a shadow administration if Spain was eventually to enter the war on the German side. His brief was to extend to North Africa and then Italy after the Allied 'Operation Torch' saw British and American troops successfully getting a toehold in North Africa. Spain now became less of an issue as the focus turned towards penetrating Axis networks along the new front. In a lecture to the East German Stasi in 1981, he would describe how easy it had been for him to get hold of files which had nothing to do with his own job. He says that he simply made friends with the archivist who managed the files by going out two or three times a week for a drink with him. Every evening, he said, he left the office with a big briefcase full of reports and documents from the archive that he would hand over to his Soviet contact. The next morning, he would return them their rightful places.

Experiencing the stresses of his daily espionage activity, Philby was also engulfed by the perennial swirling paranoia in Moscow Centre. He had received the transcript of an intercepted telegram sent by the Japanese ambassador in Berlin back home to Tokyo outlining his discussions with Hitler and von Ribbentrop. Philby duly passed this on to Moscow but Moscow discovered from another source that Philby had omitted an important final paragraph and concluded that he had done so deliberately as part of some British misdirection plot. This was never the case, but Moscow instructed its London residency to treat Philby and the other Cambridge spies with extreme caution. They even sent a special eight-man surveillance team to London to check upon them for a while.[35]

Then in May 1943, there opened up a whole new opportunity for Philby when SIS expanded its anti-communist Section IX under the leadership of John Court Curry to spy on the Soviet Union and through that increased its cooperation with the American intelligence agencies. Section IX had been set up in the first half of 1938 'to plan, prepare and, when necessary, carry out sabotage and other clandestine operations, as opposed to the gathering of intelligence'. By the following year it had established a presence at Bletchley to develop sabotage material, including incendiaries, plastic explosives and fuses.[36] Moscow urged

Philby to make every effort to take over Curry's role. It took a whole year but by October 1944, Philby, with the backing of his old friend Vivian, was in Curry's chair. Around this time, Philby met James Jesus Angleton, an American Office of Strategic Services (OSS) officer who was in England undergoing training. They became friends. Angleton claimed that it was Philby's influence that he became thoroughly consumed by the world of intelligence. The Americans looked with great admiration on the British intelligence services and held Philby, in particular, in highest esteem.

With the end of the war, the focus of much Western intelligence work was now turned on the Soviet Union. SIS trawled for defectors and found one in Istanbul, where an NKVD officer called Konstantin Volkov had approached the British Consul offering to provide information in return for asylum for himself and his wife. He claimed to have the names of two Soviet agents working in the British Foreign Office and another working in counterintelligence. When the case landed on Philby's desk, he contrived to delay flying out to Istanbul and it was a full three weeks after Volkov's approach before he laned there. By this time, Volkov had disappeared presumably having been spirited away by Moscow. A number of stories were circulated to explain how the Soviets had cottoned on to Volkov's treachery but, fortunately for Philby, none rested at his door. That did not mean that the issue would not come back to haunt him, however.

Now that Philby had inveigled his way into the heart of Western anti-Soviet operations it was important to tie up a few loose ends. He was still legally married to Litzi, who was now living in East Berlin with Georg Honigmann, but to the world, he was married to Aileen and the father of her three children. Litzi had left for Paris in late August and was in Prague by 5 September before going on to Berlin. There are varying accounts of a divorce being concluded between Philby and Litzi but few details of where and how this was arranged. Philby claimed to have gone to Paris to meet Litzi on 18 September when Litzi presented a petition for divorce based on Philby's adultery. Some writers such as Anthony Cave-Brown, however, believe that the divorce never actually happened which meant that when Philby married Aileen one week later, he was committing the prisonable offence of bigamy.

Philby was not allowed to stay with Section IX. SIS had a doleful war record and was fighting for its very existence against a hostile Labour government and other services that wanted to take it over. In February 1947, he was posted to Istanbul in what was quite a promotion on the new front line of the Cold War. By now, Philby was consuming vast quantities of alcohol on a daily basis and Aileen, left at home all with the children in a strange city was feeling the strain. Their somewhat isolated house was on the opposite side of the Bosphorus from the fashionable European part of the city. It was an idyllic old house amongst trees and undergrowth with a sweeping panoramic view of the Bosphorus but Aileen's daily life was stalked by loneliness despite the presence of her children who revelled in the luxuriant almost wild overgrown garden. A product of the English middle classes, she found it hard to adjust to the strictures of being the wife of an intelligence officer especially during those occasions when they were visited by Burgess who would monopolise her husband for hours at a time after which they would both return much the worse for drink.[37] Alcohol was such a problem for Philby now that on one occasion he was carried home from the Moda Yacht Club.

After one of Burgess' visits, Aileen was so distressed that she crashed her car one night and claimed that she had been assaulted by a stranger. When what had at first seemed to be a superficial head wound became infected she was flown to a clinic in Switzerland for treatment. Returning to Istanbul, the family now moved into a flat in Moda. Soon afterwards, while Philby was in London, Aileen was badly burned in a small house fire and was returned to the Swiss clinic. She would not live in Turkey again.

In October 1949, the weakest sector of the Soviet empire was the Balkans and it was here that the Western governments planned to undermine it. Philby, was posted as counsellor attached to the embassy in Washington, with special responsibility for liaising with the CIA, over the joint SIS-CIA operation to infiltrate exiles into Albania in an attempt to overthrow Enver Hoxha's communist government. A Committee of Free Albanians was set up in Italy as a front to recruit guerillas who were formed into small bands and infiltrated into the mountains. In what proved to be an unmitigated disaster, of the 300 who set out, more than half were killed almost immediately along with a number of locals who had been willing to welcome and help them. Their arrival had clearly been anticipated. The Americans looked sideways at Philby but SIS would not listen to any talk of his complicity. After his defection, Philby would later say that it had indeed been he who tipped off the Soviets but claimed that by doing so he had averted a major international crisis and possible war. The Albanian debacle was the first time that the new Americans intelligence agencies had looked with scepticism on SIS who they had, up to this point, revered as the great masters of espionage and the mutual trust and confidence that characterised the relations between Washington and London was about to break down.

While in Washington, Philby was acquainted with the American Venona project. Through decrypted Soviet signals, Robert Lamphere, FBI agent in charge of Russian espionage, discovered that a member of the British Embassy, codename 'Homer', was sending messages to Soviet intelligence, KGB. After a process of elimination, a list of three or four men were identified as possible suspects. One of these was Donald Maclean.

SIS was in the midst of a serious crisis in 1951. Klaus Fuchs was going to trial for divulging nuclear secrets to the Soviets. His handler, Ursula Burton had fled the country. Venona had exposed Maclean, as a possible Soviet agent but despite MI5 placing him under intensive surveillance on 25 May of that year, Maclean defected to the Soviet Union with Burgess. The two men had absconded in circumstances that suggested to the cross-departmental committee tracking the case that the pair had been warned in advance that Maclean was about to be called in for questioning.

Having been alerted by Blunt that Maclean was probably going to be recalled to London, Philby warned his handler in New York, Valery Makaev about the surveillance on Maclean and suggested that Maclean be exfiltrated without delay but said nothing about it to Maclean himself. Philby, however, did tell Burgess that in his opinion, if Maclean defected, under no circumstances was he to go with him, and from that point Philby was out of the loop. Burgess had been living with Philby in Washington in what was surely one of the most blatant examples of poor tradecraft. Not realising for a moment that Burgess was suspected, Philby had used him as a convenient courier for communications with Makayev. Burgess returned to Southampton on 7 May when he was met at the Ocean Terminal by Blunt, who was seen meeting Maclean two days later. Blunt told Yuri Modin that the net was drawing in on Maclean and Moscow drew up plans to get Maclean out. Burgess was chosen to replace Blunt as the link to Maclean. The plans were change when Maclean's interrogation was deferred to 18 June, the time of the hospital confinement of Mrs Maclean.

While it had only been planned to exfiltrate Maclean, Blunt became worried that Burgess might be taken into custody also and questioned and he had no confidence that Burgess would be able to stand up to interrogation. He suggested that Burgess should go with Maclean and Moscow agreed. When Philby heard that Burgess had fled with Maclean, he was as surprised as anyone. Pressure was building. Philby was SIS' liaison officer in Washington and it was clear that, given his close association with Burgess, suspicion would inevitably fall on him but, outside the CIA, very little was being said about any 'third man' in the affair apart from a vague and unsubstantiated rumour aired in the *Daily Express* on 21 June. The Foreign Office had claimed that it had no idea why the two men had fled or where they had fled to and certainly was not looking for an accomplice. They did, however, issue a statement on 1 June saying that the two men had been dismissed from the service. Litzi was suspected of having been a courier for another spy, Engelbert Broda, who had left Britain for Vienna in 1947. The new American intelligence agencies were starting to look sideways at the British and questioned the extent to which they could rely on their security. It was as good a time as any to rein Philby in and thoroughly investigate him but that risked further embarrassment if he was found to be guilty of any crime.

The matter of Philby's suspected involvement was not going to go away, however, and events gained momentum when, on 5 June, Menzies ordered Philby to return to London which he did on 12 June. The FBI were given the identities of the absconders on 6 June, which required MI5 chief Percy Sillitoe and his deputy Martin Jones to fly to New York to pacify them. On the day that Philby landed in England, they handed a document to Robert Lamphere at FBI headquarters that included the 'seven points' indicating Philby's possible involvement in Soviet espionage. Meanwhile on 10 June British Prime Minister Clement Atlee, had called for details of the careers of Burgess and Maclean and the Foreign Office cast a complete security blackout over the investigation. Dick White, who had started investigating Philby in April when the 'Homer' link was exposed, conducted two rather polite and low-key interviews with Philby. The first, on 12 June, was conducted as soon as Philby's feet touched British soil and a second took place two days later. On both occasions White got only evasive answers to undemanding questions.

Philby was well prepared for his meetings with White, who had no skills as an interrogator. If he hadn't already guessed, he had got a handwritten letter from the newly appointed SIS deputy director, James Easton, who was present at the interviews although only as an observer, alerting him to the reason that he was being recalled from Washington but he took it to be no more than a friendly warning and nothing to be too concerned about. White relied on what, in his own words he called, 'an element of quiet probing and deceptive gentleness' which was not going to cause Philby any discomfort. He did not, for instance, make any reference to the Volkov affair in which, by now, Philby had become a prime suspect. When faced with questions about the funding for his first trip to Spain in 1937, Philby obfuscated and at times simply lied, but White had neither the patience nor the guile to follow up on that. White's final report on his interviews with Philby, released to Menzies in November 1951, concluded little more than that Philby was probably hiding something and was definitely suspect. It made no reference to the fact that Millicent Bagot had been compiling a dossier about Philby since Maclean had been exposed as a possible Soviet mole back in April. The implication was that everything had come out about Philby as a result of the Burgess and Maclean affair. It was all part of White's plan to keep MI5 as far away from the Philby affair as possible. The question for him was how far he had succeeded in convincing the Americans of that.

Lamphere passed the 'seven points' document implicating Philby to the CIA and it landed on the desk of Allen Dulles on 15 June with an accompanying FBI report noting that it contained nothing about Gouzenko's 1945 allegations of a Soviet spy in British intelligence, a fact that Dulles was not slow to point out to Sillitoe. Menzies realised that not only Philby's days in Washington were over but his tenure at SIS was also at and end and that raised the problem of pretext for his dismissal. Menzies had plotted with White to give the CIA just enough information about Philby's background, in relation to his marriage to Litzi for instance, for them to push for Philby's removal from the intelligence services. In that way they would not find themselves the centre of a storm if a full investigation was launched in Britain and more facts about Philby emerged that even they knew nothing about.

This might have worked had not the head of MI6, John Sinclair, retained full confidence in Philby and had Easton not been determined to see Philby brought to trial. On 12 June, Easton had told then CIA in Washington that he had no reservations at all about Philby only to return to London to be presented with documents containing details of Philby's past about which he had been unaware, and which completely undermined his assurances to Washington. It was the cause of much embarrassment for him. He was particularly enraged to discover that Philby's marriage to Aileen was bigamous at a time when the couple were expecting their fourth child. He called Philby 'an accomplished liar ... capable of anything.'[38] Philby, meanwhile was on a boating holiday in Chichester with his friend Nicholas Elliot.

In his book *The Agency*, John Ranelagh claims that CIA chief, Walter Bedell Smith wrote to Menzies saying, 'Fire Philby or we break off the intelligence relationship.'[39] It was Menzies, himself, unable to resist American pressure, who personally asked for Philby's resignation and told him that he would get £4,000 severance pay in lieu of a pension. Philby took the news calmly. He doubted that the sort of evidence Menzies had against him would stand up in court and knew that the government was desperate to avoid another scandal. He was also curious to know how SIS would handle the publicity over his resignation. In the event, Menzies fudged the issue and apparently issued some kind of suspended sentence, and awaited the results of further research before confirming his decision. What he did know, however, was that Philby, still married to Mitzi, was guilty of bigamy and could be threatened with imprisonment if Menzies chose to use that as an excuse to fire him and keep him quiet.

The British Embassy in Washington was starting to feel the heat of American interest in just how much Maclean had known about Western projects to develop atomic weaponry and a wider investigation would inevitably look at Philby. Dick White took rapid steps to distance himself from any fallout and suggested an official inquiry might calm things down. The whereabouts of Burgess and Maclean remained a mystery and Menzies was still keeping the British government in the dark about any possible 'third man' suspect but things would change after the 25 October general election when the British Labour government was replaced by Winston Churchill's Conservatives.

Churchill ordered that a thorough interrogation of Philby be carried out immediately. He and Foreign Secretary Anthony Eden planned to make an early visit to Washington, and they wanted to settle the issue of cooperation with the Americans. Helenus ('Buster') Milmo QC, was selected to perform the interrogation which would begin on 12 December 1951.

Eden was prepared for a trial if the evidence warranted it, especially with the Americans peering over his shoulder but White at MI5 knew that the circumstantial evidence was such that only a full confession by Philby could lead to a conviction. Milmo was not unfamiliar with the intelligence world having worked for MI5 during the war, interrogating suspected Nazi spies, but he was not given sufficient time to acquaint himself with the huge volume of statements taken from witnesses and other papers and documents relating to the matter. Meanwhile, there had been calls for the inquiry to be expanded from the 'third man' issue to include an investigation into whether Philby had been for many years, a spy for the Russians but, in the end, Milmo was asked simply to 'undertake an official enquiry into the possibility of there having been a leakage of information to Mr Burgess and/or Maclean resulting in their subsequent disappearance.'[40]

The interrogation was a failure. Philby simply denied everything and Milmo, having had so little time to fully acquaint himself with the background to the case, was unable to put him on the spot where weaknesses in his testimony showed up. Neither had he been given access to some parts of the MI5 dossier on Litzi's activities and her relationship with Honigmann. He had not called any SIS officers to testify. The smooth implementation of Burgess and Maclean's escape through Jersey and St Malo indicated that it was not a last-minute act of desperation but one that had been weeks in the planning in Moscow and that let Philby off the hook entirely. The fact that MI5 grossly misrepresented the events leading up to 25 May suggests that they had attempted to implicate Philby as the 'third man' and get him out of their hair once and for all. The plan had failed. Dick White told the Americans that Philby was probably a spy, but that SIS would not back that claim up. Bedell Smith agreed to accept the Milmo findings at face value and everyone hoped that the press would soon find something else to write about.

MI5 had failed to pin the blame on Philby and found themselves scrambling to prevent facts emerging about the gross incompetence of both them and SIS by neglecting to pull together all the facts of Philby's activities since 1934 which would have pointed to his espionage role very much sooner. Tony Percy on *Coldspur* has made a detailed analysis of Philby's intelligence career in SIS and offers the theory about why and how Philby was protected for so long, and why SIS was so reluctant to admit that it had nourished a traitor in its corporate body. There was a sizeable body of circumstantial evidence pointing at Philby not only from the Krivitsky interviews but also from Litzi wartime activities under the pseudonym of Litzi Feabre, and her association with the German-born communist Georg Honigmann.

Honigmann, had fled Germany in 1934 and taken a job monitoring German broadcasts for the news agency Extel. In May 1940, he had been swept up in the mass arrests of aliens and shipped off to Canada but was back in England and living in London with Litzi by 1942. In 1946, the British authorities had to deal with the fact that Honigmann, a known communist and nominee for a propaganda position with the Control Commission to help with the denazifying process in the British zone of control in Berlin, had decamped to the Soviet sector leaving behind his partner, Litzi, also a communist, who was still the wife of a senior SIS officer.

Philby was banished to Beirut in August 1956, partly because of pressure brought to bear by the American counterintelligence agencies. He had been under mounting suspicion in the four years since the defection of Burgess and Maclean and had eventually been shuffled off to a place where he would be out of the limelight and out of SIS. It was an exile that many of his former colleagues deplored. The general opinion in some circles was that he had been shabbily treated and made a scapegoat for the failings of others.

Philby had been hugely popular in America and had charmed his American counterparts. FBI chief J. Edgar Hoover had been a great admirer of his and dined several times at his house while James Angleton, who would become head of CIA counterintelligence valued Philby for his advice and guidance.[41] When Philby came under suspicion, however, they were swift to turn on him. American newspapers such as the *Sunday Daily News* openly named him as a spy and the British press had picked up the story forcing the British government to debate the issue in the House of Commons. At the end of which the foreign secretary at the time, Harold Macmillan, said 'I have no reason to conclude that Mr. Philby has at any time betrayed the interests of his country, or to identify him with the so-called "third man", if indeed there was one.'[42] Within a few weeks Hoover had reluctantly closed his files on Philby after having been an unwitting instrument in forcing a public declaration of his innocence.

There was no way that SIS would leave Philby on its books but they had no qualms about using him as a freelance. It was Philby's old school friend and fellow SIS officer, Nicholas Elliot who eased Philby out of his harness and guided him into a job as stringer for *The Observer* and *The Economist*. St John Philby was living in Ajaltoun, just outside Beirut, at the time and Elliot thought Philby might join his father there and work in an area that was becoming increasingly important from a British intelligence perspective. Philby would be paid £3,000 a year plus travel and expenses through Godfrey Paulson, chief of the Beirut SIS station.

Soon after arriving in Beirut, Philby was introduced to Eleanor Brewer by her husband, *The New York Times* correspondent, Sam Brewer. She was described as a 'rangy, steady-drinking American, who looked tough and sophisticated [but] Underneath ... was a romantic, and politically naïve'.[43] In 1943, Eleanor had worked for the US government in Istanbul lobbying for Turkey to join the Allied cause and had probably done a little spying on the side.[44]

Her immediate impression of Philby was of a lonely man whose old-fashioned reserve and beautiful manners set him apart from the other journalists. Within weeks they became close friends and eventually lovers meeting secretly at little cafés in the mountains. Sam Brewer soon knew but he did not intervene, he was well used to his wife's infidelity and kept the marriage going for the sake of their daughter, Annie. The author Anthony Cave Brown believes that the CIA station chief in Beirut, Wilbur Crane Eveland, had been instrumental in bringing Eleanor and Philby together so that he could use her to spy on Philby.[45]

Meanwhile, on 12 December 1957, Aileen Philby was found dead in the bedroom of her house in Crowborough. Rumours circulated about suicide, but a coroner ruled she had died from heart failure, myocardial degeneration, tuberculosis, and influenza, all exacerbated by alcoholism. According to *The Times* foreign correspondent Richard Beeston, who met Philby in Beirut soon afterwards, he was far from devastated by the news of Aileen's death and invited Beeston and his wife to join him in a celebration. It was a wonderful escape, Philby said, that now left him free to marry again.[46]

The problem for Moscow was that Philby was not engaged in active espionage at this time. Since he was not working inside SIS, he was of little use to the Soviets but that would change in 1960 when Nicholas Elliot arrived in Beirut to take on the role of station chief. He immediately activated Philby after a couple of years during which Philby had been going through the motions as a journalist. He was now sent all across the Middle East, ostensibly on reporting assignments but in reality to gather intelligence. While his lack of access to SIS files was an obvious problem for his Soviet handlers, Philby collected a great deal of intelligence through meetings and conversations with informants that conveniently found its way to Moscow. His attitude towards Philby certainly seems to indicate that Elliot still had no suspicions about him but there is a counterargument that says Elliot's boss as head of SIS in London since 1956, Dick White, had ordered Elliot to activate Philby as a conduit for misinformation to Moscow.

In early January 1963, Philby was secretly visited in Beirut by Sir Anthony Blunt, art adviser to Queen Elizabeth II. Knowing that Moscow was pressuring Philby to 'come home', Blunt had gone to Beirut with his companion, John Gaskell, to once again urge Philby to flee. The two men were staying at the home of the British ambassador to Lebanon, Sir Ponsonby Moore-Crosthwaite. He and Blunt had been friends since school and although Moore-Crosthwaite was well aware of Blunt's left-wing sympathies he found it 'unthinkable' that Blunt would take advantage of their friendship for nefarious purposes. When later questioned about Blunt's work for Moscow, he said 'My instinct told me it was a private matter and it was better not to raise it with Anthony.'[47] Blunt would later be stripped of his knighthood after having been exposed as a Soviet spy in 1979.

It was Blunt's second visit to see Philby, the first having been eighteen months earlier just after British police had exposed and arrested the Soviet spy, George Blake, who was being interrogated. Fearful of his and Philby's exposure, Blunt had come on a fruitless mission to persuade Philby to follow the example of Burgess and Maclean and defect to Moscow. Philby, however, was working with Elliot and had felt no immediate threat at that time and decided to stay put.

What was London to do about Philby now? Could he be just left to fade into obscurity? Could Dick White be sure that he would not be exposed by a third party? Would the Soviets hang the threat of a scandal over the head of SIS to embarrass and manipulate them? If Philby really was a Soviet spy, as many believed, and there were still others yet to be exposed, what would it say about SIS' reputation if they just let the matter lie? Would the Soviet's be mocking them in Moscow and raising toasts to their ineptitude? How could they make it all go away? Ideally Philby would just disappear but it would have to be by his own hand. What pressure could London bring to bear to encourage Philby to make that decision?

When Elliot arrived in Beirut on 10 January 1963, he no longer had discretionary powers over Philby's fate. He was under strict orders from Dick White to interrogate Philby about his connections to Moscow. Initially it had been MI5 chief Roger Hollis who wanted his own men to question Philby. MI5 was convinced that Philby was a Soviet agent and had been investigating him since 1951 but Hollis was persuaded, against his better judgement, that Elliot, someone whose background made him a more convivial guest in the Philby residence, would be a better choice to draw Philby out and get a full confession out of him. Elliot made the curious decision not to order any special surveillance of Philby while he was conducting his interviews. This was remarkable given that he was going to hit Philby with an ultimatum and he could not be sure how he would react. He would later say that Philby's defection had taken him completely by surprise which, if taken at face value, casts serious doubts over Elliot's powers of perception.

Over the next few days, Elliot had a number of sessions with Philby, all of which were taped but either in a very amateurish way or in a manner deliberately designed by Elliot to obfuscate rather than elucidate. In the room where the two men talked, Elliot had opened the widows allowing the sounds of 'car horns, grinding engines [and] Arabic voices' in the street to partially obscure much of what was said.[48]

It was clear, however, that nothing Elliot said to Philby was a surprise to him. When Elliot told him there was new evidence against him, Philby did not ask what that evidence was. The implication is that he already knew and was fully prepared for Elliot's questions. Elliot assured Philby that Dick White had given his word that Philby would be given full immunity, a pardon and protection from publicity but he had to make a full and voluntary confession of his spying over the years. Philby was aware that SIS were desperate to avoid another spy scandal so soon after the Blake debacle and he demurred. Would they really take him back to England for trial and, if he was found guilty would they actually hang him? He didn't think the British government had anything to gain and much to lose by doing so. The only cards in Elliot's hand were threats to take his passport away and revoke his Lebanese residence permit. When a stalemate threatened, Elliot gave Philby twenty-four hours to decide.

The next day, Philby confessed to having worked for the Soviets during the war but claimed that he had stopped doing so in 1945. He, somewhat disingenuously, admitted to having tipped off Burgess and Maclean in 1951 allowing them to escape prosecution but only as 'an act of loyalty to friends' and not as one spy protecting another. It was something but far from enough to satisfy Elliot.[49]

The interview continued in a desultory fashion. Elliot tried to bluff by claiming to know more than he did and Philby calculating just how much he needed to tell Elliot to get off the hook. Author and ex-SIS operative, Peter Wright, who listened to the tapes of the conversations later said, 'by the end, they sounded like two rather tipsy radio announcers, their warm, classical public school accents discussing the greatest treachery of the twentieth century'.[50] Either Elliot genuinely believed that Philby was innocent of treason or he did not have the stomach to pursue a campaign against a man he had known and admired for so long. Whatever the case, the interviews stalled and no further progress was made. London was getting impatient with Elliot. They ordered him to leave Beirut and take up another assignment. When Elliot told Philby that Peter Lunn was coming to take his place, Philby asked Elliot, 'What now?' 'You have twenty-four hours head start', he replied.[51] Philby knew that Lunn would give him a much harder time and when the phone call came from the British Embassy on the morning of 23 January 1963, there would be no further prevarication. Elliot's decision not to put surveillance in place now allowed Philby time and space for Moscow to make all the arrangements necessary to expedite his extraction.

When London realised that Philby had gone, Hollis sent a memo to Hoover saying that in his judgement, Philby was telling the truth, and he had in fact given up his spying in 1945 therefore the US need have no worries that Philby had compromised their security in subsequent years. Then, three months later, intense media pressure forced British Prime Minister Edward Heath, to acknowledge that Philby had gone missing and to issue a statement to the effect that Philby had resigned from the Foreign Office in 1951 since which time he had no access of any kind to any official information. The official Soviet government newspaper, *Ivvestia* was not letting him get off so lightly, however. Philby, they said, had been divulging British secrets, and those of her allies for the last thirty years.[52]

After his disappearance, Eleanor heard hardly a word from him for months. When he did contact her, he was as cool and charmingly insouciant as ever. Eventually she joined him in Moscow, where matters ran smoothly between them until he began an affair with the wife of his fellow defector Donald Maclean. Even this affront Eleanor might have put up with. The last straw, however, landed on her already heavily burdened back when she challenged her husband to say, if he were made to choose between her and the Communist Party, who would win. He looked at her in disbelief and just said: 'The party, of course.'[53]

POSTSCRIPT

XXX was the codename given to material illegally extracted from diplomatic pouches of neutral missions in London during the Second World War. It was an MI5 operation under the leadership of Anthony Blunt that has never been officially acknowledged, and Second World War histories make no reference to it. In their book *Triplex* historian Nigel West and retired KGB officer Oleg Tsarev reveal documents from the XXX operation that, thanks to the work of the Cambridge Spies, found their way to Moscow and were later retrieved from NKVD archives when they were briefly opened up for scrutiny after the breakup of the Soviet Union. They reveal a remarkably wide range of material since each of the spies, who together had highly privileged access the whole spectrum of British intelligence, had almost complete discretion over what they thought was of most interest to their Soviet masters.

Philby, in particular, concentrated on providing intelligence that would 'ensure the powerlessness of the British Intelligence Service to neutralise the NKVD across the globe'.[1]

The files Philby selected compromised the security of every important SIS officer and amount to 'the most damningly comprehensive betrayal of any intelligence agency at any time'. Amongst them, West and Tsarev include full details of the following files, all translated from Russian.

- A resumé of Valentine Vivian's report of 6 March 1943 on the subject of Soviet penetration of British security organisations.
- A report of March 1943 on British wireless intelligence intercepts of German communications.
- An undated report concerning steps taken to break Soviet codes.
- SIS plans for anti-Soviet operations in June 1944.
- A directive issued by Sir Stewart Menzies on the work of Sections V and IX of SIS dated 26 September 1944.
- A report dated December 1944 concerning British anti-communist operations.

- A report of Philby's trip through the Mediterranean region to assess the levels of communist activity in 1944.
- An undated memo outlining British plans for the penetration of Soviet intelligence.
- A blueprint for SIS post-war operation.
- A report of SIS reorganisation after 1945.
- SIS internal structure 1946.
- A list of officers of SIS Section IX dated 16 July 1946.
- The structure and reorganisation of SIS in January 1947.

SOURCES

Andrew, Christopher and Gordievsky, Oleg, *KGB: The Inside Story of Its Foreign Operations From Lenin to Gorbachev*, (Harper Collins, 1990)

Andrew, Christopher, *The Defence of the Realm*, (Allen Lane, 2009)

Andrew, Christopher, *The Sword and the Shield: The Mitrokhin Archive and the Secret History of the KGB*, (Basic Books, 1999)

Arthey, Vin, *The Kremlin's Geordie Spy: The Man They Swapped for Gary Powers*, (Biteback Publishing, Kindle edition)

Askey, Nigel, *The 'Siberian' Divisions and the Battle for Moscow in 1941– 42*, (operationbarbarossa.net/the-siberian-divisions)

Beeston, Richard, *Looking for Trouble: The Life and Times of a Foreign Correspondent*, (Brasseys, 2006)

Berkinov, Louise, *Abel*, (Hodder and Stoughton, 1970)

Bourgeois, Guillaume, *La véritable histoire de l'orchestre rouge*, (Nouveau Monde, Kindle edition)

Brinson, Charmian and Dove, Richard, *A Matter of Intelligence*, (Manchester University Press, 2014)

Burke, David, *Family Betrayal: Agent Sonya, MI5 and the Kuczynski Network*, (The History Press, Kindle edition)

Burke, David, *The Lawn Road Flats: Spies, Writers and Artists*, (History of British Intelligence Book 3, Boydell & Brewer, Kindle edition)

Burke, David, *The Spy Who Came in From the Co-Op: Melita Norwood and the Ending of Cold War Espionage*, (History of British Intelligence Book 2,Boydell & Brewer, Kindle edition)

Carver, Tom, *Philby in Beirut*, (London Review of Books, Vol. 34, No. 19, 2012)

Cave Brown, Anthony, *Treason in the Blood*, (Houghton Mifflin, 1994)

Chang, John K., *East Asians in Soviet Intelligence*, (Intelligencer Journal of US Intelligence Studies, Vol. 29, No. 1, 2024)

Chapman, John W.M., *Richard Sorge, the GRU and the Pacific War*, (Renaissance Books, 2021)

Coppi, Hans, *Rote Kapelle im Spannungsfeld von Widerstand und Nachrichtendienstlicher*, (Tätigkeit ifz-Muenchen.de/helfarchiv, 1996)

Cortazzi, Hugh, *The Death of Melville James Cox (1885–1940) in Tokyo on 29 July 1940: Arrests of British Citizens in Japan in 1940 and 1941*, (brill.com, downloaded 20 February 2025)

Costello, John, *Mask of Treachery*, (William Morrow & Co., 1988)

Damaskin, Igor, *Kitty Harris: The Spy With Seventeen Names*, (St Ermin's Press, 2001)

Donovan, James B., *Strangers on a Bridge: The Case of Colonel Abel*, (Penguin Books, Kindle edition)

Feshun, Audrey, *The Sorge Case: Telegrams and Letters*, (Moscow, 2019)

Flicke, W.F., *Rote Kapelle, les espions de Stalin*, (Collection 'Action', Paris, 1957)

Green, John, *A Political Family: The Kuczynskis, Fascism, Espionage and the Cold War*, (Routledge, 2017)

Greenspan, Nancy Thorndike, *Atomic Spy: The Dark Lives of Klaus Fuchs*, (Penguin Books, 2020)

Hamburger, Maik, *My Mother Sonia*, (eurolitnetwork.com/the-german-riveter-my-mother-sonya-by-maik-hamburger, downloaded 18 January 2025)

Harrison, Edward, *The Young Kim Philby*, (University of Exeter Press, 2012)

Hede, Massing, *This Deception*, (Duell, Sloan and Pearce, 1951)

Henkine, Cyrille, *L'Espionage Sovietique: Le Cas Rudolf Abel*, (Fayard, 1981)

Johnson, Chalmers, *An Instance of Treason: Ozaki Hotsumi and the Sorge Spy Ring*, (Stanford University Press, 1990)

Jones, Chris, *The Spy Who Helped the Soviets Win Stalingrad and Kursk*, (Pen and Sword, 2025)

Litten, Frederick S., *Einstein and the Noulens Affair*, (The British Journal for the History of Science, Vol. 24, No. 4, 1991)

Litten, Frederick S., *The Noulens Affair*, (The China Quarterly No. 138, 1994)

Lonsdale, Gordon, *Spy: Twenty Years of Secret Service*, (Neville Spearman, 1965)

Macintyre, Ben, *A Spy Among Friends*, (Bloomsbury Publishing, Kindle edition)

Macintyre, Ben, *Agent Sonya: Lover, Mother, Soldier*, (Penguin Books, Kindle edition)

MacKinnon, Janice R. and MacKinnon, Stephen R., *Agnes Smedley*, (eFeF Verlag, 1989)

Matthews, Owen, *An Impeccable Spy: Richard Sorge, Stalin's Master Agent*, (Bloomsbury Publishing, Kindle edition)

Miller, Michael B., *Shanghai on the Metro: Spies, Intrigue, and the French Between the Wars*, (University of California Press, 1995)

Milne, Tim, *Kim Philby: A Story of Friendship and Betrayal*, (Biteback Publishing, Kindle edition)

Moss, Norman, *Klaus Fuchs: The Man Who Stole the Atom Bomb*, (Sharpe Books, Kindle edition)

Murphy, David E., *What Stalin Knew: The Enigma of Barbarossa*, (Yale University Press, Kindle edition)

Oleson, Peter C., *Richard Sorge Moscow's Spy in Tokyo*, (The Intelligencer Journal of US Intelligence Studies, Vol. 29, No. 2, 2024)

Page, Bruce, Leitch, David and Knightley, Phillip, *Philby: The Spy Who Betrayed a Generation*, (Sphere Books, 1969)

Perrault, Gilles, *L'Orchestre rouge*, (Fayard, 1967)

Price, Ruth, *The Lives of Agnes Smedley*, (Oxford University Press, 2005)

Raizen, Esther, *Cementing Strategies in Yehudit Kafri's Zosha: From the Jezreel Valley to the Red Orchestra*, (University of Texas, 2018)

Read and Fisher, *Operation Lucy*, (Coward McCann, 1981)

Ridley, Norman, *The Race for the Atomic Bomb*, (Pen and Sword, 2023)

Ridley, Norman, *The Secret War Between Hitler and Stalin*, (Pen and Sword, 2025)

Schellenberg, Walter, *Walter Schellenberg: The Memoirs of Hitler's Spymaster*, (Carlton Books, 2006)

Schimitzu, Rayotara, *Richard Sorge and the Japanese Attack on Pearl Harbor in 1941*, (Center for Military History, No. 249, 2022)

Seale, Patrick and McConville, Maureen, *Philby: The Long Road to Moscow*, (Penguin Books, 1973)

Sergeant, Harriet, *Shanghai: Collision Point of Cultures, 1918–1939*, (NewYork, 1990)

Solomon, Flora, *Baku to Baker Street*, (Collins, 1984)

Sorge, Christiane, *Mein Mann: Dr R. Sorge*, (Die Weltwoche, 1964)

Stephan, Robert W., *Stalin's Secret War: Soviet Counterintelligence Against the Nazis, 1941–1945*, (University Press of Kansa, 2003)

Stibbe, Matthew, *Jürgen Kuczynski and the Search for a (Non-Existent) Western Spy Ring in the East German Communist Party in 1953*, (Contemporary European History, Vol. 20, No. 1, 2011)

Tarrant, V.E., *The Red Orchestra*, (Turner Publishing, Kindle edition)

Tetsuro, Kato, *The Sorge Case: The End of a Myth*, (Tokyo: Heibonsha, 2014)

Trepper, Leopold, *Le Grand Jeu*, (Albin Michel, 1975)

Trepper, Leopold, *The Great Game*, (Sphere Books, 1979)

Tyas, Stephen, *SS-Major Horst Kopkow: From the Gestapo to British Intelligence*, (Fonthill, 2017)

Tyrer, William A., *International Journal of Intelligence an Counterintelligence*, Vol. 29, No. 4, (2016)

Van der Rhoer, Edward, *The Shadow Network, Espionage as an Instrument of Soviet Policy*, (Robert Hale, 1983)

Werner, Ruth, *Sonya's Report*, (Chatto and Windus, 1991)

West, Nigel, *Mortal Crimes*, (Enigma Books, 2004)

West, Nigel and Tsarev, Oleg, *Triplex*, (Yale University Press, 2009)

Whymant, Robert, *Stalin's Spy: Richard Sorge and the Tokyo Espionage Ring*, (I.B.Tauris, 1996)

Wolf, Markus and McElvoy, Anne, *Memoirs of a Spymaster*, (Pimlico, 1998)

Wright, Peter, *Spycatcher*, (Viking, 1987)

NOTES

Chapter 1: Leopold Trepper and the Red Orchestra

1. Trepper, Leopold, *Le Grand Jeu*, (Albin Michel, 1975), p.87

2. Trepper, Leopold, *The Great Game*, (Sphere Books, 1979), p.9

3. Trepper, *The Great Game*, p.11

4. Trepper, *The Great Game*, p.15

5. Tarrant, V.E., *The Red Orchestra*, (Turner Publishing, Kindle edition), p.118

6. Trepper, *The Great Game*, p.19

7. Bourgeois, Guillaume, *La véritable histoire de l'orchestre rouge*, (Nouveau Monde Kindle edition), location 654

8. Perrault, Gilles, *L'Orchestre rouge*, (Fayard, 1967), p.65

9. Bourgeois, location 818

10. *Narrative History of the Rote Kapelle The CIA's History of Soviet Intelligence and Espionage Networks in Western Europe, 1936– 1945*, (University Publications of America, 1979), p.15

11. Nelson, p.223

12. Perrault, p.126

13. *Narrative History of the Rote Kapelle*, p.22

14. Bourgeois, location 1052

15. Tarrant, p.126

16. Ibid, p.127

17. Trepper, *The Great Game*, p.276

18. Ibid, p.133

19. Tarrant, p.126

20. Perrault, p.41

21. Flicke, W.F., *Rote Kapelle, les espions de Stalin*, (Collection 'Action', Paris, 1957), p.35

22. Ibid, p.24

23. Bourgeois, location 2064

24. Perrault, p.87

25. Raizen, Esther, *Cementing Strategies in Yehudit Kafri's Zosha: From the Jezreel Valley to the Red Orchestra*, (University of Texas, 2018), p.337

26. Trepper, *The Great Game*, p.148

27. Ibid, p.157

28. Ibid, p.209

29. Bourgeois, location 2711

30. Flicke, p.46

31. Bourgeois, location 2631

32. Tyas, Stephen, *SS-Major Horst Kopkow: From the Gestapo to British Intelligence*, (Fonthill, 2017), pp.91–92

33. Trepper, *The Great Game*, p.158

34. Ibid, p.159

35. Selected excerpts by the author from an interview between Renée Barro-Scott and Clifford Davies on behalf of the USC Shoah Foundation Institute, in Boston, on 25 February 1997

36. Bourgeois, location 4456

37. Ibid, location 4587

38. PRO, KV 2/2/2068

39. Bourgeois, location 4700

40. Coppi, Hans, *Rote Kapelle im Spannungsfeld von Widerstand und Nachrichtendienstlicher*, (Tätigkeit ifz-Muenchen.de/helfarchiv 1996),

41. BA/MA Freiburg, final report of the Abwehrstelle III F Belgium dated 24 March 1943, p.26

42. Bourgeois, location 4955

43. https://maitron-fr.translate.goog/marivet-marguerite-nee-hollier-marguerite-desiree/?_

44. Trepper, *The Great Game*, p.206

45. Bourgeois, location 7119

46. Ibid, location 5088

47. Archives of Anatoli Markovitch Gourevitch report of Lieutenant Colonel Bolchakov, chief of IXe Service of the 1st Directorat of the GRU, 17 June 1943

48. Trepper 202

49. Perrault, pp.147–148

50. Report by Lieutenant Colonel Bolchakov, head of the IX Service of the I Directorate of the GRU, 17 June 17 1943

51. Perrault, p.330

52. Bourgeois, location 7462

Chapter 2: Ursula Kuczynski: The Atomic Spy

1. Green, John, *A Political Family: The Kuczynskis, Fascism, Espionage and the Cold War*, (Routledge 2017), p.252

2. Hamburger, Maik, *My Mother Sonia*, eurolitnetwork.com/the-german-riveter-my-mother-sonya-by-maik-hamburger, downloaded 18 January 2025

3. Macintyre, Ben, *Agent Sonya: Lover, Mother, Soldier*, (Penguin Books, Kindle edition), p.5

4. Ibid, p.9

5. Green, p.79

6. Ibid, p.80

7. Macintyre, p.16

8. davidmcknight.com.au/archives/2006/07/comintern-underground-shanghai, downloaded 27 February 2025

9. Burke, David, *Family Betrayal: Agent Sonya, MI5 and the Kuczynski Network*, (The History Press, Kindle edition), p.41

10. Macintyre, p.35

11. Burke, p.42

12. Matthews, Owen, *An Impeccable Spy: Richard Sorge, Stalin's Master Agent*, (Bloomsbury, Kindle edition), p.108

13. Green, p.91

14. Litten, Frederick S., *The Noulens Affair*, (The China Quarterly No. 138 1994), p.492

15. Litten, Frederick S., *Einstein and the Noulens Affair*, (The British Journal for the History of Science, Vol. 24, No. 4, 1991), p.465

16. Macintyre, p.67

17. Ibid, p.78

18. Ibid, pp.103–104

19. Burke, *Family Betrayal: Agent Sonya, MI5 and the Kuczynski Network*, p.46

20. Ibid, p.48

21. Macintyre, p.127

22. Jones, Chris, *The Spy Who Helped the Soviets Win Stalingrad and Kursk*, (Pen and Sword, 2025), p.18

23. Ibid, p.19

24. coldspur.com/sonias-radio-part-vi, downloaded 18 February 2025

25. Macintyre, p.162

26. Ibid, p.168

27. Sonia and SIS' Hidden Hand coldspur.com/sonia-SISs-hidden-hand/, downloaded 19 January 2025

28. Ibid

29. Read and Fisher, *Operation Lucy*, (Coward McCann, 1981), p.111

30. KV 2/1613-1 The National Archives, Kew, pp.23–28

31. coldspur.com/sonias-radio-part-viii/, downloaded 20 January 2025

32. Ibid

33. Ibid

34. Ibid

35. Document 47A in KV 6/41 The National Archives, Kew

36. coldspur.com/sonias-radio-part-viii/, downloaded 19 January 2025

37. KV 6/41 The National Archives, Kew

38. Burke, David, *The Spy Who Came in From the Co-Op: Melita Norwood and the Ending of Cold War Espionage*, (History of British Intelligence Book 2, Boydell & Brewer, Kindle edition), p.157

39. Burke, David, *The Lawn Road Flats: Spies, Writers and Artists*, (History of British Intelligence Book 3, Boydell & Brewer, Kindle edition), p.144

40. Macintyre, p.207

41. Burke, *The Spy Who Came in From the Co-Op*, p.102

42. Andrew, Christopher, *The Sword and the Shield: The Mitrokhin Archive and the Secret History of the KGB*, (Basic Books, 1999)

43. Macintyre, p.211

44. Brinson, Charmian and Dove, Richard, *A Matter of Intelligence*, (Manchester University Press, 2014), p.196

45. Greenspan, Nancy Thorndike, *Atomic Spy: The Dark Lives of Klaus Fuchs*, (Penguin Books, 2020), p.88

46. Ibid, p.91

47. Greenspan, p.88

48. Ridley, Norman, *The Race for the Atomic Bomb*, (Pen and Sword, 2023), p.60

49. West, Nigel, *Mortal Crimes*, (Enigma Books, 2004), p.57

50. Moss, Norman, *Klaus Fuchs: The Man Who Stole the Atom Bomb*, (Sharpe Books, Kindle edition), p.44

51. Macintyre, p.222

52. Ibid, p.228

53. Macintyre, p.366

54. Ridley, *The Race for the Atomic Bomb*, p.65

55. Wolf, Markus and McElvoy, Anne, *Memoirs of a Spymaster*, (Pimlico, 1998), p.229

56. Macintyre, p.229

57. Ibid, p.232

58. coldspur.com/sonias-radio/, downloaded 23 January 2025

59. Ibid

60. Macintyre, p.236

61. Tyrer, William A., *International Journal of Intelligence and Counterintelligence*, Vol. 29, No. 4, (2016)

62. TNA Kew KV2/1876/Minute 378, The National Archives, Kew

63. coldspur.com/sonia-SISs-hidden-hand/, downloaded 25 January 2025

64. Macintyre, p.286

65. TNA KV 6/41/170, The National Archive, Kew

66. Werner, Ruth, *Sonya's Report*, (Chatto and Windus, 1991), p.290

67. Stibbe, Matthew, *Jürgen Kuczynski and the Search for a (Non-Existent) Western Spy Ring in the East German Communist Party in 1953*, (Contemporary European History, Vol. 20, No. 1, 2011), p.62

68. MI5 to SIS, 23 January 1953, The National Archives, Kew, KV 2/1880

69. Macintyre, p.322

Chapter 3: Richard Sorge: The Tokyo Spy

1. Schimitzu, Rayotara, *Richard Sorge and the Japanese Attack on Pearl Harbor in 1941*, (Center for Military History, No. 249, 2022)

2. Andrew, Christopher, Gordievsky, Oleg, *KGB: The Inside Story of Its Foreign Operations From Lenin to Gorbachev*, (Harper Collins, 1990), p.137

3. Matthews, Owen, *An Impeccable Spy: Richard Sorge, Stalin's Master Agent*, (Bloomsbury Publishing, Kindle edition), p.21

4. Whymant, Robert, *Stalin's Spy: Richard Sorge and the Tokyo Espionage Ring*, (I.B.Tauris, 1996), p.46

5. Sorge, Christiane, *Mein Mann: Dr R. Sorge*, (Die Weltwoche, 1964),

6. Whymant, p.27

7. Feshun, Audrey, *The Sorge Case: Telegrams and Letters*, (Moscow, 2019), p.79

8. Matthews, p.78

9. Sergeant, Harriet, *Shanghai: Collision Point of Cultures, 1918–1939*, (New York, 1990), p.14

10. Miller, Michael B., *Shanghai on the Metro: Spies, Intrigue, and the French Between the Wars*, (University of California Press, 1995), p.257

11. Chang, John K., *East Asians in Soviet Intelligence*, (Intelligencer Journal of US Intelligence Studies, Vol. 29, No. 1, 2024), p.38

12. Price, Ruth, *The Lives of Agnes Smedley*, (Oxford University Press, 2005), p.180

13. Ibid, p.185

14. Police Interrogation, Richard Sorge, 24 July 1942, ID 923289, RG 319

15. Price, p.200

16. MacKinnon, Janice R. and MacKinnon, Stephen R., *Agnes Smedley*, (eFeF Verlag, 1989), p.194

17. Ibid, p.195

18. Price, p.214

19. Whymant, p.39

20. Tetsuro, Kato, *The Sorge Case: The End of a Myth*, (Tokyo: Heibonsha, 2014), pp.186–187

21. Johnson, Chalmers, *An Instance of Treason: Ozaki Hotsumi and the Sorge Spy Ring*, (Stanford University, Press, 1990), p.4

22. Whymant, p.52

23. Ibid, p.58

24. Ibid, p.61

25. Chapman, John W.M., *Richard Sorge, the GRU and the Pacific War*, (Renaissance Books, 2021), p.64

26. Whymant, p.6

27. Hede, Massing, *This Deception*, (Duell, Sloan and Pearce, 1951)

28. Chapman, p.91

29. Whymant, p.85

30. Ibid, p.87

31. Chapman, p.79

32. Oleson, Peter C., *Richard Sorge Moscow's Spy in Tokyo*, (The Intelligencer Journal of US Intelligence Studies, Vol. 29, No. 2, 2024), p.83

33. Whymant, p.96

34. Oleson, p.83

35. Whymant, p.110

36. Cortazzi, Hugh, *The Death of Melville James Cox (1885–1940) in Tokyo on 29 July 1940: Arrests of British Citizens in Japan in 1940 and 1941*, (brill.com, downloaded 20 February 2025)

37. Murphy, David E., *What Stalin Knew: The Enigma of Barbarossa*, (Yale University Press, Kindle edition), pp.85–86

38. Ibid, p.88

39. Declaration Regarding Mongolia 13 April 1941 Avalon Project at Yale University

40. Whymant, p.145

41. Murphy, p.87

42. Schellenberg, Walter, *Walter Schellenberg: The Memoirs of Hitler's Spymaster*, (Carlton Books, 2006), p.225

43. Whymant, p.184

44. Oleson, p.83

45. Whymant, p.234

46. Ibid, p.244

47. Askey, Nigel, *The 'Siberian' Divisions and the Battle for Moscow in 1941–42*, (operationbarbarossa.net/the-siberian-divisions)

48. Schimitzu, p.17

49. Whymant, p.238

50. Ibid, p.288

Chapter 4: Willy Fisher: The Geordie Spy

1. Lonsdale, Gordon, *Spy: Twenty Years of Secret Service*, (Neville Spearman, 1965), pp.62–64

2. Henkine, Cyrille, *L'Espionage Sovietique; Le Cas Rudolf Abel*, (Fayard, 1981), p.117

3. Van der Rhoer, Edward, *The Shadow Network, Espionage as an Instrument of Soviet Policy*, (Robert Hale, 1983), p.93

4. Ibid, p.95

5. Khenkin, Kirill, *Okhotnik vverkh nogami: o Rudol'fe Abele i Villi Fishere*, (Posev, 1979), p.36

6. Van der Rhoer, p.96

7. Damaskin, Igor, *Kitty Harris: The Spy With Seventeen Names*, (St Ermin's Press, 2001), pp.138–140

8. Ibid, p.141

9. Khenkin, p.126

10. Stephan, Robert W., *Stalin's Secret War: Soviet Counterintelligence Against the Nazis, 1941–1945*, (□University Press of Kansa, 2003), p.160

11. Ridley, Norman, *The Secret War Between Hitler and Stalin*, (Pen and Sword, 2025), p.177

12. Arthey, Vin, *The Kremlin's Geordie Spy: The Man They Swapped for Gary Powers*, (Biteback Publishing, Kindle edition), location 2976

13. Berkinov, Louise, *Abel*, (Hodder and Stoughton, 1970), p.17

14. Ibid, p.28

15. Donovan, James B., *Strangers on a Bridge: The Case of Colonel Abel*, (Penguin Books, Kindle edition), p.31

16. Berkinov, p.68

17. Ibid, p.98

18. Donovan, p.27

19. Ibid, p.21

20. Ibid, p.15

21. Ibid, p.2

22. Ibid, p.350

23. Arthey, location 4550

Chapter 5: Kim Philby: The Cambridge Spy

1. Macintyre, Ben, *A Spy Among Friends*, (Bloomsbury Publishing, Kindle edition), p.18

2. John Banville, Review of *Love and Deception, Philby in Beirut* by James Hanning, *The Guardian*, 18 September 2021

3. Carver, Tom, *Philby in Beirut*, (London Review of Books, Vol. 34, No. 19, 2012)

4. Page, Bruce, Leitch, David and Knightley, Phillip, *Philby: The Spy Who Betrayed a Generation*, (Sphere Books, 1969), p.30

5. Harrison, Edward, *The Young Kim Philby*, (University of Exeter Press, 2012), p.10

6. Ibid, p.11

7. Seale, Patrick and McConville, Maureen, *Philby: The Long Road to Moscow*, (Penguin Books, 1973), p.25

8. Ibid, p.27

9. Milne, Tim, *Kim Philby: A Story of Friendship and Betrayal*, (Biteback Publishing, Kindle edition), location 214

10. Ibid, location 388

11. Page, Leitch and Knightley, p.78

12. Ibid, p.82

13. Seale and McConville, p.87

14. coldspur.com/litzi-Kim-under-the-covers, downloaded 3 March 2025

15. coldspur.com/litzi-Kim-under-the-covers, downloaded 3 March 2025

16. Harrison, p.36

17. Edith Tudor-Hart, Spartacus Educational, downloaded 3 March 2025

18. Harrison, p.23

19. Arnold Deutsch, Spartacus Educational, downloaded 3 March 2025

20. Ibid

21. coldspur.com/litzi-Kim-under-the-covers/, downloaded 3 March 2025

22. Ibid

23. Page, Leitch and Knightley, p.116

24. Harrison, p.60

25. Ibid, p.63

26. Page, Leitch and Knightley, p.119

27. coldspur.com/kim-Kim-always-working-for-sis/, downloaded 6 March 2025

28. Costello, John *Mask of Treachery*, (William Morrow & Co., 1988), p.386

29. Solomon, Flora, *Baku to Baker Street*, (Collins, 1984), p.172

30. Page, Leitch and Knightley, p.135

31. Harrison, p.111

32. Page, Leitch and Knightley, p.149

33. Andrew, Christopher, *The Defence of the Realm*, (Allen Lane, 2009), p.268

34. Seale and McConville, p.201

35. Harrison, p.159

36. erenow.org/modern/the-secret-history-of-mi6/10.php, downloaded 11 May 2025

37. Seale and McConville, p.234

38. coldspur.com/kim-philby-in-1951-alarms-and-diversions, downloaded 21 April 2025

39. Ibid

40. Ibid

41. Carver, unpaginated

42. Hansard column 1483, 7 November 1955

43. Beeston, Richard, *Looking for Trouble: The Life and Times of a Foreign Correspondent*, (Brasseys, 2006), p.29

44. Banville

45. Cave Brown, Anthony, *Treason in the Blood*, (Houghton Mifflin, 1994), p.481

46. Beeston, p.29

47. Penrose, Barrie and Freeman, Simon, 'Blunt's Secret Visit to Philby in Beirut', *The Sunday Times*, 8 November 1981

48. Macintyre, p.250

49. Ibid, p.255

50. Wright, Peter, *Spycatcher*, (Viking, 1987), p.194

51. Banville

52. Macintyre, p.270

53. Banville

Postscript

1. West, Nigel and Tsarev, Oleg, *Triplex*, (Yale University Press, 2009), p.104

INDEX